Enterprise 2.0

Social Networking Tools to Transform Your Organization

Enterprise 2.0

Social Networking Tools to Transform Your Organization

Jessica Keyes

CRC Press
Taylor & Francis Group
Boca Raton London New York

CRC Press is an imprint of the
Taylor & Francis Group, an **informa** business

AN AUERBACH BOOK

CRC Press
Taylor & Francis Group
6000 Broken Sound Parkway NW, Suite 300
Boca Raton, FL 33487-2742

First issued in paperback 2019

© 2013 by Taylor & Francis Group, LLC
CRC Press is an imprint of Taylor & Francis Group, an Informa business

No claim to original U.S. Government works

ISBN-13: 978-1-4398-8043-2 (hbk)
ISBN-13: 978-0-367-38099-1 (pbk)

Library of Congress Cataloging-in-Publication Data

Keyes, Jessica, 1950-
    Enterprise 2.0 : social networking tools to transform your organization / Jessica Keyes.
        p. cm.
    Includes bibliographical references and index.
    ISBN 978-1-4398-8043-2
    1. Social networks. 2. Web 2.0. 3. Information technology. 4. Management. I. Title.

HM741.K49 2012
302.3--dc23   2012017900

Visit the Taylor & Francis Web site at
http://www.taylorandfrancis.com

and the CRC Press Web site at
http://www.crcpress.com

This book is dedicated to my family and friends.

I would especially like to thank those who assisted me in putting this book together. As always, my editor, John Wyzalek, was instrumental in getting my project approved and providing great encouragement.

Contents

Preface

You may not realize this, but the collaborative web is getting ready to radically change the face of business. Some have taken to calling this use of collaborative technologies in business Enterprise 2 (E 2.0). Wikipedia may have been the first company to popularize the phenomenon of user-generated knowledge, but this "open" encyclopedia is just the tip of the iceberg. Companies far and wide are wiki-izing. Nokia hosts a number of wikis, some of which are used internally to coordinate technology research. Dresdner Kleinwort, an investment bank, operates the largest corporate wiki. About 50% of Dresdner staff members use this wiki to make sure that all team members are on the same page.

E 2.0 is more than just wikis, of course. It constitutes the entirety of social networking applications, including blogs, discussion boards, workspaces, and anything else that is shareable or even combinable (for example, mashups). IBM uses E 2.0 for everything from collaborative document production to internal project collaboration. Nokia uses it for all-purpose teamware. A whole host of companies use it for knowledge management. Honeywell was one of the first to use E 2.0 to perform knowledge discovery, research, and sharing across miles—regardless of whether users even know each other. The University of Phoenix uses it to allow 500,000 students to communicate on topics of interest. More importantly, it uses the same social platform to allow faculty to collaborate on topical issues of import. It would appear, then, that E 2.0 using social networking technologies has wide applicability to all things business.

The goal of this book is to examine business enterprise through the spectrum of the social activities that compose it. The art of business must be fused with the sciences of psychology, sociology, and mathematics, and wrapped around the principles of knowledge engineering to develop an appropriate collaborative infrastructure (that is, tools, applications, and environments) such that an organization might achieve or maintain a competitive advantage.

This book will discuss uses of social networking in such enterprise activities as human resources, risk management, operations, and project management, as well as provide some insights into legal and performance and measurement issues. I will refer to this as social enterprising throughout the book.

Along the way you will see some text call-outs that reflect true-to-life stories as told by my *crowdsourced* workforce. What's a crowdsourced workforce, you ask? According to Wikipedia (itself a crowdsourced encyclopedia maintained via a social network), *crowdsourcing* is the act of sourcing tasks traditionally performed by specific individuals to a group of people or community (crowd) through an open call. Crowdsourcing is a distributed problem-solving and production model. In the classic use of the term, problems are broadcast to an unknown group of solvers in the form of an open call for solutions. Users—also known as *the crowd*—typically form into online communities, and the crowd submits solutions. I used Amazon's Mechanical Turk (www.mturk.com) to ask hundreds of thousands of people to help me out by identifying wonderful uses of social networking at the Enterprise level. I paid them a nominal fee, anywhere from ten cents to a dollar. You'll see the results peppered throughout this book.

Welcome to social enterprising!

About the Author

Jessica Keyes is president of New Art Technologies, Inc., a high-technology and management consultancy and development firm started in New York in 1989.

Keyes has given seminars for such prestigious universities as Carnegie Mellon, Boston University, University of Illinois, James Madison University, and San Francisco State University. She is a frequent keynote speaker on the topics of competitive strategy and productivity and quality. She is former advisor for DataPro, McGraw-Hill's computer research arm, as well as a member of the Sprint Business Council. Keyes is also a founding board of directors member of the New York Software Industry Association, and completed a 2-year term on the Mayor of New York City's Small Business Advisory Council. She currently facilitates doctoral and other courses for the University of Phoenix and is a member of the Faculty Council for the College of Information Systems and Technology. She has been the editor for WGL's *Handbook of eBusiness* and CRC Press's *Systems Development Management* and *Information Management*.

Prior to founding New Art, Keyes was managing director of R&D for the New York Stock Exchange and has been an officer with Swiss Bank Co. and Banker's Trust, both in New York City. She holds a master's degree in business administration degree from New York University, and a doctorate in management.

A noted columnist and correspondent with over 200 articles published, Keyes is the author of the following books:

The New Intelligence: AI in Financial Services (HarperBusiness, 1990)
The Handbook of Expert Systems in Manufacturing (McGraw-Hill, 1991)
Infotrends: The Competitive Use of Information (McGraw-Hill, 1992)
The Software Engineering Productivity Handbook (McGraw-Hill, 1993)
The Handbook of Multimedia (McGraw-Hill, 1994)
The Productivity Paradox (McGraw-Hill, 1994)
Technology Trendlines (Van Nostrand Reinhold, 1995)
How to Be a Successful Internet Consultant (McGraw-Hill, 1997)
Webcasting (McGraw-Hill, 1997)
Datacasting (McGraw-Hill, 1997)

The Handbook of Technology in Financial Services (Auerbach, 1998)
The Handbook of Internet Management (Auerbach, 1999)
The Handbook of eBusiness (Warren, Gorham, & Lamont, 2000)
The Ultimate Internet Sourcebook (Amacom, 2001)
How to Be a Successful Internet Consultant, Second Ed. (Amacom, 2002)
Software Engineering Handbook (Auerbach, 2002)
Real World Configuration Management (Auerbach, 2003)
Balanced Scorecard (Auerbach, 2005)
Knowledge Management, Business Intelligence, and Content Management: The IT Practitioner's Guide (Auerbach, 2006)
X Internet: The Executable and Extendable Internet (Auerbach, 2007)
Leading IT Projects: The IT Manager's Guide (Auerbach, 2008)
Marketing IT Products and Services (Auerbach, 2009)
Implementing the Project Management Balanced Scorecard (Auerbach, 2010)
Social Software Engineering: Development and Collaboration with Social Networking (Auerbach, 2011)

Chapter 1

Human Side of Technology

When the telegraph was invented, the newspaper writers of the day heralded this new technology that was then sweeping the world. They said it had the potential to revolutionize the way we live our lives and the way business was done.

When the telephone was invented more than 100 years ago, newspaper writers of the day heralded this new technology that was then sweeping the world. They said it had the potential to revolutionize the way we live our lives and the way business was done.

When the Internet was invented, newspaper writers heralded this new technology that was sweeping the world. They said it had the potential to revolutionize the way we live our lives and the way business was done.

So, is this thing we call the Internet a revolution?

In spite of the hundreds, if not thousands, of articles and books testifying otherwise, my answer would have to be no. Shocked?

Revolution is a loaded word. It's the word of journalists and business leaders who very much want us to get all excited enough to purchase their newspaper, book, product, or service. It's the word that gets us to jump on any number of bandwagons lest we appear to be old fuddy-duddies or, in the realm of all things technology (gasp!), Luddites.

The telegraph, the telephone, and the Internet are three rungs on a rather long evolutionary ladder of progress, although the rungs are unevenly spaced. But to call the Internet a revolution would be stretching it. Evolution is truly a better fit.

The modern age of invention has been a long one. In his book *What the Victorians Did for Us*, author Adam Hart-Davis makes an excellent case that our

1

own age is really an extension of what the Victorians created. They invented the lawnmower, the concept of the seaside vacation resort, nationwide weather forecasts, the modern bicycle, napkins, aspirin, the telegraph, theatres offering mass entertainment, free universal primary education, sewage systems, and toilets. Freed from the pestilence of untreated sewage and the invention of public health, and assisted by a great many labor-saving inventions, the middle class was finally able to blossom. All this led Hart-Davis to conclude that the Victorians virtually invented the modern world.

Rise of the Modern Internet

The Internet was not invented by Al Gore. Sorry, Al. Its infancy, however, was spent under the tutelage of the United States government, which invented the ARPAnet communications network in 1969 in the event that a military attack destroyed conventional communications systems. It's rather amusing to think that the Internet, which was fully embraced by weed-smoking liberals and other anti-establishment types back in the 1970s, was actually a byproduct of the "evil military industrial complex."

The Internet, as we've come to know and love it, was jump-started in 1989, and thrust into full throttle in 1993. In 1989 Tim Berners-Lee of Geneva's European particle research laboratory (CERN) proposed that a hypertext system for easy information exchange among widely dispersed research teams be created. Hypertext was actually invented back in the 1970s, but it was Berners-Lee who first thought of using hypertext to self-organize online documents that would eventually come to be called the World Wide Web. While some effort was made to develop friendly interfaces (e.g., the furry little Gopher, named after the University of Minnesota's school mascot), it wasn't until 1993 that the rest of the world sat up and took notice.

In that year, a pudgy college student named Marc Andreessen invented Mosaic, the first graphical user interface for the World Wide Web. It was clumsy, and it didn't do very much. Since it was an academic exercise, you could only get it by downloading it from the Internet itself—at the time not an easy task. But anyone who took the time to try it out instantly saw the possibilities.

Since 1993 the Internet has grown at an astonishing rate. From a dull, gray, and rather limited interface and text-based e-mail we have sprinted into full color interactivity and e-mail that has the capability of transmitting audio as well as video. The Internet age has truly arrived.

One of the most memorable telegraph transmissions was the one which was missed by the only possible ship that could have saved all the passengers of the Titanic. The most memorable telephone call was the one in which Alexander Graham Bell said, "Watson, can you hear me?" In each case the technology was new but would soon be adopted by millions and would thus be woven into the very thread of everyday life—as comfortable as an old blanket. For most of us in the

First World, there's nothing revolutionary about a telephone anymore. Nor is the Internet very revolutionary any more. It too is as comfortable as a warm blanket.

Technology Becomes an Extension of Ourselves

Technology has become our third arm. We're glued to our cell phones, and many of us would rather watch the game on TV rather than venture out in traffic to the ball park. Satellite dishes are springing up on every south-facing facade in sight, and many a church steeple has become a front for a cell phone tower. We salivate over the thought of HDTV and jump on every new tech trend even if it means we have to throw out perfectly good technology (e.g., 8-track cassettes, anyone?) that was introduced just a few years before.

People even have a tendency to humanize the things that we integrate into our lives. We give cars pet names and scream foul humanist epithets (you dirty $%$#@) at our computers when they misbehave. We trust our televisions to babysit our children and let our microwave ovens cook us up a quick meal. We even rely on our car's navigation system not to let us get lost.

We have become our technology, and our technology has become us. The Internet is the most human of all these technologies because it can actually talk back to us. One of the greatest of all human needs is the need to communicate with other people. Prisoners placed in "stir" often go crazy from the isolation, the effect called "stir crazy." Humans are nothing if not communal. From primitive times we banded together in small tribes. While protection from predators was certainly one of the best reasons to travel in packs, the most important reason was the feeling of warmth and belonging that we get when we're part of a group that understands and cares about us.

When Tim Berners-Lee developed a proposal that hyperlinked documents could be the basis for a World Wide Web of similarly themed documents, little did he realize that this one idea would spawn entire online communities. Whether your bag is UFOs, gay rights, or business, there is a community specifically geared for you—available day or night—and directly accessible from the comfort of your own home, pajamas and all.

When hunter–gatherers finally decided to end their hunting and foraging and set up agricultural communities, they radically improved on a primitive way of securing their sustenance. They did what humans do best. They invented an improvement. Fire was an invention. So was the wheel. Humans traveled to the far corners of the known world until each of these inventions was disseminated to other humans in other tribes and communities. This is called technological evolution.

So when it comes to the Internet, we shouldn't be surprised to find that folks can be quite creative in their use of the technology and everyone else quite adaptive in using it in similar or slightly different ways when they finally find out about it.

Why We Use the Web

When the web was young, it was the realm of academics, leading-edge technoids, and small businesspeople finally happy to find a cheap way to get their names in front of prospective clients—without big business competitors blowing them out of the water. Today big business all but dominates the Internet.

With the dot-com disaster a painful and rather expensive but increasingly distant memory, big business has come into its own as the major supplier of what all of us information junkies want.

> *The Internet lets me find information on anything that I want, giving me instant expertise whenever I need it. That's important because we live in an age that places a tangible value on knowledge. The ability to retrieve knowledge and put that knowledge into action ... that's how the Internet changes the way we do things.*

Over 40 years ago the personal computer was introduced. Over these past four decades we've all grown accustomed to sitting at a desk with fingers on keyboard staring into a monitor. While many among us like to brag about the brilliant kids we've spawned who seem to have been prewired for computer brilliance at birth, the truth of the matter is that today's computers are fairly simple to use and so ubiquitous that it's now second nature to sit yourself down with a cup of coffee and an Internet connection.

Cyber-cafes, kiosks in malls, and rows of Internet-enabled PCs at the public library attest to this ubiquity. And with ubiquity comes comfort—a comfort so great that even the most senior among us like to dabble. Seniors, children, and everyone in the middle are using the web, primarily for these two purposes. This is quite natural, however, since information gathering and communicating are a large part of what we have always been doing. Pre-Internet it was done in libraries, via phone, and through the mail. Today we still use these media, but as usual we are using technology, in the form of the Internet, to augment our traditional way of doing things.

The Internet is a reflection of our interests, no more and no less. It lets us be us. If we choose to it also lets us transform ourselves into the person we really wanted to be in the first place. We can be shy. We can be sexy. We can use the Internet to do good, and we can use the Internet to perpetrate fraud—and even worse. If you're good, then you will be good on the Internet. If you're evil ... well, rotten eggs are always rotten eggs.

Changed Nature of Work

When my friends commiserate with each other over the rather lousy job situation today, they like to talk about their fathers. Dad, they say, had an unwritten contract with his employer. He'd get to work for 25 or so years, and they would never think of laying him off. He had job security.

Most of our dads, in fact, did have only one job for most of their careers. I know mine did. Dad worked for CIT Financial in New York City for several decades, after stints in the army, college, and as a tour-bus hawker in Times Square during the 1940s. He moved slowly, but surely, up the corporate ladder and finally, late in his career, actually became an officer of the company. When he retired, they gave him a party, a watch, and a pension, and that was that.

Today most of us have anywhere from five to seven jobs during a career punctuated by layoffs, resignations, and generally not very good times. But it's a fantasy to think that all of our dads and granddads really had it any better.

One need only look at great literature for a record of what the "olden days" were really like. From Charles Dickens' painfully vivid description of being poor in the London of *Oliver Twist* to Upton Sinclair's sensational account of what work life was like for meatpacking workers in (1906) *The Jungle*. Both books provoked public outrage. In fact, President Theodore Roosevelt was so horrified by Sinclair's depiction of workplace amputations, lacerations, and other injuries that he launched a federal inquiry into the practices of Chicago's meatpacking industry. It wasn't until after World War II, however, that the meatpackers' union finally gave the workers in this industry what they fought so hard for: a middle class existence.

Eric Schlosser in his very fine book *Fast Food Nation* deconstructs how the meatpacking industry went from using high-paid skilled labor to largely unskilled, migrant labor in just a few short decades. The cause, according to Schlosser, was McDonald's.

Once upon a time in America, everyone could afford to eat out in restaurants. When the national highway system was built and automobile travel became ubiquitous, fast food restaurants were born to service these now car-loving Americans. Back then, however, fast food meant car hops, short order cooks, and a varied menu. If you're old enough, you might remember the shortskirted girls on roller skates who took your order; everyone else is invited to rent the now legendary movie *American Graffiti* to get a feel for the era.

All those girls and short order cooks were expensive for the owners of these first fast food establishments. Taking a cue from the assembly lines of automobile manufacturing, the fast food industry now automates and standardizes practically every facet of the business. Skilled labor need no longer apply.

As the fast food industry began to consolidate to a very few, very large players (e.g., McDonald's, Burger King, etc.), they decided that they needed to call the shots beyond their own restaurant doors. They now wanted to call the shots in the meatpacking industry. Dictating what, how, and where, they also decided to reduce the number of meatpacking firms they would work with. The ones chosen ultimately became meatpacking industry powerhouses.

In 1960, two former Swift & Company executives decided to start their own meatpacking company to compete with these giants. But it couldn't be business as usual. They need to dramatically reduce production costs to stay in the game.

To do so, they decided to apply the same techniques used at McDonald's: eliminate skilled labor. Using a combination of technology, new procedures, and cheap immigrant labor, they did just this. Not only did they successfully achieve their goal of reducing costs, they created a whole new way of packaging meat. Instead of shipping whole sides of beef, they now shipped smaller cuts, vacuum-sealed or plastic-packed. This new marketing technique virtually eliminated the need for skilled butchers in grocery stores as well.

Meatpacking isn't the only industry to be "modernized" by technology plus low-skilled labor. Farm owners are also using this combination to reduce costs. Of course, a byproduct of these techniques is the reduced demand for domestic workers.

Like the meatpacking industry, growers much prefer newly arrived immigrants. In fact, the government has a program which enables farmers to import 42,000 workers on H-2A visas to harvest crops.

So here we have it again: unskilled labor + technology = McDonaldization. Of course, this formula is not limited to meatpacking and agriculture. A variation of McDonaldization has been creeping its way into industry since the formula was created.

In my father's day, skilled workers all had the same expectations. They started out, in their twenties, as junior staffers and gradually worked their way up the ranks. No 20-something bosses here. You first had to pay your dues, and gather some experience. Pre-Internet technology started the ball rolling.

When I started my first professional job, most executives had private secretaries. Everyone else shared one or two secretaries. These were the folks that typed and mailed your letters and interoffice memos. In 1981, there was a sea change. The personal computer was introduced to office workers. Along with the hardware came a couple of revolutionary software packages including a word processor and spreadsheet. Over time, most office workers started doing their own typing, gradually reducing the need for a large pool of typists and secretarial staff.

Over the next two decades, great strides were made, and we saw the rise of complex, sophisticated "thinking" technologies such as expert systems and neural networks. While we are nowhere close to the wonders seen in Steven Spielberg's movie *A.I. Artificial Intelligence*, we do have software today that can predict the behavior of consumers, diagnose software problems, and even act as your virtual receptionist. Elimination by technology, it seems, is moving up the food chain.

Technology, globalization, and a bouncing ball economy have changed the dynamics of being an employee. In Europe, the unemployment rate hovers around 10%, although there are vast variations between individual countries—up to 20% unemployment in Spain (http://epp.eurostat.ec.europa.eu/statistics_explained/index.php/Unemployment_statistics). In the United States, the government will only admit to a 9.1% unemployment rate according to the U.S. Bureau of Labor Statistics, but most of us know otherwise. If you add in those that fall off the unemployment rolls (and are therefore not counted in the official statistics) and add in underemployed workers such as part-timers who really want full-time jobs, then the real unemployment rate has been calculated to be as high 25% according to some alternative sources (http://www.shadowstats.com/alternate_data/unemployment-charts).

Technological advances coupled with cheap labor overseas have further diminished the opportunities for American workers in several ways. When was the last time you called an 800 number for help? You're probably no longer surprised to find that a goodly number of folks that you are talking to are thousands of miles away. That sweet woman with the Midwestern accent on the other end of the phone just might be sitting in a massive call center somewhere in India. What might surprise is that an increasing number of white collar activities have also been outsourced, this includes everything from reading an x-ray, to legal discovery, to editorial, to even writing a book!

Technologically Enabled Worker

Workers, here and abroad, all have one thing in common. They are tethered to their work pretty much 24–7. How is this possible? The Internet coupled with the office intranet permits you to work anyplace, anytime. All you need is a PC, a modem (and this can be wireless or broadband), and a connection to the web. Few people can just call in sick anymore. If they have a computer at home, they can merely sit in their bathrobes with a box of tissues on the desk, and accomplish the same amount of work that they would have if they went to work with that nasty cold.

Need to write a report and send it to a dozen co-workers? Your trusty word processor coupled with a broadcast e-mail will work just fine. There are even web-enabled high-speed printers if that report needs to be collated, bound, and then distributed. You can even hold meetings and give presentations using web services. I just viewed a demonstration of a complicated PC-based software package. The demo was given using the client's PC using WebEx's (www.webex.com) real-time business meeting service. According to Stephen S. Roach, an economist often quoted in the *New York Times*, the dirty little secret of the information age is that an increasingly large slice of work goes on outside the official work hours the government recognizes and employers admit to. Electronic devices ranging from telephones and fax machines and pagers to cell phones and portable e-mail devices mean employees are connected to the workplace 24 hours a day, seven days a week.

One creative group of employees created their quarterly review by using video chat software, recording it, saving it as a podcast, and then letting their manager watch the video via the Internet. This seems to be becoming a trend. A survey found that 69% now view these sorts of videos on their PCs, with 33% viewing on their smartphones. It should come as no surprise that social networking, the focus of this book, has become the number one category of online activity that Americans engage in online according to NielsenWire (http://blog.nielsen.com/nielsenwire/online_mobile/what-americans-do-online-social-media-and-games-dominate-activity/).

Between 2009 and 2010, use of social networks grew by an astounding 43%, up from 15.8% of time spent online to 22.7%. As of 2011, nearly four out of five active Internet users use social networks, according to Nielsen's 2011 "The Social Media Report" (http://blog.nielsen.com/nielsenwire/social/). Since so many workers are already enamored of social networking, exhibiting a real facility for using it, it makes sense to leverage this level of expertise to promote enhance productivity, efficiency, and maybe even competitive advantage.

In the next chapter, we're going to delve into some of the reasons why social enterprising is probably a good idea for your company, for more than just marketing.

Key Point

Workers the world over are tethered to the Internet, for both personal and professional reasons. Savvy companies need to leverage this desire, willingness, and expertise toward increasing productivity in the workplace.

> *Social networking like Facebook is a great way for all of my co-workers to stay connected with each other. We can keep in contact with our clients through Facebook's e-mail system. It is quick and easy, and we know we won't miss a Facebook notification. Because all of the workers check Facebook regularly, it is better than regular e-mail because Facebook notifications are easier to see and do not get lost as easily. Essentially, I use social networking to stay connected with my coworkers in a fast and efficient way.*

Chapter 2

Social Enterprising Environment

Work is made up of a series of projects. You might have a project to create software, another to develop a marketing campaign, and still another to develop that new style of automobile. Yet a variety of studies have found that many projects are prone to failure. In the world of software development, the Standish Group found that only 32% of surveyed projects were considered to be successful (i.e., on time, on budget, and with the required functionality and feature set). Nearly one quarter of projects were considered to be failures. The rest were considered to be challenged, an euphemism for late, overbudget, or implemented without the full set of promised functions and features. It should be noted, however, that there are many who dispute the Chaos report findings. What's undisputed is that a large number of projects do fail.

Quite a few things can, and do, go wrong. McConnell (1996) neatly categorized these, as shown in Table 2.1.

Hyvari (2006) provides an updated view of this, as shown in Table 2.2. The names may have changed, but the problems remain more or less the same.

As you can see, there are a host of reasons that can negatively impact success, but high up on the list is the human element. It is critical that stakeholders collaborate with a clear vision of what is to be achieved, how it is to be achieved, and at what cost and in what time frame.

> *Social networking can allow employees to get to know each other better, which fosters a better relationship. Social networking connects people and creates a sense of trust and responsibility toward each other.*

Table 2.1 Classic Project Problems

People-related mistakes	Process-related mistakes	Product-related mistakes	Technology-related mistakes
Undermined motivation	Overly optimistic schedules	Requirements gold-plating—i.e., too many product features	Silver-bullet syndrome—i.e., latching onto a new technology or methodology that is unproven for the particular project
Weak personnel	Insufficient risk management	Feature creep	Overestimated savings from tools or methods
Uncontrolled problem employees	Contractor failure	Gold-plating—i.e., adding features no one asked for	Switching tools in the middle of a project
Heroics	Insufficient planning	Push me, pull me negotiation—i.e., constantly changing schedule	Lack of automated control
Adding people to a late project	Abandonment of planning under pressure	Research-oriented development—i.e., stretching the limits of technology	
Noisy, crowded offices	Wasted time before project actually starts—i.e., the approval and budgeting process		
Friction between workers and customers	Shortchanged upstream activities—e.g., adequate planning, etc.		
Unrealistic expectations	Inadequate design		

Table 2.1 *(Continued)* **Classic Project Problems**

People-related mistakes	*Process-related mistakes*	*Product-related mistakes*	*Technology-related mistakes*
Lack of effective project sponsorship	Shortchanged quality assurance		
Lack of stakeholder buy-in	Insufficient management controls		
Lack of user input	Premature or too frequent convergence—i.e., release the product too early		
Politics over substance	Omitting necessary tasks from estimates		
Wishful thinking	Planning to catch up latter		

Having the right people on a team is certainly key to the success of a project. In a large pharmaceutical company, the lead designer walked off a very important project. Obviously, that set the team back quite a bit as no one else had enough experience to do what he did. Even if the staff stays put, there is still the possibility that a "people" issue will negatively affect the project. For example, a change in senior management might mean that the project you are working on gets canned or moved to a lower priority. A project manager working for America Online Time Warner had just started an important new project when a new president was installed. He did what all new presidents do—he engaged in a little housecleaning. Projects got swept away—and so did some people. When the dust settled, the project manager personally had a whole new set of priorities—as well as a bunch of new team members to work with.

As you can see, today's dynamically changing, and very volatile, business landscape can play havoc with social enterprising efforts, and going global adds an entirely new dimension to the mix. What we need, then, is a whole new paradigm of software development that places the human aspect at the center of social enterprising.

Social Network

Social networking is a hot topic. More than 30 billion pieces of content are shared on Facebook each month, and Nielsen researchers say that consumers spend more

Table 2.2 Success/Failure Factors

Factors related to project	Size and value
	Having a clear boundary
	Urgency
	Uniqueness of project activities
	Density of the project network (in dependencies between activities)
	Project life cycle
	End-user commitment
	Adequate funds/resources
	Realistic schedule
	Clear goals/objectives
Factors related to the project manager/ leadership	Ability to delegate authority
	Ability to trade off
	Ability to coordinate
	Perception of his or her role and responsibilities
	Effective leadership
	Effective conflict resolution
	Having relevant past experience
	Management of changes
	Contract management
	Situational management
	Competence
	Commitment
	Trust
	Other communication
Factors related to project team members	Technical background
	Communication
	Troubleshooting
	Effective monitoring and feedback
	Commitment

Table 2.2 *(Continued)*   **Success/Failure Factors**

Factors related to the organization	Steering committee
	Clear organization/job descriptions
	Top management support
	Project organization structure
	Functional manager's support
	Project champion
Factors related to the environment	Competitors
	Political environment
	Economic environment
	Social environment
	Technological environment
	Nature
	Client
	Subcontractors

than five and a half hours on social networking sites per day. So I am sure it doesn't come as a surprise that social networking has made its way into the workplace.

As early as 2008, AT&T released the results of a research study they conducted in Europe. The study, conducted by Dynamic Markets, found that the use of social networking tools has lead to an increase in efficiency. About 2,500 people were surveyed in five countries, and 65% said that use of these tools has made them or their colleagues more efficient, and 46% insisted that it has sparked ideas and creativity.

Deep Nishar is vice president of products and user experience at LinkedIn. He's in charge of a group of data researchers that look at everything from data center behavior to trends in search and mobile communications. His eclectic staff has experience in such fields as brain surgery, computer science, meteorology, and poetry. According to Nishar, machine-based systems like Google can't keep up with organizing the data they are capturing. Interesting and important problems will be solved by looking at social networks.

In 1976, sic-fi author Richard Dawkins coined the term *meme*, which is an idea that moves from person to person and onward. With social networking tools, staff can check to see what ideas people are discussing within the organization. Some refer to these sorts of tools as a "meme broadcast tool." Where marketers have Twitter to communicate with people outside the company, business people can use services such as Yammer (yammer.com) to share information within the company,

Table 2.3   Social Networking Tools

Social networking	Facebook, Friendster, LinkedIn, Ning, Orkut, Bebo, KickApps, OpenACircle, Vyew, MOLI, Fast Pitch!, Plaxo, Yammer, Eurekastreams.org, researchgate.net
Publishing	TypePad, Blogger, Wikipedia, Joomla
Photo sharing	Radar.net, SmugMug, Zooomr, Flickr, Picasa, Photobucket, Twitxr
Audio	iTunes, Rhapsody, Podbean, Podcast.com
Video	YouTube, Metacafe, Hulu, Viddler, Google Video, Brightcove
Microblogging	Twitxr, Twitter, Plurk
Livecasting	SHOUTcast, BlogTalkRadio, TalkShoe, Justin.tv, Live365
Virtual worlds	There, SecondLife, ViOS, ActiveWorlds
Productivity	ReadNotify, Zoho, Zoomerang, Google Docs
Aggregators	Digg, Yelp, iGoogle, Reddit, FriendFeed, TiddlyWiki
Rich site summary (RSS)	RSS 2.0, Atom, PingShot
Search	Technorati, Redlasso, EveryZing, MetaTube, IceRocket, Google Search
Mobile	Jumbuck, CallWave, airG, Jott, Brightkite
Interpersonal	WebEx, iChat, Meebo, Acrobat Connect, Goto Meeeting, Skype

discuss relevant issues, and more (Table 2.3 lists some of the more popular social networking tools in use today.)

Bleeding-edge organizations have already figured out how to make social networking profitable for them. SolarWinds, a network management company, built a 25,000-member user community of network administrators who help each other with various problems. This allows the company to support a customer base of over 88,000 companies with just two customer support people. Cisco created employee councils and shifted decision making down to these levels. The councils are supported using collaborative technologies. Indeed, Cisco's CEO, John Chambers, insists that most of the progress made during the past two years has been because of collaborative and social technologies.

When IBM transformed an intranet into a social network, it provided each of IBM's 365,000 employees a voice and identity that not only helped increase effectiveness and productivity, it also helped workers transcend national cultures. IBM uses a variety of social networking tools. Long before Facebook graduated from college, IBM created its own internal social networking site, which they called BluePages. It lists basic information about an employee as well as views of that individual, such as who reports to them, who they report to, what organization they're in and what communities they are a part of. Employees can self-edit their listing, and even add a picture. Clicking on an entry allows someone to send an instant message.

Perhaps the most powerful feature is social tagging, also called social bookmarking. Clicking on an employee not only brings up identifying data, it also brings up the employee's tags: i.e., blog feeds, RSS feeds, communities joined, social networks joined, recent forum entries, and wiki participation. Ethan McCarty, who is former editor in chief of IBM's intranet, describes it like this, "if you think of the phases of the intranet and even Internet communication, first, it's about access to information, then it's about transacting with it—like e-business—and now it's more about people."

The people we refer to as the millennials come into the workplace with cellphone glued to their ear and fingers firmly glued to the keyboard tweeting and Facebooking to friends and strangers alike. These folks think that talking on the phone is passé. Some don't even have landlines. These folks are communicating via social networks, instant message, Twitter, and smartphones. However, it's their older brothers and sisters, Gen-Y, that is working to convince tech management of the values of these new technologies, according to a Forrester Research survey of 2000 IT professionals. This isn't all that surprising as a recent Pew report found that Internet users from all ages groups have increased their usage. While 83% of those between 18 and 33 use social networking, those 45 and older more than doubled their participation.

> *I work for a hospital, and we use Facebook, Twitter, and YouTube to update the community about new services, new equipment, new physicians, health events, fundraisers, etc.*

Enterprise Social Network

The modern work paradigm can be considered to be a social activity. Most work projects use a team model, where the work is divided among the various team members. Various studies suggest that on large projects, team members spend between 70% and 85% of their time working with others. Thus, it is important that the team members collaborate effectively to achieve their common goal.

Much of the literature on the psychology of work teams concludes that most of the social problems inherent in development teams can be solved by a critical analysis of the dynamics between the people involved. This sort of introspective analysis can be helpful to explain (1) why certain people are excluded from group decision making; (2) why there is always someone who resists the decisions of project leadership; (3) why certain kinds of people should never be grouped together, to avoid group fragmentation; (4) why groups often divide themselves into subgroups; and (5) what is the difference between the "real" chain of command and the formal one.

It is worthwhile to understand individual and social perspectives that affect product design. Individuals often worry about whether they are interested enough to be effective during the span of the project. They also worry about whether they have something relevant to add to the group, and can express it clearly so that others might understand them. On the other hand, the group is interested in hearing from a wide variety of stakeholders. Thus, the group is concerned with encouraging individuals to contribute; to prevent voices from being lost because there might be too much information; to avoid illegitimate voices; to prevent getting stuck in group think; and to eliminate sources of exclusion.

There have been a multitude of studies that discuss the vast amount of time spent on communication and collaboration with others. Modern work is an inherently collaborative and distributed process, and with teams of developers working intra- and interorganizationally and globally, it is logical that these teams would require toolsets designed specifically for the collaborative, distributed nature of their work.

> *I use social networking to keep up with fellow accountants, so that we can compare notes and ideas about work and upcoming deadlines for tax work. It helps me keep track of seminars that might be available, and other opportunities for professional development.*

Collaborative Applications

The computer-supported cooperative work (CSCW) community has been studying computer-assisted collaboration for quite some time. CSCW researchers have developed a number of frameworks that seek to categorize the requirements of the collaborative toolset. One framework categorizes these tools into four groups: (1) model-based collaboration tools, (2) process support tools, (3) collaboration awareness tools, and (4) collaboration infrastructure tools.

On the other hand, a more intriguing framework classifies tools based on the effort required to collaborate effectively. The framework consists of five layers and three strands, as shown in Figure 2.1. The layers are tools and strands are critical needs that permeate all aspects of collaboration.

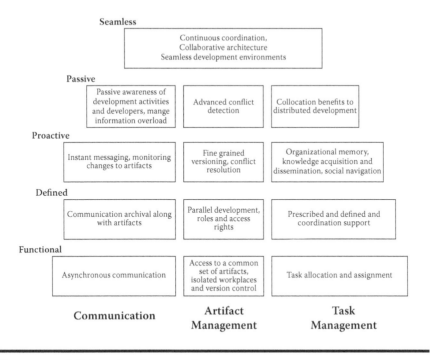

Figure 2.1 Collaboration framework.

As is often the case, many of the toolsets discussed in the literature are experimental, not offered for use by those in the field. In 2003, Booch and Brown surveyed both experimental and commercial collaborative development environments (CDEs). Their definition of a CDE is a virtual space in which all the stakeholders of a project, even if distributed in time or distance, may negotiate, brainstorm, discuss, share knowledge, and generally labor together to carry out some task. They base their requirements list on Fournier (2001). Table 2.4 shows the combined Fournier, Booch, and Brown requirements list for this sort of environment.

Web 2 technologies have finally given a voice to the collaborative needs of software developers and can lend a hand toward building the type of CDE envisioned in Table 2.4. Web 2 engages users to build collective intelligence. One of the most common examples of this is the wiki (wiki is a variant of the Hawaiian word *wicki*, which means "fast"). Wikis are so ubiquitous that the learning curve is minimal. Quite a few organizations use this tool. Studies have found that wikis really do help organization improve work processes, increase collaboration efficiency, increase knowledge reuse, and identify new business opportunities. However, wikis have their own attendant problems. Insufficient usage and decaying structure all need to be addressed if wikis are to be successful.

Table 2.4   Recommended Feature Set of a Collaborative Development Environment

Coordination
Centralized information management
Configuration control of shared artifacts
Online event notification
Calendaring and scheduling
Project resource profiling
Project dashboards and metrics (Booch & Brown)
Searching and indexing of resources and artifacts
Electronic document routing and workflow
Virtual agents and scripting of tasks (Booch & Brown)
Collaboration
Threaded discussion forums (Booch & Brown)
Virtual meeting rooms
Instant messaging
Online voting and polling
Shared whiteboards
Cobrowsing of documents
Multiple levels of information visibility (Booch & Brown)
Community Building
Personalization capabilities (Booch & Brown)
Established protocols and rituals
Well-defined scope and leadership
Self-publication of content (Booch & Brown)
Self-administration of projects (Booch & Brown)

I mainly use social networking as education for business. Via LinkedIn profiles and Facebook, specials/status updates, I can quickly find out people who are successful in what they do versus the majority who just look for a lot of friends and "likes" in the hopes of drawing business. I make sure to spend as much time and attention as I can with those that are successful, even if they're not in my line of work. There's almost always something I can learn from them and apply to my own profession.

The advent of social networking services such as LinkedIn, Facebook, and MySpace demonstrate the power of social networks and give us an insight into what could be created specifically at the enterprise level. Of course, the current state-of-the-art social networks do have some limitations. Chief among the described problems is the lack of interoperability between social networks. One way to fix this problem might be by leveraging Semantic Web technologies, one of which is ontologies. An ontology is a formal representation of specific domain concepts and the relationship between those concepts. A domain ontology describes the knowledge that might reside within a particular business unit or even across business units. Method ontologies capture the knowledge and reasoning needed to perform a task. Status ontologies, either dynamic or static, capture the status characteristics of a process or system. Intentional ontologies model the softer aspects of living things, such as beliefs, desires, and intentions. Process ontologies capture the three aspects of enterprise knowledge, that is, enterprise knowledge (i.e., processes, organizational structure, IT structure, products, customers), domain knowledge (i.e., terms, concepts, relationships), and information knowledge (i.e., document types and structures). Finally, social ontologies describes the organizational structure and the interdependencies that exist among the social actors (i.e., analyst, tester, developer, etc.).

Several ontologies (e.g., www.foaf-project.org, www.sioc-project.org, http://www.semanticdesktop.org/ontologies/pimo/) have become universally recognized, and it is expected that at some point interoperability between social networks using ontologies will become standard practice.

Key Point

Sure, we can all use Microsoft Sharepoint, Oracle Beehive, or glue together any number of social networking tools such as wikis and blogs to effect a viable software solution. We're going to discuss many of these in this book, and even show you how to use them. You'll find that there are good social enterprising tools galore. When I first began writing this book, I thought that this was a problem in search of a software solution. However, the more research I did, and the more people I spoke with, I became convinced that this is really a problem in search of a process. The goal of the rest of this book, therefore, is to fuse the way we work to the underpinnings of social enterprising: knowledge sharing and transfer.

References

Booch, G., and Brown, A. W. (2003). Collaborative development environments. *Advances in Computers,* 59: 2–29.

Fournier, R. (2001, March 5). Teamwork is the key to remote development. *Infoworld.* Retrieved from http://www.itworld.com/IW010305tcdistdev.

Hyvari, I. (2006, September). Success of projects in different organizational conditions. *Project Management Journal,* 37(4): 31–41.

McConnell, S. (1996). *Rapid development: Taming wild software schedules.* Redmond, WA: Microsoft Press.

Chapter 3

Web 2 to Enterprise 2

Most professionals, when they think of social networking at all, think in terms of Facebook and Twitter. Many managers see great potential in these kinds of tools. IBM conducted a worldwide study of 2,500 C-level managers in late 2010. The collective take on collaboration tools is that they need to be institutionalized to meet the demands of the business. Surprisingly, as we will shortly show, and with some effort, all of these can be "institutionalized" in some way to enhance employee productivity.

Given the popularity of these sorts of tools among consumers, it is no wonder that a variety of these sorts of tools have cropped up that are geared to specific business disciplines.

> *Social networks are a great way of spreading useful information to employees; some people tend to check their Facebook account more often than their e-mail; sometimes information is lost in employee e-mail accounts.*

Tools That Provide Networking Capabilities

Salesforce.com, the enterprise customer relationship management (CRM) giant, has begun to involve itself in providing social networking capabilities. Its new Chatter service is available on Salesforce's real-time collaboration cloud. Users establish profiles and generate status updates. These might be questions, bits of information and/ or knowledge, or relevant hyperlinks. All of this is then aggregated and broadcast to co-workers in their personal network. Essentially, a running feed of comments and updates flow to those in that particular network. Employees can also follow colleagues from around the company, not just in their own personal network, enabling cross-organizational knowledge sharing. Towards that end, Chatter also provides a profile database that users can tap into to find needed skills for a particular project. Chatter is accessible via desktop or mobile.

Like Salesforce.com, more than a handful of well-known software companies have developed collaboration tools, all for a fee. Oracle's Beehive provides a suite of tools such as instant messaging, e-mail, calendaring, and team workspaces. Microsoft's SharePoint is quite heavily used within many departments. Microsoft's Lync Server product, which permits users to communicate from anywhere via voice, video, or document share, is also becoming a contender. One of the first companies to dabble in the collaborative market—indeed they created it—was Lotus. Now owned by IBM, Lotus Notes brings together a wide array of tools: instant messaging, team rooms, discussion forums, and even application widgets.

There are also a wide variety of free tools available, which can be adapted for our purposes. LinkedIn has been widely used to provide networking capabilities for business people. A relevant feature is LinkedIn groups. A group can be created for any purpose, with permission granted to join. Thus, project teams can make use of the already-developed facilities LinkedIn provides. For example, the Tata Research Development and Design Centre (TRDDC) was established in 1981 as a division of Tata Consultancy Services Limited, India's largest IT consulting organization. TRDDC is today one of India's largest research and development centers in software engineering and process engineering. TRDDC has its own membership-by-request LinkedIn group. It is quite easy to create a members-only LinkedIn group for a particular project, and limited to specific members, as shown in Figure 3.1.

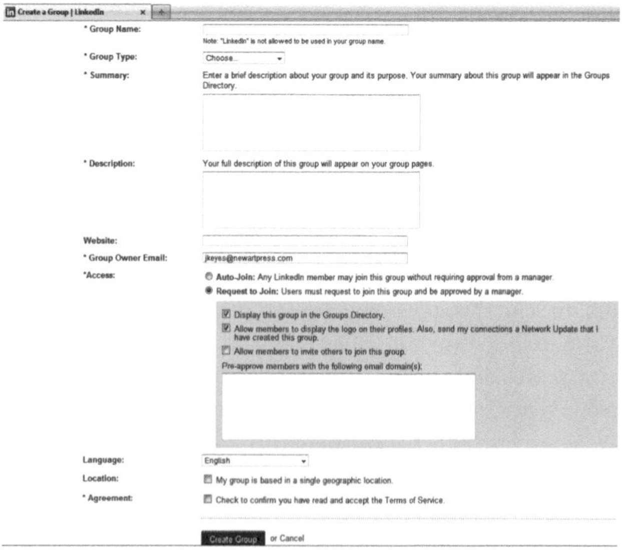

Figure 3.1 Creating a members-only LinkedIn group.

Of all of the collaborative tools available, particularly those that are free, wikis are the most prominently used. Zoho.com provides a wide range of tools, including chat, discussions, meetings, and projects, but it is their wiki tool I'd like to focus on here.

In Figure 3.2, I created a wiki to store all of the artifacts for a typical software development project—that is, project plan, systems requirement specification, analysis docs, etc. In Figure 3.3, you can see the Project Plan artifact in wiki form. Note the ability to post comments.

Twitter, a social networking app make famous by celebrities who tweet hourly updates on what they are doing (e.g., eating lunch, shopping, etc.), has morphed into an enterprise social networking application called Yammer. With the ability to integrate with tools such as SharePoint, Yammer provides a suite of tools including enterprise microblogging, communities, company directory, direct messaging, groups, and knowledge base. SunGard employees actually started using Yammer on their own to share information about projects they were working on. Now it's been rolled out to all 20,000+ employees.

Much of what Yammer offers is free with their basic service. Their Gold subscription provides such corporate niceties as security controls, admin controls, broadcast messages, enhanced support, SharePoint integration, keyword monitoring, and virtual firewall solution.

Yammer can be used by the software development team to interactively discuss any aspect of a project, as shown in Figure 3.4.

Project groups have used wikis in some creative ways: writing up personal research and making comments on others' research; asking questions; posting

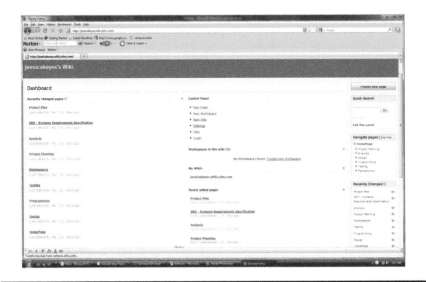

Figure 3.2   Project artifact wiki.

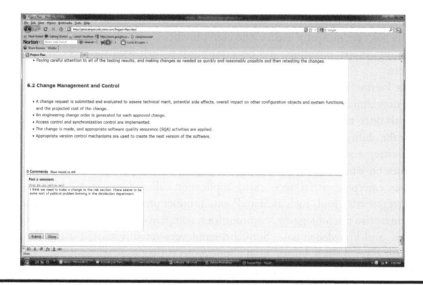

Figure 3.3   Project plan wiki, demonstrating ability to include comments.

Figure 3.4   Dynamic discussion using Yammer.

links to resources that might be of interest to others in the group; adding details for upcoming events and meetings; letting each other know what they're up to; adding comments to other team members' information and pages; and recording minutes of meetings in real time. One might think that use of these sorts of ad hoc discussion tools would degenerate into chaos. In truth, this rarely happens, even in a social network of anonymous users. Anderson (2006) talks about the fact that the largest wiki of all, Wikipedia, is fairly resistant to vandalism and ideological battles. He stresses that the reason for this is "the emergent behavior of a Pro-Am (meaning professional and amateur) swarm of self-appointed curators." This group of curators has self-organized what Anderson terms the most comprehensive encyclopedia in history—creating order from chaos. Welcome to the world of "peer production."

Wikis in Action

Intellipedia (https://www.intelink.gov/wiki) is an online system for collaborative data sharing used by the United States Intelligence Community (IC). It consists of three different wikis with different levels of classification: Top Secret, Secret, and Sensitive but Unclassified. They are used by individuals with appropriate clearances from the 16 agencies of the IC and other national-security-related organizations, including Combatant Commands and other federal departments. The wikis are not open to the public

Intellipedia includes information on the regions, people, and issues of interest to the communities using its host networks. Intellipedia uses MediaWiki, the same software used by the Wikipedia free-content encyclopedia project. Officials say that the project will change the culture of the U.S. intelligence community, widely blamed for failing to "connect the dots" before the September 11 attacks.

The Secret version predominantly serves Department of Defense and the Department of State personnel, many of whom do not use the Top Secret network on a day-to-day basis. Users on unclassified networks can access Intellipedia from remote terminals outside their workspaces via a VPN, in addition to their normal workstations. Open Source Intelligence (OSINT) users share information on the unclassified network.

Intellipedia was created to share information on some of the most difficult subjects facing U.S. intelligence and to bring cutting-edge technology into its ever-more-youthful workforce. It also allows information to be assembled and reviewed by a wide variety of sources and agencies, to address concerns that prewar intelligence did not include robust dissenting opinions on Iraq's alleged weapons programs.

Some view Intellipedia as risky because it allows more information to be viewed and shared, but most agree that it is worth the risk. The project was greeted initially with a lot of resistance because it runs counter to past practice, which sought to limit the pooling of information. Some encouragement has been necessary to spur contributions from the traditional intelligence community. However, the system appeals to the new generation of intelligence analysts because this is how they like to work, and it's a new way of thinking.

The wiki provides so much flexibility that several offices throughout the community are using it to maintain and transfer knowledge on daily operations and events. Anyone with access to read it has permission to create and edit articles. Since Intellipedia is intended to be a platform for harmonizing the various points of view of the agencies and analysts of the Intelligence Community, Intellipedia does not enforce a neutral point of view policy. Instead, viewpoints are attributed to the agencies, offices, and individuals participating, with the hope that a consensus view will emerge

During 2006–2007, Intellipedia editors awarded shovels to users to reward exemplary wiki "gardening" and to encourage others in the community to contribute. A template with a picture of the limited-edition shovel (actually a trowel), was created to place on user pages for Intellipedians to show their "gardening" status. The handle bears the imprint: "I dig Intellipedia! It's wiki wiki, Baby." The shovels have since been replaced with a mug bearing the tag line "Intellipedia: it's what we know." Different agencies have experimented with other ways of encouraging participation. For example, at the CIA, managers have held contests for best pages with prizes such as free dinners.

Chris Rasmussen, knowledge management officer at the Defense Department's National Geospatial-Intelligence Agency (NGA), argues that "gimmicks" like the Intellipedia shovel, posters, and handbills encourage people to use Web 2.0 tools like Intellipedia and are effective low-tech solutions to promote their use. Also, Rasmussen argues that social-software-based contributions should be written in an employee's performance plan.

Meaning-Based Computing

Even before the advent of social networking, the sheer amount of data needed to be processed by a worker was overwhelming. Researchers and writers talked about information overload decades ago. Now data is coming in from many more directions, much of it unstructured and unordered (e.g., e-mail, IM, video, audio, etc.). Wall Street technologies have a solution for this sort of data overload. They use powerful computers to speed-read news reports, editorials, company websites, blogs posts, and even Twitter messages. Intelligent software then parses all of this and figures out what it means for the markets. If only we could have smart software like this for our IT-oriented blog, wiki, discussion group, etc., messages!

Autonomy.com is a leader in the movement toward finding a way to add this sort of meaning to this disorganized chaos of data. Termed meaning-based computing, the goal here is to give computers the ability to understand the concepts and context of unstructured data, enabling users to extract value from the data where none could be found before. Meaning-Based Computing systems understand the relationships between seemingly disparate pieces of data and perform complex analyses on that data, usually in real time. Key capabilities of Meaning-Based Computing systems are automatic hyperlinking and clustering, which enables users to be connected to documents, services, and products that are contextually linked to the original text. To be able to automatically collect, analyze, and organize data so that this can be accomplished requires these computer systems to extract meaning.

Autonomy's Meaning-Based Computing platform, IDOL, is capable of processing any type of information from any source. IDOL can aggregate hundreds of file formats, including voice, video, document management systems, e-mail servers, web servers, relational database systems, and file systems.

Google's most recent plans for "augmented humanity" will most certainly give Autonomy.com something to think about. According to Google CEO Eric Schmidt, Google knows pretty much everything about us—that is, "We know roughly who you are, roughly what you care about, roughly who your friends are." Schmidt sees a future where we simply don't forget anything because the computer (read that Google) remembers everything. Some of this already exists if you're using Google Tasks, Contacts, Calendar, and Docs. Your searches too are stored and accessible by Google. If you are using Google e-mail and chat, all of this data lives on Google servers as well. Google's plan is to be able to suggest what you should do based on what your interests or knowledge requirements are. It intends to use this knowledge to suggest ideas and come up with solutions that you might have come up if you did the analysis on your own. Some writers are comparing this eventuality as a clone, or "your own virtual you" (Elgan, 2010). Coupled with Google's new voice synthesizer, which can replicate your voice, it's not too much of a stretch to find that one day you will go on vacation and your clone will give your team a call to set up a project meeting on something you (or it) is working on.

Semantic Web

Google cloning is actually an extension of something that exists today. Tim Berners-Lee, who invented the World Wide Web as well as HTML, also came up the idea of the Semantic Web, as shown in Figure 3.5. The Semantic Web is a synthesis of all corporate and external data, including results from data mining activities, hypermedia, knowledge systems, etc., which uses a common interface that makes data easily accessible by all (e.g. suppliers, customers, employees).

The Semantic Web is sometimes called the Defined Web and is the ultimate repository of all content and knowledge on the web. It uses XML (extensible markup language, a formalized version of HTML) to tag information on intranets, extranets, and the Internet.

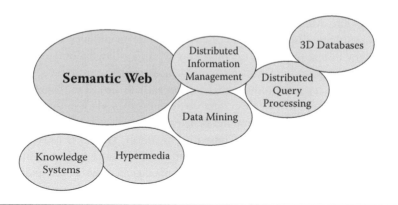

Figure 3.5 The Semantic Web.

Tim Berners-Lee explains the Semantic Web as follows:

> At the doctor's office, Lucy instructed her Semantic Web agent through her handheld Web browser. The agent promptly retrieved information about Mom's *prescribed treatment* from the doctor's agent, looked up several lists of *providers*, and checked for the ones *in-plan* for Mom's insurance within a *20-mile radius* of her *home* and with a *rating* of *excellent* or *very good* on trusted rating services. It then began trying to find a match between available *appointment times* (supplied by the agents of individual providers through their websites) and Pete's and Lucy's busy schedules.

Hewlett-Packard's Semantic Web research group frequently circulates items of interest such as news articles, software tools, and links to websites. They call these snippets, or information nuggets (Cayzer, 2004). Since e-mail is not the ideal medium for this type of content, they needed to find a way to technique for decentralized, informal knowledge management. They began a research project to create a system that was capable of aggregating, annotating, indexing, and searching a community's snippets. The required characteristics of this for this system include

1. Ease of use and capture
2. Decentralized aggregation. Snippets will be in a variety of locations and formats. It will be necessary to integrate them and perform some global search over the result.
3. Distributed knowledge. Information consumers should be able to add value by enriching snippets at the point of use by adding ratings, annotations, etc.

4. Flexible data model. Snippets are polymorphic. The system should be able to handle e-mail, web pages, documents, text fragments, images, etc.
5. Extensible. It should be possible to extend the snippet data schema to model the changing world.
6. Inferencing. It should be possible to infer new metadata from old. For example, a machine should "know" that a snippet about a particular HP Photosmart model is about a digital camera.

Some have suggested that blogs make the idea tool for this type of content and knowledge management. However, today's blogging tools offer only some of the capabilities mentioned. Traditional blogging has many limitations, but the most important limitation is that metadata is used only for headline syndication in a blog. Metadata is not extensible, not linked to a risk-flexible data model, and not capable of supporting vocabulary mixing and inferencing.

The researchers, therefore, looked to the Semantic Web for a solution. As we've discussed, the premise of the Semantic Web is that data can be shared and reused across application, enterprise, and community boundaries. RSS1.0 (web. resource.org/rss/1.0) is a Semantic Web vocabulary that provides a way to express and integrate with rich information models. The Semantic Web standard Resource Description Framework (RDF) specifies a web-scale information modeling format (www.w3.org/RDF). Using these tools, they came up with a prototype (http:// www.semanticfocus.com/blog/) for creating what they called a Semantic Blog. The prototype has some interesting searching capabilities. For example, snippets can be searched for either through their own attributes (e.g., "I'm interested in snippets about HP") or through the attributes of their attached blog entry (e.g., "I'm interested in snippets captured by Bob").

Virtual Worlds

Perhaps the most interesting of all social-based community software is Linden Labs' Second Life (http://www.secondlife.com). Though primarily used for such fun activities as fantasy role-playing (pirates, Goths, sci-fi, and all that), Second Life does have a serious side.

In 2008, IBM's Academy of Technology held a virtual world conference and annual meeting in Second Life, as shown in Figure 3.6. The virtual meeting conference space had room for breakout sessions, a library, and various areas for community gathering. IBM estimates that the ROI for the virtual world conference was about $320,000 and that the annual meeting cost one-fifth that of a real-world event.

Just think of the possibilities. Project team members near and far can use Second Life to hold virtual, but tactile, team meetings and even work with clients.

Figure 3.6   Using Second Life to host a conference.

Knowledge Management Tools

Knowledge management (KM) has been defined as the identification and analysis of available and required knowledge, and the subsequent planning and control of actions, to develop these into "knowledge assets" that will enable a business to generate profits and/or improve its competitive position. The major focus of knowledge management is to identify and gather content from documents, reports, and other sources and to be able to search that content for meaningful relationships. A variety of business intelligence, artificial intelligence, and content management methodologies and tools are the framework under which knowledge management operates.

While we will be discussing the relationship between knowledge management (KM) and social enterprising in more depth later on, it's worthwhile to briefly address the most well-known KM construct now.

Groups of individuals who share knowledge about a common work practice over a period of time, though they are not part of a formally constituted work team, are considered to be "Communities of Practice" (CoP). Communities of Practice generally cut across traditional organizational boundaries. They enable individuals to acquire new knowledge faster. They may also be called communities of interest if the people share an interest in something but do not necessarily perform the work on a daily basis. For example, in one government agency, a group of employees who were actively involved in multiparty, multiissue settlement negotiations began a monthly discussion group during which they explored process issues, discussed lessons learned, and shared tools and techniques. CoPs can be more or less structured depending on the needs of the membership (see Appendix B).

Communities of Practice provide a mechanism for sharing knowledge throughout one organization or across several organizations. They lead to an improved network of organizational contacts, supply opportunities for peer-group recognition, and support continuous learning, all of which reinforce knowledge transfer and contribute to better results. They are valuable for sharing tacit (implicit) knowledge.

To be successful, CoPs require support from the organization. However, if management closely controls their agendas and methods of operation, they are seldom successful. This is more of an issue for Communities of Practice within organizations.

Communities of Practice can be used virtually anywhere within an organization: within one organizational unit or across organizational boundaries, with a small or large group of people, in one geographical location or multiple locations, etc. They can also be used to bring together people from multiple companies, organized around a profession, shared roles, or common issues.

They create value when there is tacit information that, if shared, leads to better results for individuals and the organization. They are also valuable in situations where knowledge is being constantly gained and where sharing this knowledge is beneficial for the accomplishment of the organization's goals.

There are different kinds of CoPs. Some develop best practices, some create guidelines, and others meet to share common concerns, problems, and solutions. They can connect in different ways: face-to-face, in small or large meetings, or electronically. These virtual Communities of Practice called simply VCoPs.

VCoPs (as well as face-to-face CoPs) need a way to capture their collective experiences for online examination. Daimler AG does this using something they call the EBOK system. This is short for Engineering Book of Knowledge. It provides best practice information on pretty much everything related to the manufacture of cars. Tech CoPs share knowledge related across car processes and then consolidate this knowledge in the EBOK system.

CoPs provide a great degree of what academics refer to as "social capital." It is social capital that provides the motivation and commitment required to populate knowledge stores such as EBOK.

One of the more recent advances in CoP methodology is to take it from small team interaction to large-group intervention, although some dispute whether this can be effectively done at all. There have been some experiments where up to 300 people were brought together within a CoP to work through organizational issues. There are a variety of CoP-based designs for groups of this size. The World Café is perhaps the most well known and popular of these designs, which also includes Open Space Technology, Participative Design, and Wisdom Circles.

The World Café (http://www.theworldcafe.com) describes its process this way: it is an innovative yet simple methodology for hosting conversations. These conversations link and build on each other as people move between groups, cross-pollinate ideas, and discover new insights into the questions and issues raised. As a process, the World Café can evoke and make visible the collective intelligence of any group, thus increasing people's capacity for effective action in pursuit of a common aim.

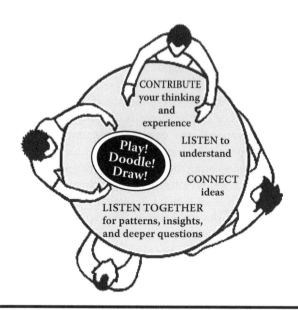

Figure 3.7   The World Café methodology.

In a face-to-face environment, the way to do this is quite simple. Tables are provided where a series of conversational rounds, lasting from 20 to 45 minutes, are held tackling a specific question. Participants are encouraged to write, doddle, or draw key ideas and themes on the tablecloths, as shown in Figure 3.7. At the end of each round, one person remains at the table as the host, while the others travel to new tables. The hosts welcome the newcomers and share the table's conversation so far. The newcomers share what they discussed from the tables they've already visited. And so on. After the last round, participants return to their individual tables to integrate all of this information. At the end of the session, everyone shares and explores emerging themes, insights, and learning. This serves to capture the collective intelligence of the whole (Raelin, 2008).

Visiting the World Café's website demonstrates how they modified this construct to suit the online environment. One of the outputs of this sort of brainstorming session might be a tag cloud, which is a visual depiction of user-generated tags based on discussions. Tags are usually single words and are normally listed alphabetically, and the importance of a tag is shown with font size or colors as shown in Figure 3.8.

Tag clouds were popularized by websites such as Flickr and Technorati. They actually serve a very useful purpose for software engineers providing a way to classify, organize, and prioritize the results of any meetings. Since individual tags can be hyperlinks, it is possible to use this as a way to store increasingly granular levels of information. Perhaps the most well known of cloud tag generators is Wordle (http://www.wordle.net/create).

Figure 3.8   Tag cloud.

Mashups

Web developers have long been engaged in what is known as service composition. This is the practice of creating value-added services by reusing existing service components. Mashups are a new emerging paradigm of Web 2.0 that enables developers, and even more talented end users, to create new web-based applications and services that address specific needs and interests.

The term *mashup* implies fast integration. This is done using open APIs and data sources to produce enriched results that were not necessarily the original reason for producing the raw source data. Mashup tools generally support visual wiring of GUI widgets, services, and components together.

Some tech leaders have since discontinued their mashup tool offerings (Microsoft Popfly in 2009 and Google Mashup Editor in 2009). However, Yahoo! Pipes (http://pipes.yahoo.com/pipes/) is still being supported. As Yahoo! describes it:

Pipes is a free online service that lets you remix popular feed types and create data mashups using a visual editor. You can use Pipes to run your own web projects, or publish and share your own web services without ever having to write a line of code. You make a Pipe by dragging pre-configured modules onto a canvas and wiring them together in the Pipes Editor. Each Pipe consists of two or more modules, each of which performs a single, specific task. For example, the Fetch module will retrieve a feed URL, while the Sort module will re-order a feed based on criteria you provide (you can find a complete list of available modules in the documentation.) You can wire modules together by clicking on one module's output terminal and dragging the wire to another module's input terminal. Once the terminals are wired together the output from the first module will serve as input to the second module. In addition to data feeds, Pipes also lets you add user input fields into your Pipe. These show up at runtime as form fields that users of your Pipe can fill in.

JackBe Corporation is a privately held software provider of enterprise mashup software. JackBe's flagship product is an Enterprise Mashup Platform called Presto (http://www.jackbe.com/products/), with support for Microsoft SharePoint. Jackbe launched its Enterprise App Store product in July 2010 as a platform for creating internal enterprise application stores. The Enterprise App Store is primarily aimed at nondevelopers, allowing them to create new business applications and then share them with other users. JackBe is a founding member of the Open Mashup Alliance (OMA), which promotes enterprise mashup interoperability and portability. JackBe was the original contributor and continues to be a key supporter of the OMA's Enterprise Mashup Markup Language (EMML).

EMML is an XML markup language for creating enterprise mashups. These are software applications that consume and mash data from variety of sources, often performing logical or mathematical operations as well as presenting data. Mashed data produced by enterprise mashups are presented in graphical user interfaces as mashlets, widgets, or gadgets. EMML is an open language specification that is promoted by the Open Mashup Alliance.

EMML is fairly easy to understand and use, as it is a derivative of the now familiar XML markup language. For example, the EMML code below joins Yahoo! News, Financial News, and Reuters feeds.

```
<merge inputvariables="$YahooRSS, $FinancialNewsRss, $ReutersRSS"
  outputvariable="$NewsAggregate"/>
```

Detailed documentation for EMML can be found on the Open Mashup Alliance website (http://www.openmashup.org/omadocs/v1.0/index.html).

Key Point

As you can see, there are a wide variety of tools out there that can support social enterprising. There are three methodologies to choose from when making the platform decision: (1) off the shelf, (2) mashup, and (3) build your own. This chapter has provided information that will get you started moving in the direction that is the most suitable for your organization.

References

Anderson, C. (2006). *The long tail.* New York: Hyperion.

Cayzer, S. (2004, December). Semantic blogging and decentralized knowledge management. *Communications of the ACM, 47*(12): 47–52.

Elgan, M. (2010, December 4). How Google plans to clone you. *Computerworld.* Retrieved from http://www.computerworld.com/s/article/9199638.

Raelin, J.A. (2008). *Work-based learning: Bridging knowledge and action in the workplace.* San Francisco: Jossey-Bass.

Chapter 4

Managing Knowledge through Social Enterprising

Social enterprising is based on effective knowledge management. So, it's worthwhile spending a bit of time delving into this paradigm so that you can fully appreciate this important relationship.

Knowledge management can be defined as the processes which support knowledge collection, sharing, and dissemination. The expectations for knowledge management are that it should be able to improve growth and innovation, productivity and efficiency reflected in cost savings, customer relationships, decision making, innovation, corporate agility, rapid development of new product lines, employee learning, satisfaction and retention, and management decision. Interestingly, these are the same expectations for social enterprising.

Many senior managers emphasize knowledge management as an important means of innovation. In organizations, it is essential to address effective knowledge flow among employees, as well as knowledge collaboration across organizational boundaries, while limiting knowledge sharing.

It is estimated that an organization with 1,000 workers might easily incur a cost of more than $6 million per year in lost productivity when employees fail to find existing knowledge and recreate knowledge that was available but could not be located. On average, 6% of revenue, as a percentage of budget, is lost from failure to exploit available knowledge.

Since knowledge is a key strategic asset for organizations of all sizes, it follows that knowledge management is critically important as it is the set of tools and processes that manages organizational knowledge. However, there are many knowledge management implementation problems. A key reason for lack of knowledge management viability is the unwillingness of employees to share their knowledge effectively with their teammates, the real focus of this chapter.

> *I have noticed that people have problems sharing with me. I always assumed that the reason was to protect their position. In other words, "knowledge is power." If they give away their knowledge, they give away their power. That was my working assumption. My peers and I would discuss, "why are they so reluctant to share information with us?" It was because they were protecting the keys to the kingdom. This was usually the older employees, who had a lot of seniority and a lot of knowledge. They didn't want to be taken over.*

Knowledge Worker

The modern work team might be agile, matrixed, or even virtual. Since teams may have different team members at different times, problems might arise as a result of this. There are four possible problems:

1. Loss of knowledge. The longer someone stays on a team, the more knowledge he or she acquires about the project, the problem domain, and the stakeholders. Loss of a team member means loss of experience and knowledge. The best approach to dealing with this problem is to make sure that the team has at least some stable team members.
2. Thinking differently. When a group of people work for any length of time together, they develop a way of synched thinking. New team members might need a bit of time to adapt to this sort of shared thinking. Use of knowledge management system and social networking technologies (e.g., knowledge bases, wikis, blogs) can greatly accelerate a new team member's trip along the learning curve.
3. Low commitment. If you know that you're a short termer on a team, it might be difficult to drum up the enthusiasm to be totally committed to that team's efforts. Motivation is the key to solving this problem. Reward systems are one method to overcome low commitment. Both positive and negative rewards can be used. While positive reward systems (e.g., days off, bonus pay, etc.) are most commonly used, negative reinforcement approaches should be considered as well.
4. Lack of cohesion. Team members might experience problems in building a sense of identification with a team whose membership is constantly changing. One solution to this is to find a way for workers identify with other people at the same company who do the same job. Some refer to these as practice centers. This is a derivative of the knowledge management technique of community of practice, where workers join together across organizational lines to discuss common goals.

Knowledge workers are considered to be the intellectual capital of a company and a key factor in its sustainable development. Managers must be able to embed more knowledge value in their decisions in order to produce a new, improved, or even better alternative than their competitors. Therefore, knowledge management has become a strategic tool in most organizations.

Siemens is an example of a company that has fully adopted knowledge management as a strategic tool. At Siemens, knowledge is regarded as the means for effective action. At companies like Siemens, knowledge management systems are considered socio-technical systems. These systems encompass competence building, emphasis on collaboration, ability to support diverse technology infrastructures, use of partnerships, and knowledge codification for all documents, processes, and systems.

Siemens is widely known as a company built on technology and was an early adopter of knowledge management. The company's goal is to share existing knowledge in a better way and to create new knowledge more quickly. Siemens' holistic approach clearly demonstrates the importance of people, collaboration, culture, leadership, and support. Absence of these critical success factors would reduce the likelihood of knowledge sharing success.

Knowledge Management and Knowledge Sharing

Knowledge can be defined as a fluid mix of framed experiences, values, contextual information, and expert insight that provides a framework for evaluation and incorporating new experiences and information. In an organization, it is embedded in the minds of its employees, as well as in organizational routines, processes, practices, and norms, sometimes referred to as socially constructed templates.

The realization of organizational knowledge depends on people who interpret, organize, plan, develop, and execute those socially constructed templates. Most importantly, organizational knowledge depends on specific situations and does not always depend on absolute truths or quantitative facts. Thus, one can conclude that organizational knowledge has some soft features, which are related to the subtle, implicit, embedded, sometimes invisible knowledge, presumptions, values, and ways of thinking that permeate an employee's behavior, decisions, and his or her actions. Ultimately, organizational knowledge is complex and always ambiguous.

Effective management of these ambiguous layers of knowledge in organizations is a primary factor for success in the knowledge economy, where harvesting knowledge is a key to remaining competitive and innovative.

Knowledge is a well-organized combination of information, assimilated within a set of rules, procedures, and operations learned through experience and practice. Knowledge can be categorized as either tacit or explicit. Explicit knowledge is knowledge that can be seen, shared, and easily communicated to others. Most explicit knowledge is in the form of raw data, such as documents that contain the work experiences of staff, descriptions of events, interpretations of data, beliefs, guesses, hunches, ideas, opinions, judgment, and proposed actions.

Tacit knowledge is more difficult to share because it is embedded in a person's memory. Tacit knowledge is often described as what we know but cannot explain. Tacit knowledge is (a) embodied in mental processes; (b) originates from practices and experiences; (c) expressed through ability applications; and (d) transferred in the form of learning by doing and watching. Knowing how to solve a problem using tacit knowledge is, therefore, a matter of personal interpretation, ability, and skill. Sharing and internalizing tacit knowledge requires active interaction among individuals, using knowledge management techniques, such as storytelling.

Knowledge management is a broad discipline, one that can be subdivided into several themes: knowledge management procedures, knowledge management techniques, knowledge management technologies and knowledge sharing issues, the last of which has ramifications for successful social enterprising.

Knowledge sharing can be compared to organizational citizenship behavior or pro-social organizational behavior. These are positive social acts carried out to produce and maintain the well-being and integrity of others. Pro-social behaviors include acts such as helping, sharing, donating, cooperating, and volunteering. Knowledge sharing is not necessarily synonymous with prosocial behavior. Indeed, knowledge sharing may involve significant effort or sacrifice. Yet, one of the critical success factors for knowledge creation, transfer, and sharing is that employees willingly contribute their knowledge or expertise to the company.

For the most part knowledge-sharing barriers can be categorized into three dimensions: (a) individual, (b) organizational and (c) technological. A study of 1,180 staff members in the regional transport union determined that its culture was not conducive to knowledge sharing for a variety of reasons, including (a) no support systems, (b) lack of training, (c) job security, (d) employee competition, (e) organizational culture, and (f) lack of recognition.

There is also a relationship between group compatibility and knowledge sharing. The more compatible a person is with the group in terms of age, gender, and other factors, the more likely he or she is to practice knowledge sharing. Conversely, individuals who perceive themselves in a minority (e.g., gender, marital status, education, etc.) are less likely to participate in knowledge sharing. Of particular note is the finding that women participants required a more positive social interaction culture before they perceive a knowledge-sharing culture as positive. The list of compatibility variables includes more than just the obvious traits of age, gender, ethnicity, and educational level. Personality differences, communication skills, and individual values also factored into the equation.

Interestingly, there is also a relationship between organizational tenure and knowledge sharing. A long organizational tenure has a negative effect on knowledge sharing. One employee commented that he felt he was being asked to give himself away when asked to share his knowledge. There are many reasons for this type of fear. For example, long-term employees might feel threatened by those they consider to be possible replacements for their positions or they might feel a level of discomfort in dealing with newer, and often younger, arrivals.

Several studies employed age as one of many variables. For the most part, researchers noted that the more *age compatible* a team is, the more likely the team will engage in effective knowledge sharing. However, there will often be teams where age diversity is present. Older workers are sometimes technology resistant or, as discussed earlier, may feel threatened by younger employees they consider rivals. A more proactive management style is recommended toward older employees to facilitate successful use of knowledge management.

Cross-Cultural Differences

There are cross-cultural differences in knowledge-sharing patterns based on three criteria: individualism versus collectivism, in-group versus out-group orientation, and fear of losing face. Individualism is the tendency of people to place their personal goals ahead of the goals of the organization's, while individuals from collectivist cultures tend to give priority to the goals of the larger collective, group, or company to which they belong. Essentially, members of individualist cultures, like the United States, view themselves as independent of others, whereas members of collectivist cultures (e.g., China, Brazil, and Russia) see themselves as interdependent with other members of their group.

Collectivists tend to distinguish sharply between in-group and out-group members. For example, some researchers have compared factors influencing knowledge-sharing behaviors between American and Chinese managers and found that Chinese nationals were much more reluctant to share with an out-group member than employees in the United States were. Individualists are generally more concerned with gaining face (i.e., impressing colleagues) than collectivists. Individuals who want to gain face are more likely to use formal communications channels to show their knowledge and ability, while those who fear losing face prefer informal communication channels. This has ramifications for use of formal knowledge-sharing systems (e.g., intranets, blackboards, social networks, etc.) because collectivists might resist using these technologies.

Organizational Culture's Effect on Knowledge Sharing

Organizational culture is the shared values, beliefs, and practices of people in an organization. Beyond the mission statement and stated values of the organization lies a deeper level of culture. This is embedded in the way people act, what they expect of each other, and how they make sense of each other's actions. Culture is rooted in core values and assumptions and is taken for granted, and is therefore often hard to articulate. Essentially, some aspects of organizational culture are confusing or even invisible to organization members.

In some organizations, there is a low awareness or realization of the value and benefit of possessed knowledge to others. Hierarchical, position-based status, and formal power issues might also act as inhibitors. In other organizations, there might be a general lack of time and resources to share knowledge. Organizational culture-related barriers can be categorized as follows: organizational relationships, organizational climate, organizational structuring, and organizational imperative.

Organizational culture influences knowledge-related behaviors in four ways: (a) culture, particularly subcultures, heavily influences what is perceived as useful, important, or valid knowledge in an organization; (b) culture mediates the relationship between levels of knowledge; that is, it dictates what belongs to the organization and what knowledge remains in control of the individual employee, determining who is expected to control specific knowledge as well as who must share it and who can hoard it; (c) culture creates a subtext for social interaction in that it represents the rules and practices that determine the environment within which people communicate, that is, the cultural ground rules; and (d) culture shapes the creation and adoption of new knowledge. Thus, organizational culture (and its related subcultures) affects the level of collaboration within an organization, and it is collaboration that is the key to successful knowledge sharing.

The collaborative climate is one of the major factors influencing the effectiveness of knowledge programs as it improves knowledge sharing and organizational effectiveness. A culture audit should be conducted to determine the extent to which organizational culture exhibits the cultural values of collaboration, empowerment, action taking, and informality.

Collaboration in most organizations usually takes the form of teaming. Team performance increases with the amount of knowledge that employees share. However, it should be noted that a positive relationship exists between individual self-interest concerns (e.g., competition, job security) and reduction in knowledge-sharing intentions.

There is a relationship between apprehension or fear that sharing might compromise or jeopardize job security and a reluctance to share knowledge. Knowledge sharing does impose costs on knowledge contributors. Under intensive competition for rewards, status, and promotions, employees often regard their unique knowledge as power in the organization. If others gain power, they fear they will lose power within the organization. It takes a great deal of trust to make an employee share this level of power. Ultimately, successful teams do overcome these fears. This might be attributed to the concept of workplace ethics, where knowledge sharing is considered the right thing to do.

Some companies might be tempted to reward knowledge-sharing behavior as a spur to successful collaboration and teaming. However, most companies do not provide individual rewards based solely on the ability to learn or to share knowledge. Interestingly, researchers find no relationship between the use of rewards and knowledge sharing. Promoting a positive attitude toward knowledge sharing causes a positive intention to share knowledge. There are a multitude of opinions on reward systems. Some recommend that the group, rather than the individual, be rewarded. Some experts think that extrinsic motivation is not an influential variable at all; thus, it should not be necessary to establish reward systems. These experts suggest that more effort should be given to reinforce employee absorptive capacity (i.e., the ability to acquire, assimilate, and use knowledge) and knowledge transmission mechanisms. Employees with closely aligned knowledge bases should work together more frequently for knowledge sharing. Greater learning performance resulting from their large absorptive capacity will lead to favorable attitudes toward knowledge sharing and outstanding sharing achievement.

Organizational factors, such as hierarchy, power, available resources, support, reward systems and, ultimately, attitude about knowledge sharing, could either impede or promote knowledge-sharing behaviors. Much of the literature stresses the potentially negative effects of power and organizational politics on the role that social capital plays in knowledge sharing. The effects of power are actually very diverse, making it a highly complex factor in knowledge sharing.

IT Support's Effect on Knowledge Sharing

Knowledge management systems are often driven by technology. Studies continually find that there is a relationship between IT support and the *perceived* relative advantage (i.e., the degree to which knowledge sharing was perceived to benefit the conduct of business) of knowledge sharing and the perceived compatibility (i.e., fits into the business process). Most importantly, there is a positive relationship between the level of information technology usage by the individual and his or her knowledge-sharing behavior. There are a wide variety of technologies thought to be knowledge-sharing and knowledge management enablers. These include ontologies, document retrieval software, groupware, intranets, knowledge-based systems, pointers to people, decision support systems, data mining, and intelligent agents—all the stuff of social networking. However, it is important to understand that organizations cannot expect uniformity in the ways in which different groups will use knowledge management tools.

A social enterprising IT infrastructure would include (a) knowledge repositories, which are databases that allow the storage and retrieval of knowledge; (b) best-practices and lessons-learned systems, which are knowledge repositories used specifically for the explication, storage, and retrieval of business best practices and in making lessons learned available to others; (c) expert networks, which are networks of individuals identified as experts and electronically accessible by others who have questions related to that expertise; (d) Communities of Practice, which are electronically enabled networks of self-organizing groups whose members share professional interests.

It is important to stress that a poor understanding of the relationships between sources of knowledge and users of knowledge, which often overlap, can result in one of two extremes: the focus on IT as the only tool or not dedicating an IT resource at all. It is feasible that cultural implications could result in IT systems that are not compatible with the environment within the organization and its structure.

Knowledge management can certainly be mismanaged from a technology perspective. The key factors here are technological ignorance, technical over-complexity, lack of technical infrastructure scalability (i.e., inability to support the required volume of users), and techno-bias (i.e., believing that technology can solve all problems).

Few new technologies are extensively used by employees who have not received training or support from management. There have been cases in which employees had no incentives to use a new system; in fact, they were afraid of giving away their expertise to colleagues who might use this knowledge to get promoted instead of them.

There are a wide variety of information technologies that fit within the knowledge management rubric. However, a variety of factors can lead to success or failure of such technology implementations, such as training, management support or even age, gender, and culture of the employees.

Techniques for Promoting Knowledge Sharing

It is a good idea to map knowledge flows across the various boundaries in an organization to yield critical insights into where management should target efforts to promote collaboration. Four relational qualities were found to promote effective knowledge sharing. Knowing what someone else knows (knowledge) is a precursor to seeking out a specific person when faced with a problem for which a solution is needed. However, knowing to whom to turn is only useful if one can gain access to that person in a timely manner. Access is influenced by the closeness of one's relationship as well as physical proximity, organizational design, and use of collaborative technology. Once access is made available, knowledge can only be shared if the expert understands the problem as experienced by the person seeking assistance (engagement). At this point, the expert can shape his or her knowledge to help solve the problem at hand. Finally, the safety of the person seeking knowledge is of utmost concern. Being able to admit a lack of knowledge and seek out assistance results in creativity and learning.

It is particularly important to identify points of knowledge creation and sharing that hold strategic relevance. Example domains that might yield this sort of benefit include senior management networks, collaborative initiatives, joint ventures and alliances, and Communities of Practice.

Communities of Practice are a common knowledge-sharing or transfer technique. In a Community of Practice, groups of individuals share knowledge about a common work practice over a period of time, although they are not part of a formally constituted work team. Communities of Practice often cut across traditional organizational boundaries. The purpose of this organizational structure is to enable individuals to acquire new knowledge more quickly. Des Moines-based Weitz Company uses Communities of Practice as a way of enabling its workforce, which exhibited a wide diversity in ages, to collaborate more effectively. Weitz invested in its employees through a variety of methods, including job rotation, shadowing programs, executive internships, and mentoring. However, older Weitz employees were suspicious that the mentoring program was designed to drain their experience before terminating them. To counter this negative feeling about mentoring, Weitz created Communities of Practice in which junior and senior employees came together to share best practices; thus, the senior employees were not just offloading knowledge.

A viable framework for creating an organization-wide knowledge-sharing information culture should include sources of knowledge, organizational learning, and business process reengineering. Organizations should provide basic resources like technology. Once the resources are made available, the organization must ensure that the basic resources are turned into a competence, that is, employees understand how to exploit these resources. Most importantly, organizational learning must be embedded in the organization. It is imperative to recognize that an organization's workforce is more than merely a collection of expert individuals. These experts must hone their skills to adapt and distribute their expertise through official and unofficial networks.

There is a major benefit from knowledge that flows freely throughout the organization. However, a variety of cultural, social, and technological barriers often limit effective flow of knowledge among workers. Age is one variable affecting knowledge sharing. In a team, persons of similar ages are likely to band together and interact more freely within the subgroup. It should also be noted that individuals who perceive themselves as being in a minority are less likely to participate in team-level knowledge-sharing processes.

The key is that management cannot just expect knowledge sharing to occur on its own. Rather, management must be the instigator of knowledge sharing within the organization.

Worker Study

I decided to put all of this to the test and interviewed 21 typical employees over the course of a one-month period. The major research questions that were addressed were as follows:

1. What are the cultural reasons that employees resist the sharing of knowledge?
2. What are the organizational reasons that employees resist the sharing of knowledge?
3. What are the key reasons employees list for not wanting to share their expertise?

The sample for this study consisted of highly educated knowledge workers with lengthy tenure within the industry and some with lengthy tenure in their organizations. This expertise was readily evidenced during the interviews. The participants were uniformly cooperative and reflective. They were knowledgeable on the subject of knowledge management and fully understood the ramifications of knowledge sharing or lack of knowledge sharing. All articulated the importance of knowledge sharing to the organization and to them. Appendix H provides the details of responses to each question.

A variety of factors affected the willingness to share knowledge in the sample population, as shown in Figure 4.1. Workers first needed to feel secure in their jobs. They needed to know that the act of sharing knowledge with their co-workers would not endanger their job in any way. Perhaps, more importantly, office politics had the potential to become a barrier to effective collaboration and knowledge sharing, dampening any eagerness for knowledge sharing. One participant even mentioned the survivor-type mentality in her office, an allusion to popular television shows where teams are pitted against teams.

Trust, respect, and comfort were mentioned as variables that also affected the willingness to share knowledge. It was stated that workers needed to trust and respect their co-workers. Given the diversity of the modern organization, one of the most important factors that affected willingness to share knowledge was the level of comfort in dealing with others. If there were language or cultural barriers, that level of comfort did not effectively exist, thereby, diminishing the level of effective knowledge sharing.

More than a few of the participants in the sample indicated that they simply did not have sufficient time to share knowledge; they were too busy getting their

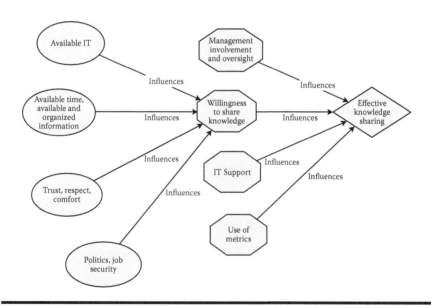

Figure 4.1   Key factors affecting knowledge sharing.

base-level work completed. Several of the participants also complained about the lack of knowledge organization within their companies. Essentially, they felt that it was difficult to find the information they needed so that they could effectively collaborate and share knowledge.

Lack of available information technology assets was another factor affecting willingness to share knowledge. Modern collaborative software, such as lessons learned databases, wikis, and other technologies, were simply not available to them. One of the participants complained about the post-9/11 enforced security restrictions that effectively rendered his network useless.

Willingness to share knowledge, discussed in the last section, is just one of four factors that affect effective knowledge sharing. The other three factors are (a) management involvement and oversight, (b) IT support, and (c) use of metrics.

Many of the participants indicated that their senior management was not actively involved in promoting knowledge management within the company; in fact, knowledge management was not mentioned at all. Other participants indicated that their senior managers stated they supported knowledge management but did little else to promote it or did little to integrate it into the organization's performance management and measurement programs. One participant suggested that one way a company could promote a more effective knowledge-sharing atmosphere was to utilize metrics to measure how it was used, when it was used, and how effective it was.

Finally, IT support was seen as critical to effective knowledge sharing. In some instances, the IT department was seen as the barrier, effectively limiting what information could be shared across teams and among members of teams. In other cases, IT was castigated for not providing modern technologies that supported knowledge sharing (e.g., wikis, whiteboards, etc.).

Figure 4.2 lists the technologies being used by the participants and the technologies that they desired to use.

It was noted that face-to-face (f2f) is still the predominant method of knowledge sharing, with e-mail coming in a close second.

Chat was less popular than expected, although many project leaders used it with their younger project teams, but not without some complaints.

However, in all cases, technology was a fundamental component of the way information was transferred within these organizations. In many cases, the participants recommended more cutting-edge technologies, such as blogs and wikis—the stuff of social networking, although none of them seemed to be aware of the many knowledge-sharing technologies and techniques available to them. Information technology (IT) support, therefore, can be said to be a critical factor in effective knowledge sharing.

The research uncovered a moderate relationship between education and knowledge sharing. While the majority of participants felt that education did not impact knowledge sharing, some of the participants felt that the higher the educational level, the more likely it was that the person would share knowledge; the lower the

	Technology desired	Technology used
Participant 1	0	f2f, online forums, email, wiki
Participant 10	blogs	email, wiki
Participant 11	wiki	f2f, bulletin board
Participant 12	0	email
Participant 13	0	f2f email, chat, whiteboard
Participant 14	wiki, repository	f2f
Participant 15	whiteboard	Sharepoint, intranet, email, cellphone
Participant 16	0	f2f, email
Participant 17	0	f2f, whiteboard
Participant 18	0	email, chat, WebEx
Participant 19	0	f2f, email, chat, intranet
Participant 2	0	email, web-based conferences, f2f
Participant 20	0	email
Participant 21	0	email
Participant 3	wiki	chat
Participant 4	0	f2f, email, web pages
Participant 5	0	f2f, email, conference calls
Participant 6	0	chat
Participant 7	0	phone, email
Participant 8	0	f2f
Participant 9	0	email, f2f, shared drive

Figure 4.2   Technology desired and in use in sample organizations.

educational level, the less likely the person would share knowledge, possibly due to fear that they could lose the only thing that made them valuable to the company.

The research uncovered a more definite relationship between age and knowledge sharing and ethnicity and knowledge sharing. Some participants felt that there was a divide between older and younger workers, with the younger workers less willing to share with older workers. Other participants indicated that senior workers, who tended to be more mature in years, felt threatened by younger workers and, as a result, did not share knowledge with them. As one participant put it, "They don't want to be taken over."

Another participant brought up an interesting issue concerning the fact that younger people are more technologically adept. For example, younger people used text messaging to stay in constant communication. Like many of the older participants, this participant preferred face-to-face and e-mail communications and feared that his lack of "technological savvy" in terms of communication mediums might keep him out of the loop.

The research found that ethnicity was somewhat a factor in knowledge sharing. The ability to understand what was being communicated and cultural mores in terms of the way different groups communicated, as well as work ethic, were cited as barriers to knowledge sharing by the participants.

Trust, comfort, and respect figured prominently in the interviews. The participants uniformly asserted that these three factors needed to be present in the cultural mix if knowledge sharing was to be successful in their organizations.

It was expected that corporate culture would have an impact on willingness to share knowledge. There were a wide variety of variables influencing this relationship: trust, management commitment, involvement, perception, rewards, leadership, resources provided, job title, tenure, and others.

The study found that there were a variety of organizational factors that either supported or impeded effective knowledge sharing within an organization. These included (a) job security, (b) use of metrics, (c) organizing (d) office politics, (e) lack of time, (f) organizational, and management issues, and (g) IT support.

Several of the participants indicated that the issue of job security was twofold, including fear of losing face if others disagreed or one provided incorrect information and the desire to control a particular situation or people by sharing or withholding information.

Office politics was another factor discussed by many of the participants. Politics could have a corrosive effect, particularly if management spearheaded the political problem or overlooked it. Lack of time and inability to organize the vast information stores these organizations possess were also cited as factors that inhibited the effective sharing of knowledge. At least one participant advised that the only way knowledge sharing could be effective was to add it to the goals of the organization and to measure its use.

Organizational issues related to management generated the most discussion. The research found that many of those in charge of companies did not effectively promote knowledge sharing. Some did not endorse it at all (e.g., by omission), and some paid it lip service but did not provide the support required for this effort. All of the participants pointed to the technology tools in use at their organizations. These ran the gamut from e-mail to collaborative whiteboards. Some of the participants pointed out problems in using these technologies, including high-level security infrastructures that precluded easy sharing of files and "being behind the curve" in the use of technologies. It was also expected that IT support would have an impact on willingness to share knowledge.

A variety of factors affected the willingness to share knowledge in the sample population. Workers first needed to feel secure in their jobs. They needed to know that the act of sharing knowledge with their co-workers would not endanger their job in any way. Perhaps, more importantly, office politics had the potential to become a barrier to effective collaboration and knowledge sharing, dampening any eagerness for knowledge sharing. One participant even mentioned the survivor-type mentality in her office, an allusion to the popular television shows where teams were pitted against teams.

Trust, respect and comfort were mentioned as variables that also affected a tendency towards willingness to share knowledge. It was stated that workers needed to trust and respect their co-workers. Given the diversity of the modern organization, one of the most important factors that affected willingness to share knowledge was the level of comfort in dealing with others. If there were a language or cultural barriers, that level of comfort did not effectively exist, thereby, diminishing the level of effective knowledge sharing.

More than a few of the participants in the sample indicated that they simply did not have sufficient time to share knowledge; they were too busy getting their base-level work completed. Several of the participants also complained about the lack of knowledge organization within their companies. Essentially, they felt that it was difficult to find the information they needed so that they could effectively collaborate and share knowledge.

Lack of available information technology assets was another factor in affecting willingness to share knowledge. Modern collaborative software, such as lessons learned databases, wikis and other technologies, were simply not available to them. One of the participants complained about the post-9/11 enforced security restrictions that effectively rendered his network useless.

Willingness to share knowledge was just one of four factors that affected effective knowledge sharing. The other three factors were: (a) management involvement and oversight, (b) IT support, and (c) use of metrics.

Many of the participants indicated that their senior management was not actively involved in promoting knowledge management within the company (i.e., knowledge management was not mentioned at all). Other participants indicated that their senior managers stated that they supported knowledge management but did little else to promote it or to integrate it into the organization's performance management and measurement programs. One participant suggested that one way a company could promote a more effective knowledge-sharing atmosphere was to utilize metrics to measure how it was used, when it was used and how effective it was.

Finally, IT support was seen as critical to effective knowledge sharing. In some instances, the IT department was seen as the barrier, effectively limiting what information could be shared across teams and among members of teams. In other cases, IT was castigated for not providing the modern technologies that supported knowledge sharing (e.g., wikis, whiteboards, etc.). It should be noted, however, that some participants indicated that IT fully supported the move into these technologies. IT support, therefore, could be a critical factor in effective knowledge sharing.

The expectations for knowledge management, and by definition knowledge sharing, are that it would be able to improve growth and innovation; productivity and efficiency reflected in cost savings; customer relationships; employee learning, satisfaction, and retention; and management decision making. Knowledge sharing could meet these goals if it were embedded in the organization using a bottom-up approach, rather than a top-down approach. Top-down approaches were usually forced upon employees and, hence, resisted or, at least, ignored. The bottom-up approach is somewhat akin to viral marketing, where one person becomes enthusiastic about a product or service and tells someone who tells someone else. By providing the tools, methodologies, training, and support on a unit or departmental level, employees are encouraged to capture, share, and archive their knowledge for the good of the organization.

However, knowledge management needs to have a focus. A number of techniques can be used to disseminate knowledge sharing practices:

1. Don't force people to adapt. They must be self-motivated.
2. Change the job of knowledge professionals. Enable everyone to carry on the task of knowledge management.
3. Consider localized knowledge bases. There is no reason why employees cannot store their domain of knowledge in their own private databases. Respect the privacy and confidentiality of people's personal information. People do not like to share what gives them their own personal competitive edge.
4. Help people connect to experts inside and outside the organization.

The current emphasis on a Balanced Scorecard and performance management and measurement might also be used as a lever to further embed knowledge sharing within an organization. A Balanced Scorecard had four perspectives to define: a set of objectives, measures, targets, and initiatives to achieve the goals of that perspective. While the learning and growth perspective was a natural fit for knowledge sharing, the remaining perspectives should also be considered. Adding goals, metrics, and others for knowledge-sharing activities is a sure way to get these departments at least to consider usage within the department.

Recommendations for Making It Work

It seems like there are so many different places where people have to go to find stuff. We're in the process of doing a consolidation and putting it on Sharepoint, but it's a tough transition right now. We're learning this product. They call it New Source. Trying to get all information on Sharepoint so people don't have to go to multiple destinations. So much knowledge within organization, people in every tenure are learning stuff every day, so it does take a while to get up to speed to find out where the knowledge is in the organization.

Given the team-focused nature of work, collaboration and knowledge sharing is necessary if a worker expects to achieve success. A good example of this was the 2006 Netflix challenge. The company offered a million dollar award to the person or team that was able to create a movie-recommending algorithm 10% better than its own. The competitors were startlingly open about the methods they were using. One even posted a complete description of his algorithm for all to see. When asked about this surprising openness, given the million dollar prize, the general response was that the primary prize was learning and interacting with other teams.

In 2006, IBM took this to the next level. In that year over 150,000 people from 104 countries participated in the IBM Innovation Jam. IBM has been "jamming" with employees since 2001, but decided to open this collaborative brainstorming session to the public. Since 2001, IBM jams, the goal of which is to review and reexamine their core values, have created a number of products and services:

1. Smart Health Care Payment System
2. Simplified Business Engines
3. Intelligent Transportation Business
4. Digital Me

Digital Me, which simplifies secure, managed, and long-term access to personal content, was utilized by the designers of the popular *Despicable Me* animated movie to enable collaborative digital media content.

Given the evident procollaboration nature of technology workers, it is suggested that this population be more thoroughly studied to determine ways in which this mindset might be transferred to other categories of knowledge workers. To promote knowledge sharing, senior management must take a more proactive and visible role in supporting the development of a knowledge management framework within their organizations. The most important aspect of this framework is the design of a process for creating and sharing knowledge. Not only should a vision and mission be developed similar to other strategic efforts, but incentives that will influence others to adopt this vision and mission must be determined. Incentives can be in the form of compensation, promotions, or giveaways. Performance measurement was also a critical success factor, as some of the study's interview participants suggested. In the Balanced Scorecard scenario, a company organized its business goals into discrete, all-encompassing perspectives: Financial, Customer, Internal Process, and Learning/Growth. The company then determined cause-effect relationships, e.g., satisfied customers bought more goods, which increased revenue. Next, the company listed measures for each goal, pinpointed targets, and identified projects and other initiatives to help reach those targets. Departments create scorecards tied to the company's targets and employees, and projects have scorecards tied to their department's targets. This cascading nature provides a line of sight between individuals, what they are working on, the unit they support, and how that impacts the strategy of the whole enterprise. Table 4.1 provides a list of recommended metrics from a sample of knowledge management artifacts.

The interviews uncovered some of the techniques that participants were using or wished to use to promote effective knowledge sharing. There are many ways

Table 4.1   Recommended Knowledge Sharing Metrics

KM Initiative	Key System Measures
Best practice directory	Number of downloads
	Number of users
	Number of contributions
	Contribution rate
Lessons learned database	Number of downloads
	Number of users
	Total number of contributions
	Contribution rate
Communities of Practice or special interest groups	Number of contributions
	Frequency of update
	Number of members
	Number of members versus number of contributors
Expert or expertise directory	Number of site accesses
	Frequency of use
	Number of contributions
	Contribution/update rate over time
Portal	Searching precision and recall
	Usability survey
Collaborative systems	Latency during collaborative process
	Number of users

for an organization to identify, store, and transfer knowledge. Some strategies will work better in one organization than another. Some may not be appropriate for specific types of content. The challenge is to identify and develop complementary ways to further knowledge management and transfer in an organization. Some of these techniques were addressed in Chapter 3 (e.g., storytelling, CoPs, etc.).

Knowledge management requires the use of computer technologies to effectively support knowledge sharing and collaboration. All participants in this study had access to e-mail, which is now universally available. However, not everyone had access to the newer collaborative technologies, such as whiteboards, corporate intranets, and innovative products such as Cisco's Telepresence. Electronic whiteboards permit two or more employees to work together synchronously on a project artifact (e.g., memo, plan, specification), even if they are thousands of miles apart.

Some of the newer software that has entered the market has been geared to the knowledge-sharing paradigm. One of the study participants discussed the use of Basecamp (http://www.basecamphq.com/). This project management software enables collaboration on internal and client projects. More importantly, the Basecamp software enables the creation of threads, where each project can be discussed online via a web-based client.

While corporate intranets are becoming increasingly popular, for the most part, they are used for human resources activities (e.g., 401k, schedule vacation time, payroll). Since the corporate intranet is web enabled and available to employees, including those not on-site, this is the perfect venue for the databases and discussion boards listed in the earlier part of this discussion. Wikis, blogs, best practices, Communities of Practice, and documenting processes, knowledge maps, and lessons learned can all be enabled on the intranet, although the information technology department would have to support its use by implementing database and knowledge base software for this purpose.

The information technology department plays a pivotal role in the transformation of information to knowledge and the resultant transformation of the company to a knowledge-based company. The information technology department needs to take a leadership role in seeking out these newer collaborative technologies, learning how to use them, implementing them, and then supporting them. For example, quite a few of the participants said that their preferred method of knowledge sharing was still face-to-face. They insisted that important communication nuances were lost when face-to-face was replaced with the collaborative technologies available today. Thus, the marketplace must be continually monitored in order that technologies that overcome these limitations might one day be introduced.

Toward this end, it is recommended that a chief knowledge officer be appointed, whose role would be to promote knowledge management with particular emphasis on knowledge sharing in the organization. This person would be responsible for implementing many of the recommendations discussed in this chapter.

Key Point

This chapter presented an attitudinal study that demonstrates what can get in the way of effective knowledge sharing within an organization, What probably surprised you (or maybe not) is that knowledge sharing isn't all that effectively done in our sample survey population. This has some major negative consequences for the effectiveness of any project team. The goal here is to impress upon readers the importance of fixing these kinds of problems before engaging in any social enterprising.

Chapter 5

Data of Social Enterprising

Working collaboratively creates a multitude of artifacts such as memos, e-mails, policies, procedures, project plans, strategic plans, implementation plans, etc. Migrating to an online social network generates even more data. Wikis, blogs, discussion boards, and other social networking toolsets can easily double the amount of data floating around.

The main problem confronting intelligent integration of information in is to access diverse data residing in multiple, autonomous, heterogeneous repositories, and to integrate or fuse that data into coherent information that can be used by developers. To make the problem even more interesting:

1. Data may by multimedia (video, images, text, and sound).
2. Data sources may store data in diverse formats (flat files, network, relational- or object-oriented databases, expert systems, blogs, wikis, etc.).
3. Data semantics data may conflict across multiple sources.
4. Data may reside outside the enterprise, perhaps in a cloud-based environment served by Google, Amazon, or Salesforce.com.
5. Data may be of uncertain quality, and the reliability of the source may be questionable.

The goal of this chapter is to address the issues of integrating the types of cross-platforms information social enterprisers will need in the course of doing business.

Intelligent Systems

Intelligent systems originally emerged from the artificial intelligence community. There was a great deal of interest in knowledge-based systems, which are rule-based intelligent systems (also referred to as *expert systems*). These systems were considered flexible because rule bases could be easily modified. However, in practice, these early systems were often monolithic rule-based systems, and as the intertwined rule base grew in size with often over 1000 interdependent rules, it often became difficult to understand and maintain.

Right around the same time a more flexible, distributed, and adaptable paradigm emerged for intelligent systems, namely, that of intelligent-agent-based systems. Agents vary considerably in their capabilities. An intelligent-agent-based system is a highly distributed system in which agents are active concurrent objects that act on behalf of users. Agents can be thought of as intermediaries. Usually, several agents participate in the problem-solving activity, communicating with each other. This leads to a more distributed and scalable environment.

Agents can be categorized in different ways, based on their mobility, based on their intelligence, or based on the roles they play in an agent-based system. One categorization is based on the following capabilities:

1. Cooperative agents communicate with other agents, and their actions depend on the results of the communication.
2. Proactive agents initiate actions without user prompting.
3. Adaptive agents learn from past experience.

Agents may combine the above three capabilities as shown in Figure 5.1. Personal agents are proactive and serve individual users—they may also be adaptive. Adaptive personal agents can search for user information in background mode and are often coupled with the Internet access. Collaborative agents are both proactive and cooperative.

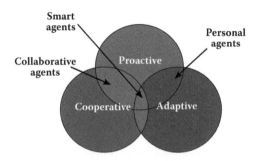

Figure 5.1   Categorization of agents.

Table 5.1   Roles of Intelligent Agents in Supporting KM-based Social Networking

KM Activities	Needs	Intelligent Agent (IA)	IA Functionality
Create knowledge	Users must be able to easily and fully represent their knowledge	User agent	Help users to create knowledge and formulate queries Remember all KM activities of users Dynamically organize content, user agendas, etc.
Combining knowledge	Users need to have the ability to assemble, customize, extend what is stored in the knowledge repository	Knowledge agent	Index knowledge Detect inconsistency Save, retrieve, and update knowledge from one or more knowledge repositories
Distributing knowledge	Users need to be made aware of dynamic changes to the knowledge repository	Knowledge manager	Monitor all changes that occur in a knowledge repository and forward them to the user agent
Retrieving knowledge	Users need to be able to intelligently retrieve knowledge (i.e., combinations of information) based on context and/or contents.	Knowledge manager	Reformulate queries based on an ontology Determine the most favored alternative based on preference weighting and ranking

Back in the late 1990s, Baek, Liebowitz, Prasad, Granger, and Lewis (1997) did some significant research on developing an agent-based conceptual framework for intelligent agents that supported processes of managing project-relevant knowledge inside of a virtual team which replicates exactly what we need to do to support social enterprising data, as shown in Table 5.1.

Oracle Beehive has moved in this direction. Beehive uses a single Oracle database store to house collaborative documents.

Semantic Standards

That which is referred to as the Semantic Web, which we first talked about in Chapter 5, is really an add-on to the current Internet in which information is given a more refined meaning, better enabling computers and people to work together. The goal of the Semantic Web is to build a global information space consisting of linked data, such as you see graphically depicted at http://richard.cyganiak. de/2007/10/lod/imagemap.html. Major web data sources such as Google, Yahoo, Amazon, and eBay have started to make their data accessible to developers. This has inspired the development of lots of interesting mashups that combine data from a fixed number of sources.

The key to the success of the Semantic Web is the development of "semantic standards." As some put it, the software industry is building an alphabet but has not yet invented a common language. This common language has appeared in the form of ontologies. An ontology is an explicit specification. The term is actually borrowed from philosophy, where an ontology is a systematic account of existence.

From a Semantic Web perspective, an ontology is an explicit, formal speci-fication of a shared conceptualization of interest. Formal means that the ontol-ogy should be machine readable, and shared indicates that the ontology captures knowledge that is not private. Essentially, ontologies represent knowledge within specific domains in a machine-readable way.

Informal ontology examples available on the Internet are Yahoo! categories, which are generalized taxonomies of "things" and the Amazon.com product cata-log. Essentially, ontologies are built to share a common understanding of the struc-ture of information among people and among software components. Ultimately, ontologies enable inferencing and reasoning on data. This permits an understand-ing of the interrelationships among data, which allows software to reason against the data to infer new information. So, you could build an ontology for human resources, marketing, sales, and whatever else requires a specificity of language.

Semantic Web technologies are being used to develop social ontologies, important in social networks (e.g., friend of a friend [FOAF] on networks such as Facebook). Data can be scraped, or mined, from various sources such as the web, e-mail, and bibliographic data. This data is then stored and enhanced, usually through some sort of reasoning, or intelligent, system. Finally, the data can be browsed and visualized, often for the purpose of social network analysis. Social network analysis views social relationships in terms of network theory consisting of *nodes* and *ties* (also called *edges*, *links*, or *connections*). Nodes are the individual actors within the networks, and ties are the relationships between the actors. The resulting graph-based structures are often very complex. There can be many kinds of ties between the nodes. Research in a number of academic fields has shown that social networks operate on many levels, from families up to the level of nations, and play a critical role in determining the way problems are solved, organizations are run, and the degree to which individuals succeed in achieving their goals. It can also be used to analyze the performance of a group or individual and observe the dynamics of community development

Enterprise Information Management

The Semantic Web is an excellent vehicle for enabling data collection and retrieval of data related to social enterprising. Some information and processes can be web based, some solely client based with both information and processes encapsulated in an executable, and some a combination of the two.

Content can be delivered to the employee in a variety of ways: bots, search, push, browsing, and portal. This is referred to as *knowledge flow*. Bots, short for robots, are automated agents that seek out information of interest and send it back to the end user by that end user's request. Push technology, or server-push as it is sometimes known, is delivery of information that is initiated by the information server rather than by the end user. The information is "pushed" from a server to an end user as a result of a programmed request initiated originally by the end user. A portal is a website that serves as a single gateway to information and knowledge. Each of these methodologies requires that the content be managed in some way. In the world of business, this is referred to as Enterprise Information Management, or EIM.

There are four major elements to EIM: correspondence management, workflow management, document management, and records management.

In a modern organization, these information assets might take the form of documents, multimedia objects, e-mails, discussion posts, wikis, blogs, technical documents, images, sounds, video, databases, knowledge bases, and any combination thereof.

All of this data is usually spread around the different varieties of EIM systems that can be implemented, as shown in Figure 5.2:

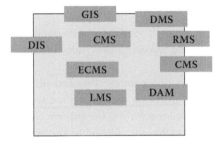

Figure 5.2   Enterprise Information System components.

1. Content management system (CMS): Usually focused on intranet-based or Internet-based corporate content including data and knowledge bases. Can be expanded to extranet or public web-based social networking sites.
2. Document management system (DMS): Focuses on the storage and retrieval of work documents (e.g., forms), in their original format.
3. Records management system (RMS): The management of both physical and electronic documents.
4. Digital asset management (DAM): Similar to RMS but focused on multimedia resources, such as images, audio, and video.
5. Library management system (LMS): The administration of a (corporate) library's technical functions and services.
6. Digital imaging system (DIS): Automates the creation of electronic versions of paper documents (e.g., PDF files) that are input to records management systems.
7. Learning management system (LMS): The administration of training and other learning resources. Learning content management systems (LCMSs) combine content management systems with learning management systems.
8. Geographic information system (GIS): Computer-based systems for the capture, storage, retrieval and analysis, and display of spatial (i.e., location-referenced) data.

Enterprise content management systems (ECMSs) combine all of the above within an organizational setting, in a variety of configurations. It is this ECMS which should provide the foundation for maintaining those valuable social enterprising artifacts.

Content Management System (CMS)

This digital content life cycle consists of six primary states: create, update, publish, translate, archive, and retire, each of which can take place on a variety of platforms. For example, an instance of digital content is created by one or more authors. Over time, that content may be edited. One or more individuals may provide some editorial oversight, thereby approving the content for publication. Once published, that content may be superseded by another form of content and thus retired or removed from use.

Content management is a collaborative process out of design and necessity. The process usually consists of the following basic roles and responsibilities:

1. Content Author—responsible for creating and editing content
2. Editor— responsible for tuning the content message and the style of delivery
3. Publisher—responsible for releasing the content for consumption
4. Administrator—responsible for managing the release of the content, ultimately placing it into a repository so that it can be found and consumed

A critical aspect of content management is the ability to manage versions of content as it evolves (i.e., version control). This is particularly important as the CMS is architected to be distributed across platforms, or certain aspects of it are pushed to the client..

Essentially, a content management system is a set of automated processes that may support the following features:

1. Identification of all key users and their roles
2. The ability to assign roles and responsibilities to different instances of content categories or types.
3. Definition of workflow tasks often coupled with messaging so that content managers are alerted to changes in content.
4. The ability to track and manage multiple versions of a single instance of content.
5. The ability to publish the content to a repository in order to support the consumption of the content.

CMSs allow end users to easily add new content in the form of articles. The articles are typically entered as plain text, perhaps with markup to indicate where other resources (such as pictures, video, or audio) should be placed. Hence, CMS systems are multimedia enabled. The system then uses rules to style the article, separating the display from the content, which has a number of advantages when trying to get many articles to conform to a consistent "look and feel." The system then adds the articles to a larger collection for publishing.

A popular example of this is the wiki, which we have been touting as a reasonable first foray into social enterprising. A wiki is a web application that allows users to add content, as on an Internet forum, but also allows anyone to edit the content. The Wikipedia encyclopedia was created in this manner. Figure 5.3 shows a typical formatted page on Wikipedia.

There are a variety of wiki "engines" including UseMod, TWiki, MoinMoin, PmWiki, and MediaWiki. A more extensive list can be found at http://c2.com/cgi/wiki?WikiEngines. What is important here is that the "intelligence" wrapped up in the social enterprising networks, which will likely be composed of wikis, blogs, discussion messages, etc., should be managed in the same way as other corporate information assets.

Document Management Systems/Electronic Document Management Systems

Document management systems (DMSs) focus on the storage and retrieval of work documents (e.g., forms, proposals, customer correspondence, etc.), in their original format. The key processes within the DMS are

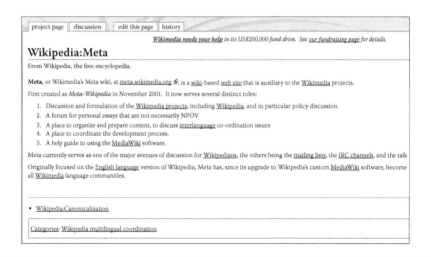

Wikipedia:Meta

From Wikipedia, the free encyclopedia.

Meta, or Wikimedia's Meta wiki, at meta.wikimedia.org ⌕, is a wiki-based web site that is auxiliary to the Wikimedia projects.

First created as *Meta-Wikipedia* in November 2001. It now serves several distinct roles:

1. Discussion and formulation of the Wikimedia projects, including Wikipedia, and in particular policy discussion.
2. A forum for personal essays that are not necessarily NPOV
3. A place to organize and prepare content, to discuss interlanguage co-ordination issues
4. A place to coordinate the development process.
5. A help guide to using the MediaWiki software.

Meta currently serves as one of the major avenues of discussion for Wikipedians, the others being the mailing lists, the IRC channels, and the talk

Originally focused on the English language version of Wikipedia, Meta has, since its upgrade to Wikipedia's custom MediaWiki software, become all Wikimedia language communities.

• Wikipedia:Canonicalization

Categories: Wikipedia multilingual coordination

Figure 5.3   Wikipedia page structure.

1. Feed—paper scanning or document importing.
2. Store—Every organization has its own particular storage needs, based on data volume, accessibility requirements, archival duration, etc. Choices include magnetic (such as typical desktop hard-drives, RAID), optical (CD, DVD, WORM), magneto-optical storage technology, or a combination of these devices.
3. Indexing—tagging each document with some code for accessibility.
4. Control—One of the main advantages of an EDMS is that all documents of all types reside in the same computing environment. Yet in the context of a company's daily operations, it is quite probable that you would want for certain groups of employees to be granted access privileges to certain types of documents, while others may not.
5. Workflow—The EDMS is capable of mapping a company's organizational rules in the form of access controls to the document databases. EDMS tool suites often provide the means to model their operational procedures in the form of workflow management utilities.
6. Security.
7. Search—An efficient EDMS will allow users to search documents via preset indices, keywords, full-text search, even via thesaurus and synonym support. A majority of the time, filters can be applied, search criteria may be nested, and Boolean and comparison operators may be used. We discuss this in more depth in the following text.
8. Access—Once you have identified the documents you wish to review, the EDMS must be capable of retrieving them fast and transparently, regardless of where they are located. Documents may be distributed in multiple databases,

in multiple locations. An efficient access strategy will give the end user the impression that the documents are all stored in one location, on one computer.

9. Share—Collaborative capabilities prevent end users from making duplicates, of the retrieved documents you have just retrieved.

The document management solution allows the user to deposit documents through multiple interfaces. Most users will access the document management system through a typical desktop configuration via a web interface or an existing proprietary application. Access can also be obtained through imaging devices or through the organization's e-mail system, which archives e-mails as historical artifacts.

Search capabilities are typically built into the functionality of the document management system. Searches can be driven by a keyword search or through other designated parameters.

The web content management interface is how documents within the document management system can be integrated into the social enterprising. Access through this Web content management interface would be independent of the access directly to a document management system, but defined accessibility and authentication would have to be established.

Originally, a document management system was a computer program (or set of programs) used to track and store images of paper documents. More recently, the term has been used to distinguish between imaging and records management systems that specialize in paper capture and records, respectively. Document management systems commonly provide check-in, check-out, storage, and retrieval of electronic documents often in the form of word processor files and the like.

Typical systems have the user scan in the original paper document, and store the image of the document in the document management system, although increasingly many documents are starting life as digital documents. The image is often given a name containing the date, and the user is often asked to type in additional "tags" in order to make finding the image easier.

Digital Asset Management

Digital asset management (DAM) is similar to RMS but focused on multimedia resources, such as images, audio, and video. DAM is still a new market with rapid technical evolution; hence, many different types of systems will be labeled as DAM systems although they are designed to address slightly different problems or were created for a specific industry. A variety of commercial systems for DAM are available, and numerous groups are trying to establish standards for DAM.

DAM systems generally support functions for ingesting, managing, searching, retrieving, and archiving of assets. DAM systems may also include version control and asset format conversion capabilities (i.e., dynamically downsizing a large, high-resolution image for display on a website). DAM systems are related to and can be considered a superset of content management systems.

DAM is a combination of workflow, software, and hardware that organizes and retrieves a company's digital assets. DAM would be useful for storing any audio or video components of various social enterprising processes, such as audio or video transcripts of meetings.

Data Mining

Data mining toolsets are the primary tool for performing business intelligence in a typical organization. Most typically used in strategic planning and other business analysis departments, data mining can certainly be utilized for the purposes we are advocating in this chapter. At this point, it is probably the best tool available.

Data mining can not only help us in knowledge discovery, that is, the identification of new phenomena, but it is also useful in enhancing our understanding of known phenomena. One of the key steps in data mining is pattern recognition, namely, the discovery and characterization of patterns in image and other high-dimensional data. A pattern is defined as an arrangement or an ordering in which some organization of underlying structure can be said to exist. Patterns in data are identified using measurable features or attributes that have been extracted from the data.

Data mining is an interactive and iterative process involving data preprocessing, search for patterns, knowledge evaluation, and possible refinement of the process based on input from domain experts, or feedback from one of the steps, as shown in Figure 5.4.

The preprocessing of the data is a time-consuming, but critical, first step in the data mining process. It is often domain and application dependent; however, several techniques developed in the context of one application or domain can be

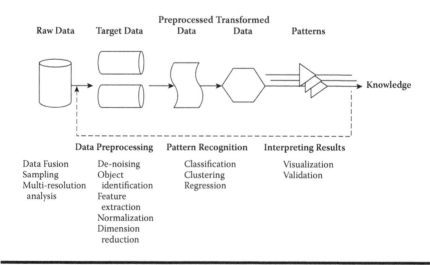

Figure 5.4   The process of data mining.

applied to other applications and domains as well. The pattern recognition step is usually independent of the domain or application

Data mining starts with the raw data, which usually takes the form of simulation data, observed signals, or images. These data are preprocessed using various techniques such as sampling, multiresolution analysis, denoising, feature extraction, and normalization.

Sampling is a widely accepted technique to reduce the size of the data set and make it easier to handle. However, in some cases, such as when looking for something that appears infrequently in the set, sampling may not be viable. Another technique is to reduce the size of the data set. With multi-resolution analysis, data at a fine resolution can be "coarsened," which shrinks the data set by removing some of the detail and extracts relevant features from the raw data set. The key to effective data mining is reducing the number of features used to mine data, so only the features best at discriminating among the data items are retained.

One great example of the value added of using data mining is in lessons learned analysis. Post implementation, the project team should spend a bit of time in creating a lessons learned document, detailing issues and problems, and their resolutions, encountered. Over time, hundreds of lessons learned should be recorded in this knowledge repository. When embarking on a new system, lessons learned should be reviewed so that the same problems can be avoided. Obviously, it would be a tedious process to review hundreds of lessons learned documents. Instead, data mining techniques can be used to pick out the lessons learned specific to characteristics of the new problem at hand.

Once the data is preprocessed or "transformed," pattern-recognition software is used to look for patterns. Patterns are defined as an ordering that contains some underlying structure. The results are processed back into a format familiar to the experts, who then can examine and interpret the results.

Key Point

Most work processes are data heavy. Social enterprising is often data light. This chapter discusses some methodologies for integrating the full spectrum of documentation required by a typical work process or project into a social enterprising framework.

References

Baek, S.L, Liebowitz, J., Prasad, S.Y., Granger, M.J., and Lewis, M. (1997). An intelligent agent based framework for knowledge management on the Web: A case study of a virtual team designing a multimedia system. *AAAI Technical Report* (WS-97-09).

Chapter 6

People Prep

The goal of any business is to produce quality products and services efficiently. The goal of social enterprising is to enhance the quality and productivity aspects of the work experience. To achieve this goal, we need to pay special attention to productivity and creativity. In this chapter, we will discuss how to do this using social enterprising.

A Question of Productivity

A lack of productivity can be caused by managerial, organizational, economic, political, legal, behavioral, psychological, and social factors. To achieve an acceptable level of productivity, as much emphasis must be placed on "people" issues as on business process issues. The human aspect provides by far the largest source of opportunity for improving productivity.

Poor management leads to a wide variety of problems. Staff might become unmotivated because their creativity is unappreciated or underutilized. There might be a lack of effective teamwork due to the inability of the manager to build and manage effective teams. The manager might engage in micromanagement, leading to inadequate delegation and ineffective organization of the team. This problem might extend itself to inadequately trained staff due to a short-sighted rather than long-term perspective.

We have already discussed knowledge-sharing problems in an earlier chapter. Teaming problems are probably one of the biggest reasons for lack of productivity. Many employees have a real desire for autonomy, and many have an unusual need for privacy. Organizational culture actually rewards individual efforts more than team efforts, so this sort of behavior is reinforced. The problem with this is that it leads to a concentration of key knowledge by just a few individuals. Aside from the fact that this can prove to be disastrous should one of these chosen few decide to leave or become ill, any teaming effort is destined to be lopsided as knowledge and expertise is bunched up in one or two of the team members.

Experts have more organizational clout and power than nonexperts, so decision making becomes problematic. For example, it is not unusual for a key team member to vote down any approach that the team member did not come up with or does not personally endorse. Thus, the team's solution might reflect the ideas and decisions of the experts, and not necessarily the best approach.

Solving these teaming problems is not all that simple to do. The best technique would be to modify organizational culture so that it condones and rewards group efforts. We should attempt to come up with some objective assessment of team contributions and tie these assessments to appropriate rewards. Most importantly, we want to make an active effort to disperse crucial knowledge across the project staff. We must couple this with improvements in communication and coordination across organizational layers. Happily, social enterprising does a good job on both fronts.

There are large performance differences between individuals, and this obvious fact negates productivity increases. There are some interesting reasons for this variability. The most obvious is misguided staffing practices. Some managers simply do not know how to hire a good person. Even if everyone has stellar credentials, it is quite possible that productivity might plummet due to ineffective management. Poor team development and an inattention to the critical role of motivation are also factors.

There are several tactics you might use when trying to increase productivity. Improved management and performance recognition, as we have already mentioned, are the more obvious techniques that can be used, with the enterprise social network a perfect place to provide the sort of recognition employees crave. Often overlooked is the importance of making sure that the right person is selected for the job. Skills testing is paramount here to make sure that what is on the applicant's resume is an actual skill rather than just a skill in progress. Why not couple the enterprise social network with a web-based testing system? You will also want to be sure that the person is matched to the correct job and that some form of career progression is being offered along with that job. Again, the enterprise social network can be used for this purpose. The corporate intranet is often used to provide do-it-yourself services to employees. Some of this functionality, such as job descriptions, can be linked to the enterprise social network. The enterprise social network can even be used to apply for that open position. Most importantly, the facilities of the social network can be used to engage employees in a discussion about that open position.

In many organizations, the corporate intranet performs much of the "people prep" functionality. Forrester Research recently release a report entitled "State of the Workforce Technology Adoption: U.S. Benchmark." While corporate intranets have become a constant in an employee's work life, as you can see

Table 6.1   How Companies Use Their Intranets

Benefits	75%
Company directory	67%
Training/development	64%
Benefit enrolment forms	55%
Payroll functionality	57%
Pension/401K	48%
Time tracking tools	39%
Employee performance review goal setting	39%
Health-related tools	36%
Search	33%
Team content	29%
Executive communications	22%
Collaboration tools	21%

from Table 6.1, few use it for collaboration. This paltry showing caused *Baseline* magazine to quip that "employees are intranets as you would expect them to use them—if it were 2002" (http://www.baselinemag.com/c/a/Enterprise-Apps/How-Companies-Really-Use-Their-Intranets-785247/).

The enterprise social network will never take the place of the corporate intranet. I am not advocating that, and neither does it currently have the facilities to do some of what is listed in Table 6.1. What the enterprise social network does provide is a set of forums for employees to engage in discussion of every topic listed in this table. Going further, it permits both organized teams (project related) and ad hoc teams (organized around an area of interest with no need to formally join the group) to collaborate more effectively.

Social-Based Creativity Development

How many of you have ever attended a trade show and walked onto the floor before the doors were open to the public? If you have ever done this, then you have been witness to some energy-boosting exercises (involving lots of arm waving and yelling) that many sales managers think lead to increased sales. Creativity-boosting techniques have some real value and can be adapted to a social network.

The most obvious technique is to use an online survey to obtain perceptions on the environment for creativity and innovation. Based on the results, an online workshop can be used to discuss ways to generate creativity within the organization, department, and team. Usually facilitated by someone outside of the organization, staff should be asked to keep a "creativity blog" in which they keep track of their creativity improvements based on all of this.

A single online workshop might be effective, but an entire online discussion forum dedicated to this same subject matter might prove beneficial. Aside from discussing ways to improve creativity, some creativity-inducing exercises can be used. Social networking software has the ability to enable discussion forums that can be facilitated by a moderator, usually referred to as a *facilitator*. An unlimited number of forums can be created for an unlimited number of discussions. Here are a few ideas for discussion forums related to boosting creativity.

An analogy is a statement about how objects, people, situations, or actions are similar in process or relationship. An online workshop facilitator can come up with one or a series of that can be used to create fictional situations for gaining new perspectives on problem definition and resolution. In the blue slip technique, online polls can be used to generate ideas for a specific chosen problem. This is usually done anonymously to make people feel more at ease so that they readily share ideas.

5Ws and H is an online variation of the journalistic approach of who, what, where, when, why, and how. Use of this technique serves to expand a person's view of the problem and to assist in making sure that all related aspects of the problem have been addressed and considered. The facilitator poses a problem—for example, why are sales stalling—asking the forum attendees to stretch their imaginations by addressing the 5Ws and H.

The strength of the Force Field analysis technique comes from its ability to identify forces contributing to or hindering a solution to a problem. This technique stimulates creative thinking in three ways: (1) it defines direction, (2) identifies strengths that can be maximized, and (3) identifies weaknesses that can be minimized. Like 5Ws and H, the facilitator moderates an asynchronous discovery discussion.

Virtually, any creativity-inducing activity can be translated to work online. Here are two more. Be creative. Come up with a way to turn these into moderated online discussions. Reversing a problem statement often provides a different framework for analysis. For example, in attempting to come up with ways to improve productivity, try considering the opposite, how to decrease productivity. Wishful thinking enables people to loosen analytical parameters to consider a larger set of alternatives than they might ordinarily consider. By permitting a degree of fantasy into the process, the result just might be a new and unique approach.

In all cases, follow-up sessions should be scheduled for reinforcement. Employees should be invited to identify results of creative activity. Alternatively, employees can use blogs to discuss their successes.

Aside from facilitated "creativity-inducing" workshops, there are also several managerial techniques that can be utilized to spur innovation, as shown in Table 6.2. In all cases, the social network can be utilized for this purpose. The

Table 6.2 Promoting Innovation

Technique	Definition/Examples
Commitment to problem solving	Ability to ask the "right questions" Build in time for research and analysis
Acceptance of "outside-the-box" thinking	Seek out and encourage different view points, even radical ones!
Willingness to reinvent products and processes that are already in place	Create a "blank slate" opportunity map, even for processes that appear to be battle tested and comfortable
Willingness to listen to everyone (employees, customers, vendors)	"Open door" Respect for data and perspective without regard to seniority or insider status
Keeping informed of industry trends	Constantly scanning business publications/trade journals, and clipping articles of interest "FYI" participation with fellow managers
Change of management policies	Instill energy and "fresh start" by revising established rules
Use of project management	Clear goals and milestones Tracking tools Expanded communication
Transfer of knowledge within an organization	Commitment to aggregating and reformatting key data for "intelligence" purposes
Use of simple visual models	Simple but compelling frame works and schematics to clarify core beliefs
Use of the Internet for research	Fluency and access to websites (e.g., competitor home pages)
Development of processes for implementing new products and ideas	Structured ideation and productization process Clear release criteria Senior management buy-in
Champion products	Identify and prioritize those products that represent best possible chance for commercial success Personally engage and encourage contributors to strategic initiatives

manager need only host his or her own forum, answering questions, sharing articles of interest, discussing policies and procedures, responding to employee's suggestions, etc.

Communications and Group Productivity

Communications can dominate productivity. Most problems arise as the result of poor communications between workers. If there are n workers on the team, then there are $n(n-1)/2$ interfaces across which there may be communications problems.

An individual working alone has no interruptions from fellow group members and, therefore, the productivity can be quite high for a motivated individual. For example, in the IT department, it is estimated that one programmer working 60 h a week can complete a project in the same calendar time as two others working normal hours, but at three quarters of the cost.

There is a point where coordination overhead outweighs any benefit that can be obtained by the addition of more staff. Statistics that support this were pioneered during the nineteenth century in work on military organizations. It was noted that as the number of workers who had to communicate increased arithmetically, from 2 to 3 to 4 to 5 and so on, the number of communication channels among them increased geometrically, from 1 to 3 to 6 to 10. From this study, it was concluded that the upper limit of effective staff size for cooperative projects is about 8. It has also been shown that when the number of staff increased to 12 or more, the efficiency of the group decreased to less than 30%. The optimum group size is between five to eight members. The group should be provided with its own private forum that they can use to bounce around ideas, upload and download group documents, as well as discuss progress. The goal here is to promote collaboration.

Promoting Collaboration

Social enterprising is more than just a set of forums for discussion. It is a composite of those forums and other online technologies such as blogs, polls, podcasts, and voice over Internet services such as WebEx and Skype. Thus, social enterprising also makes use of face-to-face, real-time collaboration. There are a few techniques that can be used to help promote this form of collaboration.

Verbal Cues

Pausing actually slows down the "to and fro" of discussion. There are fewer "frames per second" to deal with. It provides for the precious "wait time" that has been shown to dramatically improve critical thinking. Pausing and the acceptance of moments of silence creates a relaxed and yet purposeful atmosphere. Silence, however initially uncomfortable, can be an excellent indicator of productive collaboration. Pausing also signals to others that their ideas and comments are worth thinking about. It dignifies their contribution and implicitly encourages future participation. Pausing enhances discussion and greatly increases the quality of decision making.

To paraphrase is to recast or translate into one's own words, to summarize or to provide an example of what has just been said. The paraphrase maintains the intention and the accurate meaning of what has just been said while using different words and phrases. The paraphrase helps members of a team hear and understand each other as they evaluate data and formulate decisions. Paraphrasing is also extremely effective when reducing group tension and individual anger. The paraphrase is possibly the most powerful of all nonjudgmental verbal responses because it communicates that "I am attempting to understand you" and that says "I value you."

Probing seeks to clarify something that is not yet fully understood. More information may be required, or a term may need to be more fully defined. Clarifying questions can be either specific or open-ended, depending upon the circumstances. Gentle probes increase the clarity and precision of a group's thinking and contributes to trust building because they communicate to group members that their ideas are worthy of exploration and consideration.

It takes a degree of self-confidence and courage to put forward an idea, and it is vital that collaborative groups nurture such self-confidence and courage. Ideas are the heart of a meaningful discussion. Groups must be comfortable to process information by analyzing, comparing, predicting, applying, or drawing causal relationships.

Collaborative work is facilitated when each team member is explicitly conscious of self and others—not only aware of what he or she is saying, but also how it is said and how others are responding to it. Understanding how we create different perceptions allows us to accept others' points of view as simply different, not necessarily wrong. The more we understand about how someone else processes information, the better we can communicate with them.

Presuming positive presuppositions is the assumption that other members of the team are acting from positive and constructive intentions (however, much we may disagree with their ideas). Presuming positive presuppositions is not a passive state but needs to become a regular manifestation of one's verbal responses. The assumption of positive intentions permits the creation of such sophisticated concepts as a "loyal opposition," and it allows one member of a group to play "the devil's advocate." It builds trust, promotes healthy cognitive disagreement, and reduces the likelihood of misunderstanding and affective/emotional conflict.

Both inquiry and advocacy are necessary components of collaborative work. Highly effective teams are aware of this and self-consciously attempt to balance them. Inquiry provides for greater understanding. Advocacy leads to decision making. One of the common mistakes that collaborative teams may make is to bring premature closure to problem identification (inquiry for understanding) and rush into problem resolution (advocacy for a specific remedy or solution). Maintaining a balance between advocating for a position and inquiring about the positions held by others further inculcates the ethos of a genuine learning community.

Any group that is too busy to practice the skills of collaboration is also a group that is too busy to improve. Ironically, the groups that are most in need of the skills of collaboration are often those most resistant to them. Groups functioning most effectively are the same ones that recognize the need for regular collaboration training; those in trouble are very often the ones that are too busy to examine how they are working together or how they are failing to work together.

One excellent way of developing the skills of collaboration is a Round Robin Reflection Activity. The activity works best when groups are relatively small, no larger than seven or eight, and that a time limit is set, say 20 to 30 min. It is also more effective the second or third time it is used, as participants become more comfortable with the process of reflection. At first, the paraphrasing may seem forced and artificial and even tedious. However, the more it is used, the greater the likelihood that it will become part of one's unconscious repertoire of collaborative strategies.

Round Robin is an activity to get groups to think about how they are functioning as a collaborative team. Following a meeting or problem-solving discussion, a team should take 20 or 30 min to follow the steps outlined as follows:

1. Each member of the group is assigned a letter: A, B, C, etc.
2. Person A begins by briefly describing how his participation has affected the group's work. No interruptions or questions are permitted. Maximum time is 2 to 3 min.
3. Person B either asks Person A a probing question or briefly paraphrases what A has said. Again, no interruptions or questions are permitted.
4. Person B briefly describes how his or her participation has affected the group's work. Again, no interruptions or questions are permitted.

This activity continues in a "Round Robin" fashion until all members have had an opportunity to describe how their participation affected the group. Following the Round Robin, the group should briefly discuss what has been said. Minutes of the session can be stored in the group forum, and group members can blog the results.

Best Practices

Best practices are the identification and use of processes and practices that result in excellent products or services. Best practices, sometimes called *preferred practices*, often generate ideas for improvements in other work units. Best practices are ways of doing business, processes, methods, strategies, etc., that yield superior results. They have been implemented and honed over time to a point where they are viewed as exemplary and should or could be adopted by others. A formal "benchmarking" process is often used to identify best practices.

Identifying and sharing best practices is an important way to incorporate the knowledge of some into the work of many. Organizational structures tend to promote "silo" thinking where particular locations, divisions, or functions focus on maximizing their own accomplishments and rewards, keeping information to themselves and thereby suboptimizing the whole organization. The mechanisms are lacking for sharing of information and learning. Identifying and sharing best practices, particularly within the enterprise social network, helps build relationships and common perspectives among people who do not work side by side.

Best practices can also spark innovative ideas and generate suggestions for improving processes, even if a practice cannot be used in its entirety. The process of identifying them can also benefit employee morale. By highlighting or showcasing people's work, employees get organization-wide recognition for their work.

Expert Interviews

Expert interviews are sessions where one or more people who are considered experts in a particular subject, program, policy, or process, etc., meet with others to share knowledge. Expert interviews can be used in many ways, including capturing knowledge of those scheduled to leave an organization, conducting lessons learned debriefings, and identifying job competencies, or even videotaping a multiday session where recent retirees reflected on the reasons for success and failure.

Expert interviews are a way of making tacit knowledge more explicit. A person can describe not only what was done but why, providing context and explaining the judgment behind the action. Interviews are often easier for the experts than having them write down all the details and nuances. Learners can ask questions and probe more deeply to ensure understanding.

Making time for these sessions is probably the biggest challenge for both the experts and the learners. If the session is more formal with a large group of learners, some may be intimidated and need coaching.

Expert interviews can be used in many situations. The best place to begin is with people who have unique knowledge developed over a long period and who have the potential for leaving the organization soon. The next step might be to identify mission-critical processes or programs where only one or two staff have a high level of technical knowledge.

This process is probably most effective when someone facilitates the experience, setting the stage with participants, facilitating the exchange of any information prior to the interview, and handling scheduling or other logistics. Identify the people and knowledge you want to start with, both the experts and the learners. Discuss with the experts the reasons for the interviews, who will be involved, and what you would like to focus on. If the learner needs to prepare for the session, the expert can identify how to do this and what resource materials would be helpful. It is also essential to ask the learners what they think they would like to know from the experts. If they have specific questions, provide these to the expert in advance so he or she can be prepared. In all cases, this online meeting should be recorded and archived.

Job Aids

Job aids are tools that help people perform tasks accurately. They include checklists, flow diagrams, reference tables, decision tree diagrams, etc., that provide specific, concrete information to the user and serve as a quick reference guide to performing a task. Job aids are not the actual tools used to perform tasks, such as computers, measuring tools, or telephones.

A job aid can take many forms, but basically it is a document that has information or instruction on how to perform a task. It guides the user to do the task correctly and is used while performing the task, when the person needs to know the procedure.

Types of job aids include

1. Step-by-step narratives or worksheets sequencing a process
2. Checklists, which might show items to be considered when planning or evaluating.
3. Flowcharts, leading the user through a process and assisting the user to make decisions and complete tasks based on a set of conditions
4. Reference resources, such as a parts catalog or telephone listing

Job aids are usually inexpensive to create and easy to revise. Using job aids can eliminate the need for employees to memorize tedious or complex processes and procedures. Storing these jobs aids within the social enterprise network can help increase productivity and reduce error rates.

Job aids need to be written clearly and concisely, with nothing left to interpretation. They also need to be updated and kept current. Finding the time to create job aids can be a challenge; however, creation of good job aids produces benefits over the long term.

Consult with knowledgeable users to identify what job aids to develop. Create job aids that include only the steps or information required by the user. Keep the information and language simple, using short words and sentences. Do not include background information or other information extraneous to actual performance of the task; put that in another location. Use graphics or drawings, when appropriate, to more clearly demonstrate detail. Use bold or italicized text to highlight important points. Use colors to code different procedures or parts of a process.

Job aids are most appropriate for tasks that an employee does not perform frequently, or for complex tasks. Tasks with many steps that are difficult to remember, or tasks that, if not performed correctly cause high costs, can benefit from having readily accessible job aids. Also, if a task changes frequently, a job aid would save time and reduce the chance for errors.

Job aids can be a good supplement to classroom training. Users can learn tasks in a classroom but will likely need something to rely on when on the job.

Knowledge Fairs

Knowledge fairs can showcase information about an organization, department, topic, or project. They can be used internally, to provide a forum for sharing information, or externally, to educate customers or other stakeholders about important information.

A knowledge fair is an event designed to showcase information about an organization or a topic. It can be organized in many ways using speakers, demonstrations or, more commonly, booths displaying information of interest to the attendees. One example is the Xerox Corporation's annual "Team Day" that showcases the work of various quality-improvement teams. As you can probably figure out by now, a knowledge fair is pretty easy to convert to an online event. Demos can be videotaped and posted "YouTube" like to the enterprise social network for asynchronous viewing. Booths can be translated to discussion forums where information is posted and someone is made available for Q&A. WebEx-type online meeting software can be used to host "live" speakers.

A large amount of information can be made available, and attendees can focus specifically on what they are interested in learning. Attendees can interact directly with the presenters, getting immediate answers to their specific questions. They also can establish contacts for further exploration of topics if needed.

Attendees often network with one another and booth developers often strengthen their teamwork. Knowledge fairs also provide opportunities to draw attention to best practices and recognize employee and team achievements.

Depending on the scope and size of the event, it can require a large amount of staff time for creating booths, putting information together to display, and for organization and logistics. The costs for space, materials, and resources can be high. The potential exists for participants to become overwhelmed with information.

Consider a knowledge fair when there is a lot of information to share with a lot of people and participants need a broader perspective, as well as an opportunity to interact on a one-on-one basis on specific topics. A knowledge fair is an alternative to traditional presentations when more interactive experiences are desirable.

Knowledge Maps and Inventories

I use Facebook to create social networks of people who are interested in my writing and consulting. It's a very subtle form of advertisement which makes people view me as nonthreatening. Rather than me advertising myself, I simply share my expertise and allow them to see for themselves that I'm qualified.

Knowledge maps and inventories are used to catalog information/knowledge available in an organization and where it is located. They point to information but do not contain it. The result should be stored in the social enterprise network.

An example is an Experts or Resource Directory that lists people with expert knowledge who can be contacted by others in need of that knowledge. Knowledge mapping is particularly useful for the analysis phase of the software development life cycle.

Knowledge mapping is actually a process of surveying, assessing, and linking the information, knowledge, competencies, and proficiencies held by individuals and groups within an organization. Organizations use knowledge maps for many different uses. Some use it to compile company locators to find internal and external resources. Others use them to identify knowledge-sharing opportunities or knowledge barriers within cross-functional work groups. Many organizations use knowledge mapping before developing formal Communities of Practice.

Knowledge mapping is a process that actually never ends with a goal toward illustrating or (road) mapping how knowledge flows throughout an organization. The process consists of the following steps:

1. Discover the location, ownership, value, and use of knowledge artifacts
2. Learn the roles and expertise of people
3. Identify constraints to the flow of knowledge
4. Highlight opportunities to leverage existing knowledge

A knowledge map describes what knowledge is used in a process, and how it flows around the process. It is the basis for determining knowledge commonality, or areas where knowledge is used across multiple processes.

The knowledge map describes who has the knowledge (tacit), where the knowledge resides (infrastructure), and how the knowledge is transferred or disseminated (social). Knowledge mapping is used to focus on both the strategic as well as tactical knowledge assets of an organization. On an enterprise level, it should be focused on strategic, technical, and market knowledge as well as the cross-functional linkages between divisions and business groups. On the tactical level, it should focus on the working group and the processes within that group.

At all levels, the knowledge map provides an assessment of existing or required knowledge and information, as follows:

1. What knowledge is needed?
2. Who has this knowledge?
3. Where does this knowledge reside?
4. Is the knowledge tacit or explicit?
5. Is the knowledge routine or nonroutine?
6. What issues does it address?

The APQC's (American Productivity & Quality Center) Road Map to Knowledge Management (www.apqc.org) consists of five stages of implementation: Stage 1: getting started; Stage 2: develop strategy; Stage 3: design and launch KM initiatives; Stage 4: expand and support; and Stage 5: institutionalize KM. Within this context, knowledge mapping is recommended in stage 2 or stage 3.

Process knowledge mapping analyzes a business process or method to identify

1. Design milestones (where knowledge is needed)
2. Knowledge requirements (what knowledge is needed)
3. Routes for access and retrieval of knowledge (through people and technology)
4. Gaps between required skills and current skills

Questions that are asked during this process include

1. What do you need to know?
2. Where does the knowledge come from?
3. Who owns it?
4. What knowledge, tools, and templates exist today?
5. What knowledge, tools, and templates should be created?
6. What barriers or issues exist?

The method for mapping the process/focus area consists of the following:

1. Review critical processes.
2. Identify individual process steps within each process.
3. Determine routine/nonroutine tasks.
4. Identify key decision points, hand-offs.
5. Locate owners of and stakeholders in high-value processes.
6. Follow the knowledge pathways through the organization using the interview methodology and brainstorming.
7. Inventory types of knowledge utilized and needed. Categorize the knowledge content (explicit, tacit, embedded), the social capital (trust, interpersonal relationships, cultural norms), and infrastructure (processes, tools, roles and responsibilities, incentives).
8. Identify gaps, lack of connectivity, and information overload.
9. Develop a plan for collecting, reviewing, validating, storing, and sharing knowledge and information.
10. Create measurement criteria for each critical process step.

Once the maps have been completed, they should be analyzed. For each process step, review the knowledge resources and determine

1. Do we leverage this today?
2. Is the knowledge available and accessible to everyone who needs it?
3. Are decisions made with all the right knowledge?
4. Where should we focus our improvement efforts?
5. Summarize the analysis for creating a list of key strengths and key opportunities.

Learning Games

Learning games are structured learning activities that are used to make learning fun and more effective, provide a review of material that has already been presented in order to strengthen learning, and evaluate how much learning has occurred.

Games can also be used to

1. Help people prepare for learning by testing current levels of knowledge.
2. Apply a newly learned skill.
3. Learn as they play the game.
4. Practice what has been presented to reinforce the learning.

Games improve knowledge transfer by

1. Increasing participation among all involved.
2. Improving the learning process by creating an environment where people's creativity and intelligence are engaged.
3. Destressing learning by making it fun.
4. Addressing the different ways in which different people best learn—through movement, hearing, and seeing.
5. Adding variety to a training program, which helps to keep people actively involved.

When games are used as an end in themselves and not a means toward an end, they waste time and can hamper learning. In addition, using too many games can destroy learning effectiveness. Games are usually used in conjunction with other learning methodologies, such as presentations and discussions. When you use them, or if you use them at all, depends on the learning you are trying to convey and whether games will help you meet your learning objectives.

Games used at the beginning of a program can measure existing knowledge and build immediate interest in the training material. Games used during a program can help people discover the learning themselves (which strengthens recall and commitment), practice using new knowledge or skills, or reinforce initial learning. Games used near the end of a program can test knowledge gained and people's ability to apply it in their work settings.

For games to be effective, they must

1. Be related to the workplace by providing knowledge, reinforcing attitudes, and initiating action that is important to job success.
2. Teach people how to think, access information, react, understand, and create value for themselves and their organizations.
3. Be enjoyable and engaging without being overly simplistic or silly.
4. Allow for collaboration between learners.
5. Be challenging but not unattainable.
6. Permit time for reflection, feedback, dialog, and integration. In other words, games should be debriefed.

Examples of games, all of which can be architected to run within an enterprise social network, include

1. Quizzes
2. Scavenger hunts
3. Quiz show games, including those modeled on television game shows such as *Jeopardy* or *Family Feud*
4. "Name that" games
5. 20 questions

Lessons Learned Debriefings

These debriefings are a way to identify, analyze, and capture experiences, what worked well and what needs improvement, so others can learn from those experiences. For maximum impact, lessons learned debriefings should be done either immediately following an event or on a regular basis, with results shared quickly among those who would benefit from the knowledge gained. Hewlett-Packard refers to their lessons learned sessions held during and at the end of projects in order to share knowledge as "Project Snapshots."

Sessions are conducted at the completion of a project or activity, or at strategic points during a project or work team's ongoing work, where members of the team or group evaluate the process used and the results. They identify what was done right and what could be done better the next time.

These sessions identify and capture the things that went well and the things that could be improved so that team or work group members are aware of and can use the broader team/group's learning in their future projects or work activities. Results can also be shared with future teams or other work groups so they can learn from the experiences of others.

Making the time to conduct lessons learned debriefing sessions and documenting the results are the biggest challenges. The sessions should be done as soon as possible after the completion of the project or activities, but no more than 30 days later. They could also be done at any strategic point during a project.

Lessons learned sessions work best when they are done as a formal review session in a functional meeting room, using facilitators, and an assigned note taker. Develop ground rules for the session, for example, listen for understanding, respect others' contributions, no blaming, full participation, etc.

Include appropriate people such as

1. Project sponsor
2. Project or work unit manager
3. Project team or work unit staff
4. Customers
5. Stakeholder representatives, including the manager with responsibility for the project oversight
6. Other appropriate executive management
7. Others, depending on the nature of the project or work, for example, maintenance, information systems, technical services, and operations staff

Make sure lists of lessons learned are process oriented and are directed toward improving the work process, not individual performance. Do be sure that feedback is constructive and to identify actions and behaviors that would be more effective. Most importantly, do recognize positive contributions.

As an alternative, have groups of 6–10 people answer the following questions and consolidate responses for all the groups. You may want to consider the commonality or strength of agreement on the responses. Select questions from the following or develop your own questions. Open-ended questions usually elicit the best responses.

1. What worked best on the project or activity?
2. What could have been better on the project or activity?
3. How can we improve the methodology to better assist in the successful completion of future projects or work activities?
4. What parts of the project or work resulted in meeting the specified requirements and goals? What helped ensure these results?
5. What parts did not meet specifications and goals? What could have been done to ensure that these were met?
6. How satisfied was the customers with results? What was particularly good? What could have been done to improve customer satisfaction?
7. Were cost budgets met? Why or why not? What helped or hindered staying within budget?
8. What contributed to the schedule being met? What hindered it?
9. What appropriate risks were identified and mitigated? What additional risks should have been identified and what additional actions should have been taken to mitigate risks?

10. What communications were appropriate and helpful? What additional communications would have been helpful?
11. How did the project or activity management methodology work? What worked particularly well? What could have been done to improve it?
12. What procedures were particularly helpful in producing deliverables? What could have been improved? How could processes be improved or streamlined?

Another method is to develop, post, and use a list of 8–10 items or objectives considered most important for success. The team leader or work unit leader and facilitator could develop this list ahead of time or with participants at the beginning of the session. Possible items to help keep the discussions focused include

1. Customer expectations are met.
2. All specifications are achieved.
3. Completed on time.
4. Completed within budget.
5. Return on investment achieved.
6. Organizational goals are met.
7. Positive experience for project or workgroup members.

Identify how well these items were accomplished (fell short, met, exceeded expectations). Identify actions that contributed to or hindered the accomplishment of each of these objectives. See the following text for a possible meeting notes template.

Another strategy is to identify 8–10 major strategies, activities, or processes that helped the project or work unit and 8–10 major problems encountered during the project or activity and what could be done to address or prevent the problems in the future.

Online surveys can also be used instead of or to supplement a meeting. The goals of the survey are to review product delivered against baseline requirements and specifications, and:

1. Determine how well the needs of the customer have been met.
2. Determine whether the product or service was delivered effectively and efficiently and ultimately determine what could be improved.

Storytelling

Storytelling involves the construction of fictional examples or the telling of real organizational stories to illustrate a point and effectively transfer knowledge. An organizational story is a detailed narrative of management actions, employee interactions, or other intra-organizational events that are communicated informally within the organization. When used well, storytelling is a powerful transformational tool in organizations.

Storytelling uses anecdotal examples to illustrate a point and effectively transfer knowledge. There are two types of storytelling:

1. Organizational stories (business anecdotes) are narratives of management or employee actions, employee interactions, or other intra-organizational events that are communicated within the organization, either formally or informally.
2. Future scenarios create a future vision for the enterprise that describes how life will be different once a particular initiative, change, etc., is fully implemented. They provide a qualitative way of describing the value of the initiative even before it starts.

Storytelling has many benefits:

1. Stories capture context, which gives them meaning and makes them powerful.
2. We are used to stories. They are natural, easy, entertaining, and energizing.
3. Stories help us make sense of things. They can help us understand complexity and assist us in seeing our organizations and ourselves in a different light.
4. Stories are easy to remember. People will remember a story more easily than a recitation of facts.
5. Stories are nonadversarial and nonhierarchical.
6. Stories engage our feelings and our minds and are, therefore, more powerful than using logic alone. They complement abstract analysis.
7. Stories help listeners see similarities with their own backgrounds, contexts, fields of experience, etc., and, therefore, help them to see the relevancy of their own situations.
8. Stories can be a powerful transformational tool.

Stories are only as good as the underlying idea being conveyed. Since stories are usually orally presented, the person telling the story must have good presentation skills.

Stories are seldom used alone, but rather they are combined with other approaches such as quantitative analysis, best practices, knowledge audits, etc. They impart meaning and context to ideas, facts, and other kinds of knowledge derived from other knowledge management tools. Stories can be used to support decision making, aid communications, engage buy-in, or market an idea or approach. If being used to illustrate the value of a way of thinking, or explaining an idea, they are best used at the outset, to engage the listener and generate buy-in.

In using storytelling, the message, plot, and characters must be considered. Determine what underlying message is to be conveyed (e.g., importance of organizational goals, impact on an individual of a change effort, end benefits associated with a change effort, how a process works, and so on). How does the story illustrate the underlying message (plot)? Who was involved in the story (characters)?

Think about the audience for the story. At whom is the story aimed? What will each audience listening to the story do with the story's message? What message will be told to each audience? How do we tell each desired story?

Four different structures for using stories have customarily been used:

1. Open with the springboard story, and then draw out its implications.
2. Tell a succession of stories. The telling of multiple stories can help enhance the chances that the audience will co-create the follow-up. Two examples: You want to describe the benefits of a proposed change effort. Tell a story that only partly serves your purpose, and then extrapolate with an anecdote (e.g., a future scenario) that describes how the story will play out when the change effort is fully in place. Or, tell a series of related stories that, taken together, illustrate various ways in which the change effort is leading to payoffs for colleagues.
3. Accentuate the problem. Start with describing the nature of a problem, tell the story, and draw out the implications.
4. Simply tell the story. This is useful when time is very limited and you want to plant a seed.

The story should

1. Be relatively brief and have only enough detail for the audience to understand it; too much detail and the listener gets caught up in the explicit story and not its message.
2. Be intelligible to a specific audience so it hooks them. It must be relevant to them.
3. Be inherently interesting, maybe because the problem presented is difficult, the "old" way of resolving the problem won't work, there is tension between characters in the story, there are unexpected events, or an element of strangeness exists.
4. Embody the idea you are trying to convey and provide an easy mental leap from the "facts" of the story to its underlying message.
5. Have a positive ending, to avoid people being caught up in a negative, skeptical frame of mind.
6. Have an implicit change message, especially if the audience is skeptical or resistant, since the audience can then discover the change message on their own and, therefore, make it their own idea.
7. Feature a protagonist with which the audience can identify.
8. Deal with a specific individual or organization.
9. Have a protagonist who is typical of the organization and its main business.

True stories are generally more powerful than invented stories, and can serve as jumping-off points for future scenario stories. Stories should be tested on individuals or small groups before being tried on large groups or in high-risk settings.

The stories must be simple, brief, and concise. They should represent the perspective of one or two people in a situation typical of the organization's business, so that the explicit story is familiar to the audience. Similarly, the story should be plausible; it must ring true for the listener. It needs to be alive and exciting, not vague and abstract. By including a strange or incongruous aspect, the listener can be helped to visualize a new way of thinking or behaving. Stories, therefore, should be used to help listeners extrapolate from the narrative to their own situations.

Finally, storytellers must believe in the story (own it) and tell it with conviction. Otherwise, the audience will not accept it.

Adapting storytelling to an online medium is also fairly easy and straightforward. It's understanding how to go about creating and then relaying the story that is difficult. Readers are directed to Steve Denning's website (http://www.stevedenning.com/Storytelling-in-the-News/default.aspx), where he has ample storytelling samples for review.

Key Point

It always amazes me that management seems to throw people together on a team without adequate preparation of the team, and the respective members of that team, for the difficult task of working collaboratively. In this chapter, we covered the problems of people preparation, and hopefully offered you some good solutions for improving productivity and enhancing creativity.

Chapter 7

Business Process Social Enterprising

From marketing to risk management to any other operational business unit, it is quite likely that, if used effectively, social enterprising can be used to promote enhanced teamwork and more effective collaboration with employees, customers, clients, and suppliers. There are some first movers in this area, as shown in Table 7.1.

We will focus on effective use of social enterprising for various business purposes in this chapter.

Marketing to the Masses

As you probably expect, the most common use of social networks is for marketing to consumers. Nowadays social networks, such as LinkedIn, Facebook, and MySpace, have become popular platforms where one can share values, ideas, and friendships. It has transformed the social structure where one can discuss or popularize marketing strategies, likes, dislikes, trading concepts, etc. Some of the social networks have a great influence in solving critical issues and can guide individuals to achieve their goals and dreams.

Even major political parties utilize the popularity of such social networks. We have seen the great effects of social networks in the last U.S. Presidential election, where each candidate's presence was much felt on all the social network sites. Half of the election campaigns were done through social networks. It indicates the widespread popularity of these modern social forums.

Table 7.1 Forward-Thinking Companies

At Getty Images, 1,800 employees in over 100 countries use Socialtext to share expertise, resources, and information through tagging, microblogging, blogging, and wikis.
Lisbon-based Mota-Engil uses tech from Telligent and WeListen for project management collaboration among 20,000 employees in 17 countries; participation is rewarded.
Government agencies are incorporating capabilities ranging from internal knowledge sharing to emergency communication capabilities and geolocation services.
The FDA's Office of Regulatory Affairs uses Triple Creek for mentoring; employees use threaded discussions, messaging, task lists, polls, and learning resources.
Police, firefighters, and others in Fort Worth and Tarrant County, Texas, use tools including text messaging with integrated file and document sharing to coordinate across 40 agencies.
The NYC Fire Department is combining business intelligence with social media; inspectors share information across the department and with other agencies.

Source: http://www.baselinemag.com/c/a/Enterprise-Apps/A-Quick-Guide-to-Social-Media-Within-the-Enterprise-870757/.

Social networks have always been a vital aspect of people's social lives and communications. Thus, there is a growing educational and commercial interest in the role of *virtual* social networks in the field of brand advertising. Present-day users of social networks range from the inhabitants of Second Life (a virtual reality meeting place) to the modish, youthful users of Facebook, to the business users who post their experiences with different kind of IT products/services on business social networking websites such as LinkedIn. Such networking websites create an excellent scope for brand advertising as they are trendy, fresh, extensively covered in the press, used by tech-savvy folks, and symbolize both an opportunity and a threat to conventional advertisers.

> *Social networking is crucial to my business. Through social networks I can reach my customers, conduct researches about new trends, and read from the very people who can be interested in my services what they are looking for and what they do expect from the future. Keeping in touch with customers, being able to talk to them in an informal way, without using something as invasive as telephone has been a great improvement to my relations with customers and helped me tune my business to satisfy customers more and more.*

Consumers have started to distrust traditional advertising and the information that is pushed at them with the motive of influencing buying outcomes. People are abandoning not only traditional advertising, but mass media as well. Internet and gaming activities have replaced television to a great extent, which had itself replaced afternoon newspapers. Even if an advertiser or television network is fortunate enough to catch the attention of the viewer, the viewer usually channel surfs to an alternative or fast-forwards if viewing via TiVo or similar time-shifting technology—just to keep away from viewing the advertisements.

Since people are not watching traditional ads through traditional media, it is important to give them new ads through a new medium. Products are recommended among friends, for a fee, or products can be directly recommended to the users who can be targeted when they are in a shopping sort of mood, resulting in viral marketing at warp speed. In essence, the users are trading their "attention" to ads in exchange for the services they use.

Social networks provide the ability to geo-target any member with advertisements that would meet that person's needs based on their profile information. Thus, social networks provide any advertiser the ability to target a very specific audience.

Second Life, with millions of registered users registered with it, must be the first to be included on the list. Some companies have even set up virtual shops here, as shown in Figure 7.1.

Another social network, Flickr, allows its users to upload thousands of photos, to be viewed and commented on by other registered users. Social networking websites allow users to post their impressions and respond to the postings of others, on topics as varied as their attitudes toward the IT industry, or may be a discussion on the latest in technology and IT products/services.

These websites resonate with the actual interests of their users. Whether the interest group is all newly admitted freshman of a local technical university, or

Figure 7.1   A virtual store in Second Life.

all serious users of IT products/services, or those interested in learning how to deal with new business problems with the use of IT, or how to cope with a newly invented technology, or those interested in learning how an IT product functions, these websites provide meaning for their users.

Word-of-Mouth Marketing (WOMM), which is essentially what these social networks offer, is a type of marketing strategy that functions through an individual's personal recommendations of a particular product/service or brand. WOMM spreads outside a formalized setting from one person to another, without any kind of involvement of advertisers.

A recommendation from a person whom one is familiar with and someone whom one can trust is the easiest pathway to a product/service sale, link, or new subscriber. This is because recommendations are usually supposed to be incentive free, in contrast to the apparent driving force of advertisers, who usually overpromise in a bid to boost sales.

If a company wants to sell more of its products/services, it should acquire a greater number of affiliate commissions or simply increase the number of new supporters for its site, WOMM is one the most potent ways to do so. There is not a better method to swell the brand than to encourage a crowd of supporters continually chatting about or referencing it offline or online, through links or conversations.

WOMM strategies include

1. *Leverage existing social networks.* Online social networks have a strongly interwoven set of members who can assist in increasing a product's brand awareness. Example—Facebook, Orkut, MySpace, etc.
2. *Target the influencers.* Search for persons who are authorities or trendsetters in a specified domain. These people should generally be folks having a large and loyal audience and a plethora of personal connections. Once these people spread the message you want, the site or product/service will effortlessly be spread across the targeted audience. Example—celebrities, popular webmasters and bloggers, power users on social networks, etc.
3. *Exclusivity and scarcity.* Launching virally by offering a restricted quantity of website invites, temporal discounts, or limited edition products, in combination with influencer marketing, is an excellent way to increase brand awareness for new products/services. Curiosity is generated by exclusivity, and a consistent demand and conversation results from scarcity in production.
4. *Micromarket.* Providing individuals with highly customizable products along with scarcity and use of social networks can generate word-of-mouth exposure.
5. *Industry marketing.* Focusing on the people who have the potential to build your brand instead of focusing directly on customers. Making your mark within a niche community to leverage connections and build relationships. One needs to become a reputable brand that is recommended by other players in the same industry.

P&G Tremor creates and implements proprietary WOM promotion campaigns. Driven by P&G's marketing and consumer insight expertise, they have the potential to

1. Identify people who are most likely to discuss products/services with others
2. Determine significant customer insights that form the basis of discussions customers are most likely to share
3. Develop a plan with 10 to 12 customer touch-points (both offline and online) that facilitates customers to slot in with and "own" the product/service scheme
4. Generate outcomes of large scale using their panels of hundreds of thousands of participants
5. Measure the impact of tremor on the client's business by using control markets

BzzAgent was launched in 2001 with an aim of helping marketers harness the power of WOM. This company allows people to get early knowledge of new products/services, share their opinions about them with persons they know, and report such actions and opinions so marketers could directly see the results. This community brings marketers and consumers together to systematize and track WOM. It has a three-step methodology:

1. Selection of a challenge medium such as TV, print, radio, etc., to measure against BzzAgent.
2. Execution of the WOMM campaign.
3. Measuring results in terms of brand awareness, brand favorability, purchase intent, and purchase.

Virtual Trade Shows

Like roughly everything else these days, trade show producers are using the web to get in touch with a larger audience of global viewers. For IT products/services, virtual trade shows become even more important as most of the targeted audience already spends a lot of their time on the Internet. A virtual trade show allows participants no matter where they are located geographically to connect and exchange information with each other via the Internet through an online environment that exists online for a restricted time period. Thus, virtual trade shows are actually a specific, short-term, instance of a social network.

While the wizardry of avatars and three-dimensional graphics gave virtual trade shows a "wow" appeal in their early days, companies have shifted their priorities to improving usability for participants and measurability for exhibitors, which makes virtual trade shows much more attractive nowadays.

Companies such as IBM, Cisco, and others are taking their trade shows and conferences virtual. Some, like IBM, have used the virtual world Second Life for such events, but virtual trade shows take it a step further. Unlike Second Life shows, events are more professional and created for a business environment—there are no actual avatars. However, participants can upload a picture, chat with booth representatives, and attend sessions.

After submitting an online registration, participants are provided online name badges. Various other control features limit and/or monitor traffic flow and participation. The advancement in technology allows virtual entities to actually imitate real-world trade show booths with displays and company information. Thus, companies try to digitally replicate everything a customer would get at a face-to-face event. Tailored content is uploaded by the exhibitors to appeal to their target viewers. Communication can be established with the exhibitor with the click of a mouse through e-mail, instant messaging, or a voice-call. Seminars and product demonstrations can be given with the help of multimedia.

Elliot Markowitz, Nielsen Business Media's editorial director of webcasts and digital events, says "First, we have three to four webcasts, because the content drives the audience. Second is the virtual trade show floor, where exhibitors can house anything they would house in a regular booth, as long as it is downloadable. Third, we facilitate live interaction through chat between attendees and exhibitors, but the attendee, not the exhibitor, must initiate the conversation in the booths. Finally, we create networking opportunities, such as live forums, so attendees can meet and talk to one another."

A major advantage of a virtual trade show is that these can save a lot of money over conventional trade shows as they can be conducted anywhere in the world just by the use of a computer without the expenditure of convention centers, lodging, travel, meals, trade show displays, etc. Bottom line—virtual events are cheaper than flying in customers or team members from around the world. Other advantages include

1. The market of accessible customers. A business may be local, but the customers may be global.
2. Business on the Internet is 24/7. This allows a company to service their customers when they are not physically present. Work while you sleep takes on a new meaning when a company takes this new route of doing business on the Internet.
3. Tired of answering the same questions over and over? A website helps to move customers smoothly along the presales process because it will answer the most frequently asked questions posted already on the website. All content created for online events become mini websites in themselves, and user's questions, social media elements such as blogs, etc., are very valuable to leverage to other marketing arenas.
4. At conventional trade shows, customers can only review the products by looking at them at the show location. Using the virtual trade show format, information is available to anyone 24 hours a day.
5. Additional dimensions can be added to the business as products/services can be described in a better way through sound, pictures, and electronic files. Virtual shows can comprise a display hall with trade show displays and booths to display information and products/services much similar to conventional

trade shows. These shows can host virtual seminars, web conferences, and educational presentations. The web allows for limitless scenarios with combinations of sound, video, and text.

6. Participants also have the benefit of live interaction between company representatives and other users.
7. Virtual trade shows are excessively transparent. Every mouse click can be tracked and, thus, measured.

Public Relations

Consider the communications issues surrounding the Exxon Valdez events. On March 24, 1989, an Exxon tanker ran aground and was dumping gummy crude oil into the water just outside of Valdez, Alaska. The first message was sent when CEO Lawrence Rawl decided against making a trip immediately to Valdez, and instead opted to stay in New York. The second message rang loud and clear, but was not until one week following the spill. Exxon's words were then too little, too late, and the message mostly blamed others in defensive, argumentative language. Now this is noted as a communications textbook case of what not to do when messages are needed in a crisis.

A crisis is not the only time messages must be clear. Planned communications must include plenty of planning around the *what*—the message. One of the new key trends in messaging is personalization. Marketers are always striving toward relevance (creating meaningful messages that add value for each customer). Proctor & Gamble is one consumer products company on the edge of messaging in a personalized way. Central to P&G's online branding efforts is the idea of relevance. They have used micro-sites and personalization techniques to communicate with their target markets. For instance, one of P&G's brands, Cover Girl, asks consumers questions around hair and cosmetics that generate personal profiles, and then offers specific advice and promotions via the web based on those profiles.

> *We use social networking often for our business. We monitor Twitter constantly to read our customers @ responses and comments they make about our company and try to send everyone a message back, regardless of whether their comments were negative or positive. We also have a Facebook page that we update daily. Our goal is to keep the lines of communication open with our customers and make them feel comfortable with the people in our office. Also, as an event-based company, we also employ a "Street-team" to help spread word of mouth about our upcoming events. They use social media in all its forms to complete their assignments.*

Most modern companies have dedicated staff assigned to both Facebook and Twitter, the virtual equivalent of the press release. Consumers have 24/7 access to company announcements as well as a forum to asking questions, requesting support, and venting complaints, as shown in Figure 7.2

Figure 7.2   Using Twitter for customer care.

Marketing Control

With good marketing strategies and plans, the marketing manager and the organization are prepared for a marketing effort. However, for a *successful* marketing effort, good implementation (putting plans into operation) is critical. An important aspect of implementation is establishing measurements and controls. These provide feedback that helps the marketer understand the effectiveness of plans and implementation and to plan for the future. Advances in information technology are allowing marketers faster access to information, leading to better implementation and control. Marketing control has been set as a basic activity referred to as "reverse side of planning," focusing on the use of accounting and financial data.

Control is accomplished by continuous feedback known as *feedback control*, but it is important to realize that control reports will not affect change in performance as change will take place only when managers will take relevant actions. An extension of the feedback method is *adaptive control*. This is the variance between results and preset standards. Plans must be modified to reduce this variance.

While Marketing Decision Support Systems (decentralized) allow managers to maintain the records of the marketing program, social enterprising techniques can be used to collaborate with marketing team members on the gist of the marketing campaign, its costs, successes, and issues. If each marketing campaign had its own forum, with a set of facilitated "discussion threads," then the following can be accomplished:

1. Developing a list of critical success factors for the campaign and then monitoring and discussing those metrics. Constantly evaluating contribution margin, so appropriate adjustments can be made to product mix.
2. Producing regular dashboards/scorecards to monitor/review with management and finance regarding spend, effectiveness, and impact.
3. Making sure that the risk of exceeding thresholds is managed and mitigated.
4. Assessing impact and making changes when a situation arises.

Many marketing departments use marketing audits to make sure the campaign stays on track. The forums provide the level of transparency the auditors have long required.

Social Marketing

One way to look at marketing is to consider it as a cycle that includes a range of activities, as shown in Figure 7.3. We have already discussed marketing, customer care, sales, and public relations. Let us take a quick look at some of the other marketing activities, as shown in Figure 7.3.

Figure 7.3 The marketing cycle.

Research: The process of marketing should begin with research. Research includes tasks such as determining information about the organization's target markets—including customer demographics, psychographics, and competitive intelligence. Some say that a market can be created. Others insist that marketing is purely a response to an identified market need. In other words, pioneers create the "need," while followers try to jump on the bandwagon. Research assists in distinguishing between these two viewpoints. External social networks such as Facebook and Twitter can be used to collect this sort of information. Internal social networks can be used to collaboratively evaluate and interpret this data.

Strategy and planning: Data collected during the research activity are input into the strategic planning process. A strategic marketing plan will be created. A series of tactical plans (e.g., promotional, advertising) will be derived from the strategic plan. Strategic plans are usually created by teams of individuals. What better place to hone ideas for the plan than the social network?

Branding: Building a brand involves marketers' examining the market positioning of the product (or firm) in the marketplace and establishing how they would like the product to be perceived by consumers. For example, Donald Trump has become a billionaire by essentially branding himself in the United States. Sony has branded itself as a global leader in consumer electronics. Branding is often done in committee, facilitated by an outside advertising or marketing form expert in this area. Again, the social network has a role to play in both asynchronous as well as synchronous discussions. Keep in mind that technologies do exist that permits teams to communicate graphically. PaperShow (http://www.papershow.com/us/) does just this. Each team member has a pen and a tablet of virtual paper. The team can draw their ideas like a virtual flipchart.

Product development: Product development is usually initiated after research has been conducted. For example, an automobile company's market research finds that there is an untapped opportunity for hybrid sport-utility vehicles (SUVs). The product development initiative involves research and development and careful attention to innovation management within the company—all using electronic whiteboards, social network discussions, etc.

Pricing: Determining price is not easy, but it is the easiest factor to adjust. Price communicates to the market the company's intended value positioning of its product or brand. Think Mercedes Benz versus Ford and Rolex versus Timex. One of the interesting features included in most social network software is the ability to run polls. Rather than just assign an arbitrary price, why not poll stakeholders for their viewpoints on this?

Distribution: Building a product is only half of the equation. Getting it to the consumer is the other half. The distribution strategy consists of packaging, use of channels and affiliates, retailing, wholesaling, and even e-commerce. Facebook and other social networks are beginning to really drive sales. On my Facebook page I count six ads. Essentially, Facebook, with its 800 million users, lets you build a community around your product or business.

The great thing about Facebook is the Like button. Get your product, service, and/or company "liked" by lots of people, and there should be a positive impact on your profitability. There are two good reasons to use the Like button, according to the experts at InternetMarketingSolutions who specialize in Facebook advertising (http://www.adsforfacebook.com/): (1) the Facebook brand carries with it a sense of safety, authority, trust, and familiarity. Having their logo and a connection to them on your website will make your site look and feel more legitimate and trustworthy in the eyes of Facebook users. This is massive in building credibility, increasing traffic, and driving sales. (2) Your website has a chance to go "viral" as friends recommend you to their friends who then recommend it to other friends, etc. As the saying goes: "birds of a feather flock together" and this can be a fantastic way to penetrate your niche and have your customers spread the word in a low commitment way for them that can build amazing results for you around your business.

> *First, we can put up advertisements on social networking sites so that people know more about the business. Next, in sites like Facebook, we can put contests that can only be accessed when you "like" the page. This will lead to your site being known to the user's friends as well. We can also put up different schemes or information about the business. And last, we can also create events (in Facebook) which people are asked to join, thus showing the popularity of the business.*

Risk Management

Risk management addresses the following questions:

1. Are we losing sight of goals and objectives as the project moves forward?
2. Are we ensuring that the results of the project will improve the organization's ability to complete its mission? The result should be an improvement over previous processes.
3. Are we ensuring that sufficient funds are available, including funds to address risks?
4. Are we tracking implementation to ensure "quicker/better/cheaper" objectives are being met?
5. Are we applying appropriate risk management principles throughout the project?
6. Are we taking corrective action to prevent or fix problems, rather than simply allocating more money and time to them?
7. Have changes in the environment created new risks that need to be managed?

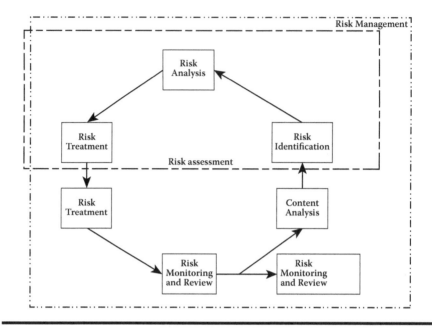

Figure 7.4   Risk management feedback loop.

A proactive risk strategy should always be adopted, as shown in Figure 7.4. It is better to plan for possible risk than have to react to it in a crisis.

Note the communication box on the lower right-hand side of the diagram. Think risk social network as you read through the following. Sound risk assessment and risk management planning throughout project implementation can have a big payoff. The earlier a risk is identified and dealt with, the less likely it is to negatively affect project outcomes. Risks are both more probable and more easily addressed early. By contrast, risks can be more difficult to deal with and more likely to have significant negative impact if they occur later in a project. As explained below, risk probability is simply the likelihood that a risk event will occur. Conversely, risk impact is the result of the probability of the risk event occurring plus the consequences of the risk event. Impact, in laymen's terms, is telling you how much the realized risk is likely to hurt.

The propensity (or probability) of project risk depends on the project's life cycle, which includes five phases: initiating, planning, executing, controlling, and closing. While problems can occur at any time during a project's life cycle, problems have a greater chance of occurring earlier due to unknown factors.

The opposite can be said for risk impact. At the beginning of the project, the impact of a problem, assuming it is identified as a risk, is likely to be less severe than it is later in the project life cycle. This is in part because at this early stage there is much more flexibility in making changes and dealing with the risk, assuming it is recognized as a risk. Additionally, if the risk cannot be prevented or mitigated, the resources invested—and potentially lost—at the earlier stages are significantly lower than later in the project. Conversely, as the project moves into the later phases, the consequences become much more serious. This is attributed to the fact that as time passes, there is less flexibility in dealing with problems, significant resources have likely been already spent, and more resources may be needed to resolve the problem.

The entire process of risk management and mitigation can be performed collaboratively via the social network:

1. The first thing that needs to be done is identify risks. Get a group of stakeholders together in a social network forum to come up with a set of risks.
2. The group should then categorize the risks—for example, project, business, technical, and also known, predictable and unpredictable.
3. The group can then jointly figure out the probability of the risk occurring and assess the impact of that risk, as shown in Table 7.2

All risks above the designated cut-off line must be managed and discussed. Factors influencing their probability and impact should be specified.

Once the risks are collaboratively determined, the team should start work on a risk mitigation, monitoring, and management plan (RMMM), which is a tool to help avoid risks. Causes of the risks must be identified and mitigated. Risk monitoring activities take place as the project proceeds and should be planned early. The team could collaborate on the creation of a risk information sheet for each identified risk as shown in Table 7.3.

**Table 7.2 A Typical Risk Table
(Think Networked Discussion or via Whiteboard)**

Risks	Category	Probability	Impact
Risk 1	PS	70%	2
Risk 2	CU	60%	3

Impact values:

1 — catastrophic
2 — critical
3 — marginal
4 — negligible

Category abbreviations:

BU — business impact risk
CU — customer characteristics risk
PS — process definition risk
ST — staff size and experience risk
TE — technology risk

Table 7.3   A Sample Risk Information Sheet

Risk Information Sheet
Risk id: PO2-4-32 Date: March 4, 2012 Probability: 80% Impact: High
Description: Over 70% of the software components scheduled for reuse will be integrated into the application. The remaining functionality will have to be custom developed.
Refinement/context: Certain reusable components were developed by a third party with no knowledge of internal design standards Certain reusable components have been implemented in a language that is not supported on the target environment
Mitigation/monitoring: Contact third party to determine conformance to design standards Check to see if language support can be acquired
Management/contingency plan/trigger: Develop a revised schedule assuming that 18 additional components will have to be built Trigger: Mitigation steps unproductive as of March 30, 2012
Current status: In process
Originator: Jane Manager

Risk Avoidance

Of course, the best way to handle risks is to avoid them. The best way to avoid them is to have a group of people dedicate a portion of their time. Risk avoidance can be accomplished by evaluating the critical success factors (CSFs) of a business or business line.

One technique that can be adapted to be collaboratively run within the social network, called Process Quality Management or PQM, uses the CSF concept. IBM originated this approach, which combines an array of methodologies to solve a persistent problem: how do you get a group to agree on goals and ultimately deliver a complex project efficiently, productively, and with a minimum of risk?

PQM is initiated by gathering online a team of essential staff. The team's components should represent all facets of the project. Obviously, all teams have leaders, and PQM teams are no different. The team leader chosen must have a skill mix closely attuned to the projected outcome of the project. For example, in a PQM team where the assigned goal is to improve plan productivity, the best team leader just might be an expert in process control, although the eventual solution might be in the form of enhanced automation.

The first task of the team is to develop, in written form, specifically what the team's mission is. With such open-ended goals as, "Determine the best method of employing technology for competitive advantage," the determination of the actual mission statement is an arduous task—best tackled by segmenting this rather vague goal into more concrete subgoals.

In a quick brainstorming session, the team lists the factors that might inhibit the mission from being accomplished. This serves to develop a series of one-word descriptions

It is at this point that the team turns to identifying the CSF, which are the specific tasks that the team must perform to accomplish its mission. It is vitally important that the entire team reach a consensus on the CSFs.

The next step in the IBM PQM process is to make a list of all tasks necessary to accomplish the CSF. The description of each of these tasks, called *business processes*, should be declarative. Start each with an action word such as: study, measure, reduce, negotiate, eliminate, etc.

Table 7.4 and Figure 7.5 show the resulting Project Chart and Priority Graph, respectively, that diagram this PQM technique. The team's mission, in this example, is to introduce just in time (JIT) inventory control, a manufacturing technique that fosters greater efficiency by promoting stocking inventory only to the level of need. The team, in this example, identified 6 CSFs and 11 business processes labeled P1 through P11.

The Project Chart is filled out by first ranking the business process by importance to the project's success. This is done by comparing each business process to the set of critical success factors. A check is made under each critical success factor that relates significantly to the business process. This procedure is followed until each of the business processes have been analyzed in the same way. The PaperShow virtual flip chart software we talked about earlier in this chapter, coupled with networked discussions threads, is a methodology that is hard to beat.

The final column of the Project Chart permits the team to rank each business process relative to current performance, using a scale of A = excellent, to D = bad, and E = not currently performed.

The Priority Graph, when completed, will steer the mission to a successful, and prioritized, conclusion. The two axes to this graph are Quality, using the A through E grading scale, and Priority, represented by the number of checks noting each business process received. These can be lifted easily from the Project Chart for the Quality and Count columns, respectively

Table 7.4 CSF Project Chart

#	Business Process	1	2	3	4	5	6	Count	Quality
								Critical Success Factors	
P1	Measure delivery performance by suppliers	x	x					2	B
P2	Recognize/reward workers					x	x	2	D
P3	Negotiate with suppliers	x	x	x				3	B
P4	Reduce number of parts	x	x	x	x			4	D
P5	Train supervisors					x	x	2	C
P6	Redesign production line	x		x	x			3	A
P7	Move parts inventory	x						1	E
P8	Eliminate excessive inventory buildups	x	x					2	C
P9	Select suppliers	x	x					2	B
P10	Measure				x	x	x	3	E
P11	Eliminate defective parts			x	x	x		3	D

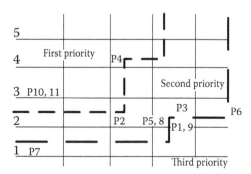

Figure 7.5 CSF priority graph.

The final task as a team is to decide how to divide the Priority Graph into different zones representing first priority, second priority, and so on. In this example, the team has chosen as a first priority all business processes, such as "negotiate with suppliers" and "reduce number of parts," that are ranked from a quality of fair degrading to a quality of not currently performed and having a ranking of three or greater. Most groups employing this technique will assign priorities in a similar manner.

Determining the right project to pursue is one factor in the push for competitive technology. It is equally as important to be able to "do the project right," which can greatly reduce risk.

Project Management

Project management is a natural for social networking. New ideas are wonderful things. However, it takes a lot of planning to get that idea through production and out to the public. The very first phase of a typical project, the concept phase, is the point at which various stakeholders meet for the first time. This is where the scope and objectives of the project are fleshed out in a very high-level document. Meetings can be face to face, but in today's distributed, global environment, this is really becoming hard to do. Feasibility needs to be researched and discussed, and ideas whiteboarded. Ultimately, a project plan needs to be created, which speaks to things such as business case, objectives, scope, budget, schedule, key deliverables, milestones, issues, risks, and critical success factors. The process of creating the project plan and then monitoring the ongoing project can have some online components. Stakeholders can gather online via the network to discuss cost, schedule, and resource issues. Once a draft of the project plan has been created, it can be disseminated via the network for review and, ultimately, approval. Finally, the social network can be used to track progress and keep in daily contact with the project team.

Project staff can use the social network for a wide variety of purposes: brainstorming with other team members, maintaining project documents, storing status reports, etc. Podcasts, blogs, and audio/video can all be combined to provide a rich experience.

I chair most of my meetings online. Everyone I know does this as well. There are a variety of methods to do this, some of which even enable meeting attendees to "see" each other. In all cases, whiteboards, flipcharts, and other usually tactile meeting tools have all been virtualized, so the virtual project meeting is as rich an experience as a face-to-face meeting.

Example

At this point I think it would be a good idea to walk you through applying social networking software to a particular department. I have chosen the IT department, as it is the one I am most familiar with. However, an IT project is fairly similar to any other type of project, so what you read about here is equally applicable to the projects you might be working on.

Socialtext 4.5 (http://socialtext.com) is representative of Enterprise (E 2.0) social networking software that is making its way into the marketplace. Socialtext's People Profiles enable staff to pinpoint just who has the expertise within an organization. It lets folks get to know each other, so to speak. Microblogging enables groups to stay in touch so that they are all on the same page, while internal blogs can be used to create and share knowledge across the organization or across teams. Teams are able to carve out their own private real estate in the social network through the use of groups. Wiki Workspaces are group-editable workspaces that will enable the team to brainstorm and then store the results of whatever they come up with. Social spreadsheets can serve many purposes, one of which is to enable the team to dynamically and collaboratively keep track of their deliverables and schedules. The Dashboard is essentially a social intranet homepage for the group, across groups, or for the entire organization.

Scrum is an agile methodology that is used by software developers who often have to tackle large, complex projects. According to the Scrum Alliance (scrumalliance.org), Scrum is made up of three roles, four ceremonies, and three artifacts, each of which will be described here in turn. The Product owner is the person or persons responsible for the business value of the project. The person who ensures that the team is functional and productive is referred to as the ScrumMaster. Finally, the team, the focus of the Scrum methodology, self-organizes to get the work done.

If the project starts with the ScrumMaster, then he or she is the person who might want to use social networking people profiles to populate the team with those who have the skillsets most suitable for the particular project. It would be important to keep the profiles current with the education and skillsets of everyone in the company, not only IT. Even though, in the parlance of this particular methodology, the Product owner is the person responsible for the business value of the project, the team will invariably need to tap into multiple levels of business expertise to build the assigned system. Just picking any available end user is a sure road to project failure. Having the ability to pick just the right people is critical if the project is to be successful.

The Product owner and the end users involved need to be tightly integrated into the project team. Informational updates can be done via microblogging, as it permits blogging via group channels. If the entire company needs to be kept in the loop, then an internal blog can be used. Since this form of blogging permits a two-way, open dialog, input from wide swathes of employees, and even those outside of the company, is quite possible.

Getting the actual work done involves four processes, called *ceremonies in Scrum speak*. During Sprint planning, the team meets with the product owner to choose a set of work to deliver during a sprint. A virtual, asynchronous meeting can be of help via the Socialtext Group or Wiki Workspace. In either the Group or Wiki Workspace, user stories can be discussed and selected at this point. The stories selected are the ones the team believes it can complete during the sprint. These stories are decomposed into tasks, and estimates are provided for each of these tasks. The resulting task schedule can be loaded to the Social Spreadsheet, where it can be dynamically updated.

Once the team starts work, it meets every day via a Wiki Workspace to discuss progress and problems. Typically, three questions are asked and answered: what did you do yesterday, what will you do today, and do you have any roadblocks. This is referred to as the *Daily Scrum*. Anyone may attend one of these meetings, but only team members may speak. With Socialtext Workspace, people do their work on group-editable web pages that are visible to authorized users. Team members that are away may contribute via e-mail, the contents of which can be posted to a Workspace by including the e-mail address of the Workspace in the address bar of the e-mail.

Periodically, the team will show the product owner what it has accomplished during the current sprint. This is referred to as a *sprint review*. The Product owner and end users can be notified of the sprint review via blog and/or via an announcement on the Dashboard. If the product under development is standards based, it is quite possible that Socialtext Connect can be used to integrate the system under development, or prototype, into the Socialtext environment.

Finally, the team will get together during a sprint retrospective to discuss ways to improve both process and product, again a process that can be done virtually via a Wiki Workspace or Group. A sprint itself will usually last between 2 to 4 weeks. Throughout its entirety, the ScrumMaster keeps the team focused on the goal and keeps track of the progress via the Social Spreadsheet.

This process repeats until enough items in the product backlog have been completed, a deadline arrives, or the budget has been depleted. The goal of Scrum is to make sure that the most valuable work has been completed when the project is terminated.

As is the case with all methodologies, there is a variety of documentation types that evolve during the development of a product, and its associated sprints. The product backlog is a list of desired project features (i.e., requirements) and can well be stored in a Social Spreadsheet. The product backlog is dynamic. That is, items may be deleted, changed, or added at any time. Essentially, there is no such thing as scope creep, a problem common in traditional project management methodologies. However, the product backlog is prioritized, thus ensuring that the highest priority items are always completed first. A sprint backlog is that set of features from the product backlog that the team has agreed to work on during a particular sprint. This is further broken down into discrete tasks. The burndown chart is a visual, again something that can be reproduced using the Socialtext set of tools, that shows all of the work remaining.

Collaborative Development Environments (CDEs)

A group of scientists from the University of Manchester and the University of Southampton developed a portal that makes it easy to find, use, and share scientific workflows and other research objects, and to build communities. While primarily for researchers, myExperiment (http://www.myexperiment.org/) is worth a mention as its approach is quite similar to what I am espousing in this chapter.

The myExperiment project team followed a user-driven, agile approach of scientific software design. This approach consists of six key principles: fit in, don't force change; jam today and more jam tomorrow; just in time and just enough; act local, think global; enable users to add value; and design for network effects. As explained by the developers, a range of mechanisms and tools are used to help myExperiment team members to collaborate with the goal of delivering value quickly. Some of these are face-to-face meetings, and others are computer mediated to cope with distributed team work. To coordinate activities day to day, the developers working from different sites have a 1-hour Skype chat daily at 5 p.m. to test changes, discuss and review technical strategies, priorities, and schedule changes, and review new requirements and various options for realizing or rejecting them. The topics are based on the developers' daily activities, informing each other of their progress, making sense of problems together, and solving them. It usually begins with greetings and social chat, and then goes into the main topic. The conversation flow is fast paced with participants very used to typing and instant messaging. It is interesting to note that the project team prefers typing over talking when using Skype. One reason may be that Skype, in this case, functions like a shared wall/whiteboard, allowing participants to draw on information from as many sources as possible (e.g., URLs, multimedia objects, copy and paste e-mail texts).

Weekly meetings are held during which core members in managerial positions track development and re-evaluate priorities. Monthly team meetings allow a wider team membership to take part and meet face to face. Since members are located in different places, collaboration tools such instant messaging are used, as well as for ad hoc interactions on a daily basis. A wiki provides a persistent and shared semiformal record for notes, task lists, and decisions. Additionally, team members have frequent virtual meetings with users.

Two mailing lists (one open for general discussion, one limited to the core team) and a wiki (with open and secure area) are also available. The open mailing list has a dual role, serving as a mechanism for users to comment on existing features and raise new requirements, and for developers to announce progress and discuss in an open way with users how new requests will be dealt with.

Retrofitting a Methodology to Incorporate Social Networking

In this section, we will retrofit the base methodology—the software development lifecycle (SDLC) using the traditional linear approach. Rather than talk about a specific product, as I did in the last section on agile technologies, let us just use the term *group workspace* to mean any combination of group discussion board, wiki, blog, etc. Any of the tools already mentioned, or listed in Appendix A, can be used, including a full-blown "social network maker" such as Socialgo, as shown in Figure 7.6.

The group workspace will have the following capabilities: ability to store documents; ability to store multimedia, such as audio/video transcripts, podcasts; ability to make comments; whiteboarding; ability to launch a survey (i.e., Q&A); link to external resources such as databases and other file systems.

Figure 7.6 Using a social network "making" tool to create a social network on the fly.

The "idea" phase of the SDLC is the point at which the end user, systems analyst, and various managers meet for the first time. This is where the scope and objectives of the system are fleshed out in a very high-level document. Meetings with end users usually utilize a brainstorming format. Using the IBM approach, a virtual environment such as Second Life can be used for this purpose. Since this is not feasible for most, face-to-face meetings can be enhanced with use of the group workspace, where notes and documents can be stored.

Next, a team composed of one or more system analysts and end users tries to determine whether the system is feasible. There are many reasons why systems are not feasible: too expensive, technology not yet available, and not enough experience to create the system are just some of the reasons why a system will not be undertaken. Reasons for and against can also be documented in the workspace or wiki, with interested stakeholders providing responses to any questions raised or commenting on any negative or positive findings. All of this becomes input into a formal feasibility study that can then be published online and/or make its way up the corporate channels for approval.

Once the system is determined to be feasible, systems analysis is initiated. This is the point when the analysts try to ferret out all the rules and regulations of the system. What are the inputs? What are the outputs? What kind of interface is required? What kind of reports would there be? Will paper forms be required? Will any hookups to external files or companies be required? How shall this information be processed?

Normally, this information is obtained using one or more information-gathering techniques. The most common of these techniques is the interview. Questionnaires can also be used. Other techniques include observation and a review of any available documentation (i.e., policy documents, memos, e-mails, etc.). Almost all of this can be done virtually. The only two that are not straightforward are observation and review of available documentation. However, since almost everything is done online nowadays, it is quite possible to use technology to "observe" what it is an end user does online using keystroke loggers, screen capture software that records as videos screen and audio activity (i.e., http://camstudio.org/, http://www.zdsoft.com/), and some quality assurance tools that automatically generate test scripts (e.g., HP Quality Center software). It is also a no-brainer to get access to all available documentation, as it is probably the case that most of it is available online. In all cases, this data should be feed right into the group workspace for review and discussion.

Once all the unknowns are known and are fully documented in the requirements specification, the systems analyst can put flesh on the skeleton by creating both high-level and then detailed designs. All along the way, the accuracy of all of these documents are checked and verified by having the end users and analysts review and discuss all of these documents, which are posted to the group workspace.

Once a complete working design is delivered to the programmers, implementation can get underway. At this point, a new group of stakeholders become active in the group workspace. Up until this point, the programmers were monitoring the group workspace, but not actively involving themselves in the discussions. Their goal was to familiarize themselves with the system so that their learning curve could be reduced to as close to zero as possible.

The detailed design document, which is also posted to the group workspace, contains the details (and all associated diagrams, database descriptions, screen designs, etc.) for the system, along with a task list itemizing human resources assigned to each task, and start and stop date of each task. Many organizations use Microsoft Project for project planning. The server version of Microsoft Project is built on SharePoint, which is integrated to at least one of the social networking platforms we discussed (i.e., socialtext.com).

Programmers will use the group workspace for a variety of purposes: code, which can then be reviewed and discussed by the programming team (i.e., the "walk-through"); status report so that the end users and managers know the status of the development effort; Q&A; and even links to interim deliverables for end-user review. Of course, it is expected that end users will monitor the group workspace on a frequent, if not daily, basis. In this way, they can quickly respond to any questions and make comments on any deliverables they have been asked to review.

At some point, the coding is done. It is now time for testing. There are several different types of testing. Programmers will first do some unit testing to make sure that what they code adheres to the directions they were given. Systems testing, parallel testing, and integration testing are all forms of testing that need involvement from end users, managers as well as the programmers. Again, the group workspace will be used for this purpose. Test scripts should be developed on a joint basis, and the results of the testing of these scripts reviewed collaboratively as well. Many companies have QA (Quality Assurance) departments that use automated tools to test the veracity of systems being implemented. The QA department, therefore, needs to have access to the group workspace as well.

Once the system has been fully tested, it is turned over to production (changeover). Usually, just prior to this, the end-user departments (not just the team working on the project) are trained and manuals distributed. Modern manuals are not usually paperbound. Online manuals and help facilities are now the norm. Of course, it is expected that these will be stored in the group workspace and reviewed before publication.

By now, it is probably obvious to you that I am going to recommend that some, if not all, training be done online. One only has to browse through Youtube.com to see how ubiquitous training videos have become. Short (minutes only) videos tied to specific functionality in the system are recommended. It is also probably obvious that these videos also should be stored in the group workspace.

Key Point

So, let us look at the sum of all of this from a knowledge perspective. At the end of the development effort, the group workspace contains all of the information nuggets that constitute the effort—from specs to brainstorming sessions, from questions and answers to training videos. Ultimately, it can be expected that a "lessons learned" log be added to the mix. The lessons learned log is basically a discussion of what went right and what went wrong with the project. If there is anything that should be reviewed at the outset of the next project undertaken by the organization, it is the lessons learned logs.

However, the sum total of all of this information is really a goldmine of knowledge if all of it is made accessible for future iterations of the project (maintenance) as well as new endeavors. Some of the social networking toolsets do just this, at least in a modified fashion. While no one yet has the ability to do what those Wall Street traders do with their intelligent news-sniffing software, Socialtext's integration to Sharepoint, its API, which can enable an organization to build its own "news-sniffing" tool, or Yammer's ability to turn all "conversations" into a fully searchable knowledgebase, comes close to social enterprising nirvana.

Chapter 8

Social Performance Measurement and Management

Robert S. Kaplan and David P. Norton developed the Balanced Scorecard approach in the early 1990s to compensate for their perceived shortcomings of using only financial metrics to judge corporate performance. They recognized that in this new economy it was also necessary to value intangible assets. Because of this, they urged companies to measure such esoteric factors as quality and customer satisfaction. By the mid-1990s, the Balanced Scorecard became the hallmark of a well-run company. Kaplan and Norton often compare their approach to managing a company to that of pilots viewing assorted instrument panels in an airplane cockpit—both have a need to monitor multiple aspects of their working environment.

In the scorecard scenario, as shown in Figure 8.1, a company organizes its business goals into discrete, all-encompassing perspectives: financial, customer, internal process, and learning/growth. The company then determines cause-effect relationships (e.g., satisfied customers buy more goods, which increases revenue). Next, the company lists measures for each goal, pinpoints targets, and identifies projects and other initiatives to help reach those targets.

Departments create scorecards tied to the company's targets, and employees and projects have scorecards tied to their department's targets. This cascading nature provides a line of sight between each individual, the project they are working on, the unit they support, and how that impacts the strategy of the enterprise as a whole.

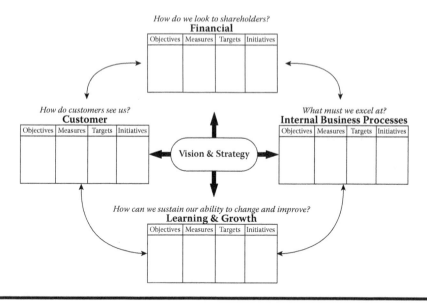

Figure 8.1 The Balanced Scorecard.

We are going to presume that most enterprise uses of social enterprising will be project based (e.g., software development project, marketing project, etc.). For project managers, the Balanced Scorecard is an invaluable tool that permits the project manager to link a project to the business side of the organization using a "cause and effect" approach. Some have likened the Balanced Scorecard to a new language, which enables the project manager and business line managers to think together about can be done to support and improve business performance.

A beneficial side effect of the use of the Balanced Scorecard is that when all measures are reported, one can calculate the strength of relations between the various value drivers. For example, if the relation between high implementation costs and high profits levels is weak for a long time, it can be inferred that the project, as implemented, does not sufficiently contribute to results as expressed by the other (e.g., financial) performance measures.

Adopting the Balanced Scorecard

Kaplan and Norton (2001) provide a good overview of how a typical company adapts to the Balanced Scorecard approach:

> *Each organization we studied did it a different way, but you could see that first they all had strong leadership from the top. Second, they translated their strategy into a Balanced Scorecard. Third, they cascaded the high-level*

strategy down to the operating business units and the support departments. Fourth, they were able to make strategy everybody's everyday job, and to reinforce that by setting up personal goals and objectives and then linking variable compensation to the achievement of those target objectives. Finally, they integrated the Balanced Scorecard into the organization's processes, built it into the planning and budgeting process, and developed new reporting frameworks as well as a new structure for the management meeting.

The key, then, is to develop a scorecard that naturally builds in cause-and-effect relationships, includes sufficient performance drivers and, finally, provides a linkage to appropriate measures, as shown in Table 8.1.

At the very lowest level, a discrete project can also be evaluated using the Balanced Scorecard. The key here is the connectivity between the project and the objectives of the organization as a whole, as shown in Table 8.2. Possible goals related to social enterprising have been bold-faced.

The internal processes perspective maps neatly to the traditional triple constraint of project management, using many of the same traditionally used measures. For example, we can articulate the quality constraint using the ISO 10006:2003 standard. This standard provides guidance on the application of quality management in projects. It is applicable to projects of varying complexity, small or large, of short or long duration, in different environments, and irrespective of the kind of product or process involved.

Quality management of projects in this international standard is based on eight quality management principles:

1. Customer focus
2. Leadership
3. Involvement of people
4. Process approach
5. System approach to management
6. Continual improvement
7. Factual approach to decision making
8. Mutually beneficial supplier relationships

Sample characteristics of these can be seen in Table 8.3. Those characteristics with a tie-in to social enterprising have been bold-faced.

Characteristics of a variable (e.g., quality, time, etc.) are used to create the key performance indicators (KPIs), or metrics, used to measure the "success" of the project. Thus, as you can see from Tables 8.1 through 8.3 above, we have quite a few choices in terms of measuring the quality dimension of any particular project, as well as directly tie in the social enterprising aspects of all of this. More specifically, the perspective that best fits the social enterprising paradigm is learning and growth. Possible metrics are shown in Table 8.4.

Table 8.1 Typical Departmental Sample Scorecard

Objective	Measure/metrics	End of FY 2010 (projected)
Financial		
Long-term corporate profitability	% change in stock price attributable to earnings growth	+25% per year for next 10 years +20% per year for next 10 years
Short-term corporate profitability 1. New products 2. Enhance existing products 3. Expand client-base 4. Improve efficiency and cost-effectiveness	Revenue growth % cost reduction	+20% related revenue growth Cut departmental costs by 35%
Customer		
Customer satisfaction 1. Customer-focused products 2. Improve response time 3. Improve security	Quarterly and annual customer surveys satisfaction index Satisfaction ratio based on customer surveys	+35%—raise satisfaction level from current 60% to 95% +20%
Customer retention	% of customer attrition	−7%—reduce from current 12% to 5%
Customer acquisition	% of increase in number of customers	+10%
Internal		
Complete M&A transitional processes Establish connectivity Improve quality Eliminate errors and system failures	% of work completed % of workforce full access to corporate resources % saved on reduced work % reduction of customer complaints % saved on better quality	100% 100% +35% +25% +25%

Increase ROI Reduce TCO	% increase in ROI % reduction of TCO	+20%–40% –10%–20%
Increase productivity	% increase in customer orders % increase in production/employee	+25 +15%
Product and services enhancements	Number of new products and services introduced	5 new products
Improve response time	Average # of hours to respond to customer	–20 minutes. Reduce from current level of 30–60 minutes to only10 minutes or less
Learning and Innovations		
Development of skills Leadership development and training	% amount spent on training % staff with professional certificates Number of staff attending colleges	+10% +20 18
Innovative products Improved process R&D	% increase in revenue Number of new products % decrease in failure, complaints	+20% +5 –10%
Performance measurement	% Increase in customer satisfaction – survey results % projects to pass ROI test % staff receiving bonuses on performance enhancement % Increase in documentation	+20 +%25 +25% +20%

Table 8.2   A Simple Project Scorecard Approach

Perspective	Goals
Customer	Fulfill project requirements Control cost of the project Satisfying project end users **Collaborating with end users**
Financial	Provides business value (e.g., ROI, ROA, etc.) Project contributing to organization as a whole **Reduction in costs due to enhanced communications**
Internal processes	Adheres to triple constraint: time, cost, quality including a **reduction in the time it takes to complete projects**
Learning and growth	Maintaining currency Anticipate changes Acquired skillsets **Promote collaboration and knowledge sharing**

Table 8.3   ISO 10006 Definition of Quality Management for Projects

Quality characteristic	Subcharacteristic
Customer focus	1. Understanding future customer needs 2. Meet or exceed customer requirements **Social enterprising promotes close collaboration with the various stakeholder groups**
Leadership	1. By setting the quality policy and identifying the objectives (including the quality objectives) for the project 2. By empowering and motivating all project personnel to improve the project processes and product, and **Social enterprising might promote leaderful teams**
Involvement of people	1. Personnel in the project organization have well-defined responsibility and authority 2. Competent personnel are assigned to the project organization
	The use of collaborative social technologies is naturally involving, which will hopefully lead to improve product and process

Table 8.3 *(Continued)* **ISO 10006 Definition of Quality Management for Projects**

Quality characteristic	Subcharacteristic
Process approach	1. Appropriate processes are identified for the project 2. Interrelations and interactions among the processes are clearly identified
	Social enterprising environments enable the team to more effectively and quickly articulate business processes and provides an excellent means for documenting those processes
System approach to management	1. Clear division of responsibility and authority between the project organization and other relevant interested parties 2. Appropriate communication processes are defined
	Social enterprising provides a systematized method for more effective management of project, as well as enhanced communication amongst the various stakeholder groups.
Continual improvement	1. Projects should be treated as a process rather than as an isolated task 2. Provision should be made for self-assessments
	Social enterprising provides the means for constant assessment via the group workspaces.
Factual approach to decision making	1. Effective decisions are based on the analysis of data and information 2. Information about the project's progress and performance are recorded
	Social enterprising provides the ability to easily track project progress and performance.
Mutually beneficial supplier relationships	1. The possibility of a number of projects using a common supplier is investigated
	Social enterprising provides the ability to work more collaboratively with suppliers.

Table 8.4 Representative Social Enterprising Metrics

Learning and growth	
	Number of blogs
	Number of group workspaces
	Number of wikis
	Number of collaborative documents
	Number of teams using social networking
	Number of team members using social networking
	Maturity of collaboration
	Degree of communication efficiency
	Collaborative lessons learned

Attributes of Successful Project Management Measurement Systems

There are certain attributes that set apart successful performance measurement and management systems, including the following:

1. *A conceptual framework is needed for performance measurement and management systems.* A clear and cohesive performance measurement framework that is understood by all managers and staff and that supports objectives and the collection of results is needed.

2. *Effective internal and external communications are the keys to successful performance measurement.* Effective communication with stakeholders is vital to the successful development and deployment of performance measurement and management systems.

3. *Accountability for results must be clearly assigned and well understood.* Managers must clearly identify what it takes to determine success and make sure that staff understand what they are responsible for in achieving these goals.

4. *Performance measurement systems must provide intelligence for decision makers, not just compile data.* Performance measures should relate to strategic goals and objectives, and provide timely, relevant, and concise information for use by decision makers—at all levels—to assess progress toward achieving predetermined goals. These measures should produce information on the efficiency with which resources (i.e., people, hardware, software, etc.) are transformed into goods and services, on how well results compare to a program's intended purpose, and on the effectiveness of activities and operations in terms of their specific contribution to program objectives.

5. *Compensation, rewards, and recognition should be linked to performance measurements.* Performance evaluations and rewards need to be tied to specific measures of success, by linking financial and nonfinancial incentives directly to performance. Such a linkage sends a clear and unambiguous message as to what's important.

6. *Performance measurement systems should be positive, not punitive.* The most successful performance measurement systems are not "gotcha" systems, but learning systems that help identify what works—and what does not—so as to continue with and improve on what is working and repair or replace what is not working.

7. *Results and progress toward program commitments should be openly shared with employees, customers, and stakeholders.* Performance measurement system information should be openly and widely shared with employees.

You will note that quite a few of attributes listed earlier seem to be made for social enterprising environments. Performance measurement systems should be communicated openly throughout the company and what better place for it than the enterprise social networking environments we have been touting in this book. In all cases, however, for the Balanced Scorecard to work it has to be carefully planned and executed.

Measuring Project Portfolio Management

Most organizations will have several ongoing programs all in play at once—all related to one or more business strategies. It is conceivable that hundreds of projects are under implementation, all in various stages of execution. Portfolio management is needed to provide the business and technical stewardship of all of these programs and their projects, as shown in Figure 8.2.

Portfolio management requires the organization to manage multiple projects at one time, thus creating several thorny issues, the most salient ones among which are shown in Table 8.5.

Many of the issues listed in Table 8.5 can be resolved using the social enterprising techniques discussed in this book. Inter- and intraproject communications would be quite possible, as would maintaining motivation across project teams. Maintaining all of the project documentation online means that it would now be possible to record lessons learned. Thus, the knowledge gleaned during past projects would no longer be lost. Finally, information would be able to move through the system quickly and reach team members without delay or loss.

Portfolio management is usually performed by a Project Management Office (PMO). This is the department or group that defines and maintains the standards of process within the organization. The PMO strives to standardize and introduce

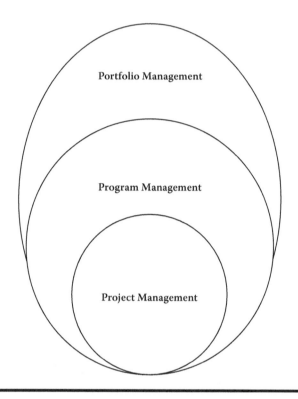

Figure 8.2 Portfolio management.

Table 8.5 Multiple Project Management Issues

Responsibility	Issue
Alignment management	Balancing individual project objectives with the organization's objectives
Control and communication	Maintaining effective communications within a project and across multiple projects
	Maintaining motivation across project teams
	Resource allocation
Learning and knowledge management	Inability to learn from past projects
	Failure to record lessons learned for each project
	Lack of timely information

economies of repetition in the execution of projects. The PMO is the source of documentation, guidance, and metrics on the practice of project management and execution. While most PMOs are independent of the various project teams, it might be worthwhile to assign to the PMO oversight of the social enterprising effort to ensure that there is some degree of standardization in terms of usage throughout the company.

A good PMO will base project management principles on accepted, industry-standard methodologies. Increasingly, influential industry certification programs such as ISO9000 and the Malcolm Baldrige National Quality Award; government regulatory requirements such as Sarbanes–Oxley; and business process management techniques such as the Balanced Scorecard have propelled organizations to standardize processes.

If companies manage projects from an investment perspective—with a continuing focus on value, risk, cost, and benefits—costs should be reduced with an attendant increase in value. This is the driving principle of portfolio management.

A major emphasis of PMO is standardization. To achieve this end, the PMO employs robust measurement systems. For example, the following metrics might be reported to provide an indicator of process responsiveness:

1. Total number of project requests submitted, approved, deferred, and rejected
2. Total number of project requests approved by the Portfolio Management Group through the first Project Request Approval cycle (this will provide an indicator of quality of project requests)
3. Total number of project requests and profiles approved by the Portfolio Management Group through secondary and tertiary Prioritization Approval cycles (to provide a baseline of effort versus ROI for detailed project planning time)
4. Time and cost through the process
5. Changes to the project allocation after Portfolio Rebalancing (total projects, projects canceled, project postponed, projects approved)
6. Utilization of resources: percentage utilization per staff resource (over 100%, 80% to 100%, under 80%, projects understaffed, staff-related risks)
7. Projects canceled after initiation (project performance, reduced portfolio funding, reduced priority, and increased risk)

We will want to compare some of these statistics for projects using social enterprising and those that are not to determine productivity and quality gains based on this process.

Interestingly, PMOs are not all that pervasive in industry. However, they are recommended if the organization is serious about enhancing performance and standardizing performance measurement. Implementation of a PMO is a project unto itself, consisting of three steps: take inventory, analyze, and manage:

1. A complete *inventory* of all initiatives should be developed. Information such as the project's sponsors and champion, stakeholder list, strategic alignment with corporate objectives, estimated costs, and project benefits should be collected.
2. Once the inventory is completed and validated, all projects on the list should be *analyzed*. A steering committee should be formed that has enough insight into the organization's strategic goals and priorities to place projects in the overall strategic landscape. The output of the analysis step is a prioritized project list. The order of prioritization is based on criteria that the steering committee selects. This is different for different organizations. Some companies might consider strategic alignment to be the most important, while other companies might decide that cost-benefit ratio is the better criterion for prioritization.
3. Portfolio management is not a one-time event. It is a constant process that must be *managed*. Projects must be continually evaluated based on changing priorities and market conditions.

It is in the analyze step that the Balanced Scorecard should be created. The scorecard should be fine-tuned in the prioritize step and actually used in the manage step.

In all likelihood, the PMO will standardize on a particular project management methodology. There are two major project management methodologies. The Project Management Body of Knowledge (PMBOK), which is most popular in the United States, recognizes five basic process groups typical of almost all projects: initiating, planning, executing, controlling and monitoring, and closing. Projects in Controlled Environments, PRINCE2, which is the de facto standard for project management in the United Kingdom and is popular in more than 50 other countries, defines a wide variety of subprocesses, but organizes these into eight major processes: starting a project, planning, initiating a project, directing a project, controlling a stage, managing product delivery, managing stage boundaries, and closing a project.

Both PRINCE2 and PMBOK consist of a set of processes and associated subprocesses. These can be used to craft relevant social enterprising metrics, as shown in Table 8.6.

Since the PMO is the single focal point for all things related to project management, it is natural that the project management Balanced Scorecard should be within the purview of this department.

Project Management Process Maturity Model (PM)² and Collaboration

The PM² model determines and positions an organization's relative project management level with other organizations. There are a variety of project management process maturity models, and they are all based on work done by the Software

Table 8.6   Sample Social Enterprising-Related Metrics

Process	Subprocess	Associated sample metric
Initiating a project (IP)	IP1 Planning quality	Number of collaborative planning sessions using social enterprising
	IP2 Planning a project	% resources devoted to planning and review of activities that used social enterprising
	IP3 Refining the business case and risks	% collaborative sessions were risk was assessed

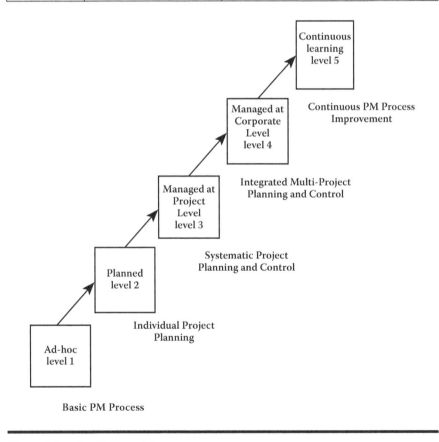

Figure 8.3   The PM² model.

Engineering Institute at Carnegie Mellon on improving the quality of the software development process.

The PM² model defines five steps, as shown in Figure 8.3.

Unfortunately, quite a good number of organizations are still hovering somewhere between the ad hoc level and planned levels. Companies that are serious about improving performance strive to achieve level 5: continuous learning. To do this requires a company to compare itself to others in its peer grouping, the goal of a model such as PM[2.]

In the PM[2] model, key processes, organizational characteristics, and key focus areas are defined, as shown in Table 8.7. Each maturity level is associated with a set of key project management processes, characteristics of those processes, and key areas on which to focus. When mapped to the four Balanced Scorecard perspectives, PM[2] becomes a reference point or yardstick for best practices and processes.

Table 8.7   Key Components of the PM[2] Model

Maturity level	Key PM processes	Major organizational characteristics	Key focus areas
Level 5 (Continuous Learning)	PM processes are continuously improved	Project-driven organization	Innovative ideas to improve PM processes and practices
	PM processes are fully understood	Dynamic, energetic, and fluid organization	
	PM data are optimized and sustained	Continuous improvement of PM processes and practices	
Level 4 (Managed at Corporate Level)	Multiple PM (program management)	Strong teamwork	Planning and controlling multiple projects in a professional manner
	PM data and processes are integrated	Formal PM training for project team	
	PM data are quantitatively analyzed, measured, and stored		

Table 8.7 *(Continued)* **Key Components of the PM² Model**

Maturity level	Key PM processes	Major organizational characteristics	Key focus areas
Level 3 (Managed at Project Level)	Formal project planning and control systems are managed	Team oriented (medium)	Systematic and structured project planning and control for individual project
	Formal PM data are managed	Informal training of PM skills and practices	
Level 2 (Planned)	Informal PM processes are defined	Team oriented (weak)	Individual project planning
	Informal PM problems are identified	Organizations possess strengths in doing similar work	
	Informal PM data are collected		
Level 1 (Ad hoc)	No PM processes or practices are consistently available	Functionally isolated	Understand and establish basic PM processes
	No PM data are consistently collected or analyzed	Lack of senior management support	
		Project success depends on individual efforts	

Thus, measurement across collaborative, distributed partners must be considered in any measurement program. Several interest groups and partnerships in the automotive industry were formed to develop new project management methods and processes that worked effectively in a collaborative environment. The German Organization for Project Management (GPM e.V.), the PMI automotive special interest group, the Automotive Industry Action Group (AIAG), and others have embarked on projects to develop methods, models, and frameworks for collaborative product development, data exchange, quality standards, and project

Table 8.8 Representative Drivers and KPIs for a Standard Project

Balanced scorecard perspective	Drivers	KPIs
Finances	Project budget Increase of business value Multiproject categorization Project management	Human resources Share of sales Profit margin Savings ROI Expenditure
Customer	Customer satisfaction	Cost overrun Number of customer audits Change management Process stability
Process	Adherence to schedules Innovation enhancement Minimizing risks Optimization of project structure Quality	Adherence to delivery dates Lessons learned Number of patent applications External labor Quality indices Duration of change management Product maturity Percentage of overhead Number of internal audits Project risk analysis
Development	Employee satisfaction Employee qualification enhancement	Rate of employee fluctuation Travel costs Overtime Index of professional experience Continuing education costs

management. One recent output from this effort was the ProSTEP-iViP reference model to manage time, tasks, communications in cross-company automotive product development projects (http://www.prostep.org/en/).

A set of drivers and KPIs for a typical stand-alone project can be seen in Table 8.8. Using guidelines from ProSTEP reference model, Niebecker, Eager, and

Table 8.9 Drivers and KPIs for a Collaborative Project (CP)

Balanced scorecard perspective	Drivers	KPIs
Finances/ project	Project cost Increase of business value Categorization into CP management Project maturity	Product costs Production costs Cost overruns Savings Productivity index Turnover Risk distribution Profit margin Feature stability Product maturity index
Process	Adherence to schedules Innovation enhancement Minimizing risks Adherence to collaboration process Quality	Variance in schedule Changes before and after design freeze Duration until defects removed # and duration of product changes # of postprocessing changes Continuous improvement process Project risk analysis Maturity of collaboration process Frequency of product tests Defect frequency Quality indices
Collaboration	Communication Collaboration	Number of team workshops Checklists Degree of communication efficiency Collaborative lessons learned Maturity of collaboration Degree of lessons learned realization
Development	Team satisfaction Team qualification enhancement Trust between team members	Employee fluctuation Project-focused continuing education Employee qualification

Kubitza (2008) have reoriented the drivers and KPIs in Table 8.8 to account for the extra levels of complexity found in a project worked on by two or more companies in a networked collaborative environment. This suits the social enterprising construct quite nicely, as shown in Table 8.9.

Niebecker, Eager, and Kubitza's recommendations expand upon the traditional Balanced Scorecard methodology, providing an approach for monitoring and controlling cross-company projects by aligning collaborative project objectives with the business strategies and project portfolio of each company. Appendix F provides an extensive set of scorecard metrics, which incorporate the collaborative aspects of social enterprising.

Key Point

I am sure you have all heard this old adage, "you can't know where you're going unless you know where you've been." That pretty much wraps up why it is important to measure. In this chapter, we advocated use of the Balanced Scorecard, tied to knowledge management and social enterprising performance metrics.

References

Kaplan, R.S. and D.P. Norton (2001, February). On balance. (Interview). *CFO, Magazine for Senior Financial Executives.*

Niebecker, K., Eager, D., and Kubitza, K. (2008). Improving cross-company management performance with a collaborative project scorecard. *International Journal of Managing Projects in Business, 1*(3): 368–386.

Chapter 9

Mobile Social Enterprising

iPads, iPhones, and all things mobile are best sellers during most holiday seasons. It is now become hard to find anyone without a smartphone or two or four. Some have even predicted the imminent death of the PC, to be replaced by the ubiquitous smartphone. Gartner, the king of all IT research firms, estimates that 1.2 billion people were using smartphones as of the end of 2010.

One would think that a smartphone is just too small to handle enterprise-level computing, let alone enterprise-level social networking. Innovations taken to market, or soon to be taken to market, include touchscreens that touch back, putting virtual controls on your forearm, eye tracking for mobile control, mobile phone mind control, computers that run on light instead of electricity, and cloud services that let small devices act like much more powerful ones. It is no wonder that some call this the fifth wave of computing.

Since modern smartphones have morphed into tiny, full-fledged computers, compete with some pretty sophisticated features and thousands of apps to choose from, we will spend some time in this chapter talking about mobile social enterprising.

Pervasive (Ubiquitous) Computing

Some time ago I wrote a book that talked about something called the "extended Internet." I talked about some exciting innovations. We are not exactly there yet, but I thought I would introduce some of these technologies to you so that you can see for yourself the direction we might be moving in, which will undoubtedly provide expanded capabilities for workers using smartphones.

Sony and Philips are coinventors of near field communication (NFC). NFC works by magnetic field induction. It operates within the globally available and unregulated RF band of 13.56 MHz. With one tap of a mobile device equipped with an NFC chip, a user can make purchases, access information and services, set up conference calls with colleagues, and much more. It is all done without menus, wires, or complex setups. According to Philips, touching is the clearest way to tell a device what to connect to. For example, if you touch a stadium's turnstile, it means "let me in." If you touch a band's "smart poster," it means "let me hear a sample." If you touch a book, it means "read me a sample."

In Germany, people are using NFC-enabled cell phones to buy, store, and use tickets on mass transit systems. In the Netherlands, football fans have turned in their club cards for NFC phones. They are using them to get into the stadium, to buy food and drinks, and to purchase souvenirs. In France, residents are using their phones to pay for shopping and parking, pick up tourist information, and download ringtones and bus schedules from smart posters. At the Philips Arena stadium in Atlanta, Georgia, a major NFC-based trial is allowing fans to get onto the grounds with a wave of their NFC phones. And with another wave, they can buy goods at concession stands and apparel stores just as easily.

There are many forces pushing us to adopt the extended Internet, which is just another way of saying interconnectivity everywhere. VoIP (Voice-Over Internet Protocol) is catching on in many companies. Computer telephony integration, where information is passed seamlessly from a telephone to a customer service representative's computer, is now becoming standard practice. The eXtensible Business Reporting Language (XBRL) is now making it possible to exchange business data between systems on the Internet without rekeying. Broadband over Power Lines (BPL) may bring high-speed Internet access to any location that has access to a power grid. This means that any device plugged into the power grid has the potential for Internet connectivity. The goal is for almost everything to have some sort of link to the Internet.

Japan is on the leading edge of mobile Internet capabilities. In Japan, more non-PC devices are now connected to the Internet than are PCs. The reason for this is Japan's successful implementation and early adoption of 3G (third-generation technology). 3G provides the ability to transfer both voice data (e.g., phone call) and non-voice data (e.g., e-mail, instant messaging). Japan's push into 4G, which is now just becoming more widely available in the United States, enables them to connect all kinds of objects and devices to their "truly ubiquitous network."

Japanese telecoms have introduced a variety of services, some requiring a refinement of the handsets being used by subscribers. NTT (Nippon Telegraph and Telephone) DoCoMo launched the i-mode service in 1999, which required a handset specifically geared for downloading e-mail, and accessing services such as Internet banking and ticket reservation. In 2001, DoCoMo launched the first Java-enabled handsets offering the i-appli service. This service enables the subscriber to download and run small Java applets. Some are stand-alone, such as games that can be saved in the handset. Others, such as stock quotes, require a connection to a server.

Location-based services in Japan were introduced by NTT in the late 1990s. Ima-doko (which translates to "where are we") uses technology that estimates a caller's distance from a wireless transmission tower. DoCoMo's i-area service provides weather, dining, traffic, and other information for 500 areas in Japan, based on location-service technology.

Japanese companies and researchers are investigating and/or using a wide variety of other pervasive technologies, aside from cell phones:

1. *Electronic tags.* These are currently being used as alternatives to bar codes for the purposes of physical plant distribution management. However, a study group was formed to develop measures to promote the advanced use of electronic tags in fields such as health care and education.
2. *Chips.* RFID (radio frequency identification tags) are tiny chips that act as transponders (i.e., transmitters/responders). The chip continuously waits for a radio signal to be sent by a transceiver. When a transponder receives one, it responds by transmitting a unique ID code. RFID tags are widely used to track the location of a tagged item. In Japan, this technology has also been used to great acclaim in a library. This permits the staff to locate a book even if it has been removed from the shelf. DoCoMo's R-Click service delivers information specific to a subscriber's location using RFID tags. The prototype of R-Click has three modes. Koko Dake Click enables the user to stand in one of 10–20 areas (cells) in the test area. The user can click a button on their device to receive information about that area. Mite Toru Click enables the user to receive information about a product or service that is advertised on an electronic board that is showing commercials. Buratto Catch automatically e-mails area information as it detects the user moving around the test area. The system actually anticipates the user's movements and e-mails the information before the user enters it.
3. *Codes.* The 2D code developed by Japan's DENSO Corporation allows for fast reading of large amounts of text. DoCoMo has released several phones that use this technology, which uses the phone's digital camera to scan text. Japan's T-Engine Forum [http://www.t-engine.org], a nonprofit organization that is open to companies from all countries, has developed the UC (Ubiquitous Communicator) for business use. It can communicate in a variety of ways, including TCP/IP, VoIP, Bluetooth, infrared, etc.

So, how can all of this be adapted for social enterprising use? Electronic tags and chips, or RFID tags, can be used to asset-manage anything physical (e.g., hardware, documentation, etc.) generated by or used by a project. 2D codes have been popularized on app-driven smartphones by companies such as Microsoft (tag.microsoft.com). Tags can be placed on anything physical (e.g., books, documents, etc.). When folks scan a Tag on their smartphones using the free Tag app, it can take them to a mobile site, show a video, download an app, add contact details to their address book, or even dial a phone number.

Sensors

The Rutgers University Wireless Internet Network Laboratory (WINLAB) (http://www.winlab.rutgers.edu/pub/Index.html) is working on a multimode wireless sensor (MUSE). It is a multichip module that includes a sensor, RF communications circuitry, a modem, a CPU, and supporting circuits. In addition, WINLAB also developed a wireless sensor network. SOHAN (self-organizing hierarchical ad hoc network) offers significant capacity improvements over conventional ad hoc wireless networks.

The European MIMOSA consortium (http://www.mimosa-fp6.com) has developed an overall architecture specification for a mobile-device centric, open technology platform for ambient intelligence. In the MIMOSA vision, the personal mobile phone is chosen as the intelligent user interface to Ambient Intelligence and a gateway between the sensors, the network of sensors, the public network, and the Internet.

According to Allan (2006), wireless sensor techniques will eventually mature to permit the seamless interconnection of the physical and virtual worlds. Wireless network technologies such as WiMedia Ultra-Wideband (UWB) (http://www.wimedia.org/en/index.asp) will enable end users to download an entire television show in just 1 minute. High data rate UWB can enable wireless monitors, the transfer of data efficiently from digital camcorders, enable wireless printing of digital pictures from a camera without the need for an intervening personal computer, and the transfer of files among cell phone handsets and other handheld devices such as personal digital audio and video players.

Mobile Social Networking

Gartner (http://www.gartner.com) researchers predict a surge in mobile collaboration. They see a world dominated by communication and social interaction taking place within communities, although requiring careful coordination. Communication will not be limited to voice. Instead, video, shared documents, messaging, e-mail, and mobile virtual (tele)presence will become commonplace. To achieve all of this, Gartner is predicting nothing less than a complete re-architecting of our communication and collaboration platforms by the year 2020. New device types and user interfaces will be needed to support such applications as object recognition, biometrics, gesture, body area networks, multi-screens, photo-conferencing, mobile virtual worlds, and proactive contextual notification based on location and context

We are not quite there yet, but there are some available apps that can be loaded to corporate smartphones that do some of the collaborative processing Gartner talks about. Some smartphone makers are actually building in the "smarts" for collaboration. The Samsung Strive enables users to create groups of fellow texters to exchange messages with everyone simultaneously. Texts will show up as "chat-style" threaded messages for easy conversational reading. However, if an organization is going to proceed down this path, they need to carefully coordinate and structure a secure mobile portal.

Given the number of instant messaging streams, those engaged in social enterprising might be involved in a service such as BeeJive (http://www.beejive.com/) might be useful. BeeJive is a multiprotocol instant messaging client that connects the mobile user to the major instant messaging networks. The BeeJive app, which is available for a wide range of mobile devices, weaves together the different messaging services. So, if you start a discussion on Facebook, you will be able to continue it on Yahoo! messaging. Currently, BeeJive supports AIM/MobileMe, MSN/Windows Live, Yahoo!, GoogleTalk, Facebook, MySpace, and Jabber. Of course, this is only useful if these are the services being used. I would expect the ability to integrate private networks via an API sometime in the future, either in BeeJive or from a more enterprise-level competitor. Virgin Mobile is in the game too. Virgin's Connect enables users to link to Facebook, MySpace, YouTube, Flickr, and more all at the same time.

Perhaps the most interesting app of all is Viewdle (http://www.viewdle.com), which was demonstrated at the Consumer Electronics Show (CES) in early 2011. Viewdle uses the phone's camera to pick out faces, using a novel compressed face-print technology, and tag them with names on the fly. It then links these names with social networks and other online sources so that their latest bits of information can be displayed beneath their image. Imagine taking a photo of Sam, a project stakeholder, and then having all of Sam's published wisdom quickly appear beneath his picture. So, as you can see, there is a real movement toward connectivity and integratability via a single device.

There are a variety of ways that collaboration vendors are providing mobile access. We have already talked about Socialtext. Rather than building native, downloadable applications for the iPhone, the BlackBerry, and other devices, the Palo Alto California company has created a mobile website that works on all smartphones. The mobile version of Socialtext includes almost all the features found in its downloadable application. You are able to read colleagues' Twitter-style comments and post your own comments in Socialtext Signals, follow co-workers' activity streams, view their profiles, and also read and edit content in Socialtext's Wiki Workspaces. Similarly, solutions such as Microsoft SharePoint, IBM's LotusLive suite, and more recently Chatter from Salesforce.com are increasingly being delivered as cloud-based services and accessed via a desktop browser or mobile application.

Aepona (http://www.aepona.com), a UK-based company, talks about mobile network-enablement. They stress that it is important to be clear about the distinction between "mobile enablement" and "mobile network-enablement." Mobile enablement means the simple rendering of an existing web or desktop application on a mobile device. Mobile network-enablement means embedding on-demand network capabilities into the application to increase its utility, whether the application itself is web/desktop-based or mobile device based.

Enterprise collaboration services augmented with mobile cloud-based network enablers create additional value that goes well beyond the simple act of making an existing application portable. So, you could think of a cloud collaboration service such as Chatter being augmented with network-derived location and presence information, allowing members of a group to see each other's real-time whereabouts and current status and making decisions on the best way to interact with each other based on this information. Then, using the Messaging and Call Control capabilities of the mobile network, set up an instant or scheduled group call without the hassle of booking a conference bridge and distributing dial-in details and passcodes.

Aepona's solution is to extend the base enterprise collaboration service using APIs provided either by mobile operators or cross-network mobile cloud providers. The advantage of enablement via the mobile cloud providers lies in the ability to reach all employees regardless of which mobile operator they are a subscriber of.

As smartphones become increasingly common, and the workforce becomes more and more mobile, spending a significant amount of time on the go and away from the office, it is important that employees have access to vital information regardless of their location. AHG's (http://www.ahg.com) Absolutely! mobile knowledge management software enables employees to access and contribute information from anywhere.

Absolutely! combines benefits of a traditional KMS (organization and distribution of knowledge), with collaboration and integration of wiki and social networks. Integration with Google Apps provides immediate access to the power of cloud computing, and enables collaborative synchronous work on documents along with sophisticated sharing options and a powerful editing interface. Absolutely! allows employees to collaborate on creating/editing knowledge base articles, that can include

Most, if not all, of the collaborative tools we have been discussing so far have been, or soon will be, ported to many mobile environments, or at least the cloud equivalent of it. So, you should be able to socialtext, yammer, or chatter away on any smartphone available to you. Many more are certain to be in the offing. We can expect all key tech players to jump on the bandwagon, if they have not done so already. However, it is recommended that you look a little further a field than just the traditional tech companies. You might find some solutions that will surprise you.

FirstClass (http://ww.firstclass.com), by OpenText, is primarily a tool for academic institutions looking to provide distance education to their students. Distance education has been around for at least a decade and there are a few good industrial-strength tools out there, all of which provide many of the capabilities business users are actually looking for. FirstClass Mobile offers quite a few intriguing features. At the core of FirstClass' collaboration capabilities are FirstClass Conferences (for large groups or departments) and WorkSpaces (for smaller project teams) which are permission-based shared spaces that facilitate topic-based discussions, e-mail, group calendars, knowledge bases, Communities of Interest, document repositories, peer-to-peer networking, and more.

Software Platforms

Organizations intent on building proprietary social enterprising applications that take advantage of the mobile platform have a few feature-rich, extensible operating systems that support third-party applications to chose from. Each of these software platforms provides a set of APIs, programming tools, and a software emulator that permits testing without the need for the physical device.

Symbian OS is supported by several large cell phone companies, including Nokia (http://symbian.nokia.com), Ericsson, and Samsung. The Symbian OS defines several user interface (UI) reference models for different types of devices. The Symbian OS is a real-time, multithreaded preemptive kernel that performs memory management, process and thread scheduling, hardware abstraction, inter-process communications, and process-relative and thread-relative resource management. Symbian OS uses EPOC C++ as the supporting programming language for both system services implementations and APIs. It also allows Java applications for mobile devices to run on top of a small Java runtime environment.

The Windows Phone 7 mobile OS is built upon existing Microsoft tools and technologies such as Visual Studio, Expression Blend°, Silverlight, and the XNA Framework (http://create.msdn.com/en-us/home/getting_started). Developers already familiar with those technologies and their related tools will be able to create new applications for the Windows Phone without a steep learning curve, as shown in Figure 9.1. Here you see how easy it is to populate the UI of the application with the

Figure 9.1   Populating the UI of a Microsoft Phone using Visual Studio.

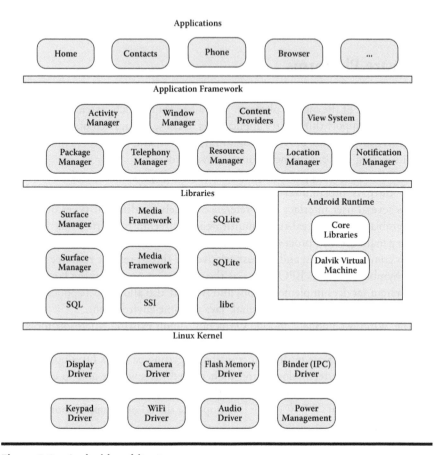

Figure 9.2 Android architecture.

familiar TextBlock, TextBox, and Button controls by dragging the controls from the Toolbox onto the design surface of Visual Studio 2010.

Android is a software stack for mobile devices that includes an operating system, middleware, and key applications, as shown in Figure 9.2. The Android SDK (http://developer.android.com/sdk/index.html) provides the tools and APIs necessary to begin developing applications on the Android platform using the Java programming language. The Google API's add-on extends your Android SDK to give your applications access to Google libraries such as Maps. Using the Maps library, you can quickly add powerful mapping capabilities to your Android applications. Android Cloud to Device Messaging is a service that allows you to send lightweight messages from your application server to an Android application on a device. You can use the service to tell the application to contact the server for updates, for example.

Security

We all use our smartphones as if there are absolutely no security issues to be concerned about. We do address this in Chapter 10, but it is worth a mention here as well. Your smartphone is not secure, not the one you use personally and not the one you might use for any mobile social enterprising.

In 2010 Nicolas Seriot, a Swiss software engineer, published a paper on the topic of iPhone privacy (http://seriot.ch/resources/talks_papers/iPhonePrivacy.pdf). In the paper, he described the software he wrote to access private data on the iPhone, including the 20 most recent searches on the Safari web browser, the user iPhone ID, and e-mail address and a history of connections to a wireless server that reveals data about a user's location.

Given this, it would be a good idea to limit what folks can access via mobile devices.

Key Point

The world is going mobile. So, the IT department needs to morph to support what the mobile platforms developers and users will expect. In this chapter, we addressed the technologies and issues raised by supporting social enterprising via smartphone.

References

Allan, R. (2006, March 30). Wireless sensing spawns the connected world. *Electronic Design, 54*(7).

Chapter 10

Legal, Privacy, and Security Issues

There is a potential for failure of security in both personal and business contexts. While many sites take precautions to keep any of these cases of harassment, cyber-stalking, online scams, and identity theft to an absolute minimum, you still may never know.

Does this concern you?

1. When you buy a Microsoft Kinect, you are bringing into your home or office a telescreen that can recognize who is in the room and interpret body language.
2. A joint effort by a British university and a Canadian security company will bring to a theater near you the ability to monitor facial expressions.
3. Cisco commissioned a survey of 2,600 workers and IT professionals in 13 countries. 20% of IT leaders said that their relationship with their employees is dysfunctional—demonstrating a disconnect between IT, employees, and policies.
4. A recent survey of 1,100 mobile workers found that 22% of employees had breached their employers strict smartphone policies when using nonmanaged personal smartphones to access corporate information.
5. One in eight malware attacks is via a USB device, according to security firm Avast Software.
6. The US Department of Defense estimates that over 100 foreign intelligence organizations have attempted to break into networks of U.S. bases (government, university, and businesses). Every year, hackers steal enough data to fill the Library of Congress many times over.

7. Viruses can come from any connected device (e.g., MP3 players, cameras, fax machines, and even digital picture frames). In 2008, Best Buy found a virus in the Insignia picture frames that they were selling.
8. Companies outsourcing data storage (to a cloud) are responsible for any data that has been breached. So, do make sure the cloud provider or data service provider you use is carefully vetted.
9. Cybercriminals are getting smarter. They invented poisoned search results, rogue antivirus, social networking malware, malicious advertisements, and even built-in instant messaging clients that are used to notify criminals when the mark has logged into his or her online bank account.

Social networkings raise some issues around content use, infringement, defamation, attribution, tort liability, privacy, and securities While most of these relate to public social networking sites such as Facebook and LinkedIn, some of the issues are still relevant to internal social enterprising, particularly if public platforms are integrated into the toolsets.

Website Legal Issues

Defamation/torts. Wikis, blogs, workspaces, etc., provide ample opportunity for defamation (i.e., harming the reputation of another by making a false statement to a third person.) These resources should be monitored for this as well as for possibility of other tort liability. Examples of this would be intentional infliction of emotional distress, interference with advantageous economic relations, fraud, or misrepresentation.

Trademarks. Trademark or service mark notices should be notably displayed wherever the marks appear. If a mark is registered with the U.S. Patent and Trademark Office (http://www.uspto.gov), the ® symbol should be displayed; otherwise, the ™ or ᔆᴹ symbols should be displayed in connection with trademarks or service marks, respectively. Organizations should be vigilant in protecting their trademarks and service marks. They should be equally vigilant that they do not infringe on the trademarks of others. Content that resides on the organization's servers need to be audited to make sure that no trademark infringement is taking place.

Copyrights. A copyright is a form of protection provided to the authors of "original works of authorship" including literary, dramatic, musical, artistic, and certain other intellectual works such as software, both published and unpublished. The 1976 Copyright Act generally gives the copyright owner the exclusive right to reproduce the copyrighted work, to prepare derivative works, to distribute copies or audio recordings of the copyrighted work, to perform the copyrighted work publicly, or to display the copyrighted work publicly.

The copyright protects the form of expression rather than the subject matter of the writing. For example, a description of a machine could be copyrighted, but this would only prevent others from copying the description; it would not prevent others from writing a description of their own or from making and using the machine.

It is important that the organization audit data residing in its social networks to make sure that any content, data, and information is not violating anyone else's copyright. For example, be careful about dynamically accessing Google and downloading research results to a social network. Because Google's content is copyrighted to Google, you would need to take care that you are not violating any copyrights.

Using any third-party content with permission can result in both criminal and civil liability, including treble damages and attorney fees under the U.S. Copyright Act. Essentially, the best course to take is to periodically review all content, screening for possible copyright violations.

Computer Fraud and Abuse Act. Most organizations have provided their employees with PCs capable of wireless Internet access. Many companies and home users have installed wireless Internet connectivity in their offices and homes. It is not usual for people to seek out unsecured "hot spots," as these wireless connections have come to be known. Several computer equipment manufacturers have even developed inexpensive, small hot-spot locaters for this purpose. The Computer Fraud and Abuse Act (CFAA) makes punishable whoever intentionally accesses a computer without authorization. Organizations will have to develop a very clear policy warning employees against using corporate-supplied PCs in this manner.

Corporate Content. Not that long ago, a Congressman made a secret trip to Iraq. When he got there, he tweeted that he had just landed. Secret no more. While we have not focused on the use of Twitter as a social enterprising tool, we expect this tool, or Yammer, its corporate equivalent, to be used. Since these sorts of tools enable almost instantaneous communication with an entire network of people, external as well as internal, users need to take care on what exactly they are communicating.

Developing Your ePolicy

It is important that the organization develop an ePolicy that addresses how employees use e-mail, the Internet, and all things social networking. The ePolicy should be comprehensive and included as part of the employee handbook. This should be reviewed with each new employee. It would also be a good idea to refresh everyone's memory on a yearly basis by sending out an e-mail instructing employees to review the ePolicy. The ePolicy should be stored on the corporate intranet as well. It is recommended that one person be assigned as the main point of contact for the ePolicy, should any questions or problems arise.

Some of the points that should be addressed in the ePolicy include

1. Whether employees may use the Internet for personal use.
2. Whether external social networking services such as Facebook, LinkedIn, or Yammer may be used.

3. Information on whether or not e-mail is being monitored (it should be). Let employees know that e-mail and any social networking system used is owned by the organization and it can be expected that management or others might access e-mail, workspaces, blogs, wikis, etc.
4. Specifics about the type of content that can be maintained within any social networking site (external or internal)—for example, copyrighted materials, etc.
5. Netiquette policies for e-mail and use of social networking websites.
6. Specifics on corporate discrimination and sexual harassment policies, particularly as it pertains to online environments.
7. The fact that individual employees are expected to respect the privacy of the individuals whose information they have access to, and to use all available security methods to preserve the integrity and privacy of information within their control.
8. A directive that specifies that employees are not to engage in any activity that alters or damages data, software, or other technological-related resources belonging to the organization or to someone else, compromising another individual's ability to use technological-related resources, or intentionally disrupting or damaging corporate technological-related resources.
9. A stipulation that individuals are expected to report potential abuse that they might have observed for appropriate resolution.

Security Issues

Not too long ago Cisco commissioned a study on security in the workplace. Their findings are probably not all that surprising to you:

1. One out of five employees altered security settings on work devices to bypass IT policy, so they could access unauthorized websites. More than half said they simply wanted to access the site, while one-third said "it's no one's business" which sites they access.
2. Seven out of ten IT professionals said employee access of unauthorized applications and websites ultimately resulted in as many as half of their companies' data loss incidents. This belief was most common in the United States (74%) and India (79%).
3. Two out of five IT pros dealt with employees accessing unauthorized parts of a network or facility. Of those who reported this issue, two-thirds encountered multiple incidents in the past year, and 14% encountered this issue monthly.
4. One out of four employees admitted verbally sharing sensitive information with nonemployees, such as friends, family, or even strangers. When asked why, some of the most common answers included, "I needed to bounce an idea off someone," "I needed to vent," and "I did not see anything wrong with it."
5. Almost half of the employees surveyed share work devices with others, such as nonemployees, without supervision.

6. Almost two out of three employees admitted using work computers daily for personal use. Activities included music downloads, shopping, banking, blogging, and participating in chat groups. Half of the employees use personal e-mail to reach customers and colleagues, but only 40% said this is authorized by IT.

7. At least one in three employees leave computers logged on and unlocked when they are away from their desk. These employees also tend to leave laptops on their desks overnight, sometimes without logging off, creating potential theft incidents and access to corporate and personal data.

8. One in five employees store system log-ins and passwords on their computer or write them down and leave them on their desk, in unlocked cabinets, or pasted on their computers.

9. Almost one in four employees carry corporate data on portable storage devices outside of the office.

10. More than one in five employees allow nonemployees to roam around offices unsupervised. The study average was 13%, and 18% have allowed unknown individuals to tailgate behind employees into corporate facilities.

As you can see, information systems are vulnerable to many threats that can inflict various types of damage, resulting in significant losses. This damage can range from errors harming database integrity to fires destroying entire systems centers.

Problems can stem from inside the company (wayward employees) to the more common scenario, those outsiders who would do the company harm. All manner of hardware and software is at risk, including mobile devices. In 2010, we all awoke to the news that iPad users' e-mail address and device IDs were exposed. In 2009, security experts identified 30 security flaws in the software and operating systems of smartphones. In 2010, two European university researchers extracted an entire database of text messages from an iPhone, including those that had been deleted, using a corrupt website they controlled.

Losses from these exploits can stem, for example, from the actions of supposedly trusted employees defrauding a system, from outside hackers, or from careless data entry. Organizations should develop an Information Systems Security Program to implement and maintain the most cost-effective safeguards to protect against deliberate or inadvertent acts, including

1. Unauthorized disclosure of sensitive information or manipulation of data
2. Denial of service or decrease in reliability of critical information system (IS) assets
3. Unauthorized use of systems resources
4. Theft or destruction of systems assets

Appendix J contains an extremely detailed DoD (Department of Defense)-originated best practices for security checklist that encompasses the following areas: access control, confidentiality, integrity, availability, non-repudiation, protection, detection, reaction to incidents, configuration management, vulnerability management, personnel security, physical security, security awareness, and training. All of these should be reviewed upon initiation of any social enterprising program to set the parameters for use of that program. The checklist should also be used on a periodic basis to ensure the security of the social enterprising platform on an ongoing basis.

The organization should develop an IS security plan to meet the following goals:

1. Achieve data integrity levels consistent with the sensitivity of the information processed
2. Achieve systems-reliability levels consistent with the sensitivity of the information processed
3. Comply with applicable state and federal regulations
4. Implement and maintain continuity of operations plans consistent with the criticality of user information processing requirements
5. Implement and follow procedures to report and act on IS security incidents

Organizations should conduct periodic security to ensure that

1. Sufficient controls and security measures are in place to compensate for any identified risks associated with the program/system and its environment.
2. The program/system is being operated cost-effectively and complies with applicable laws and regulations.
3. Program/systems' information is properly managed.
4. The program/system complies with management, financial, information technology (IT), accounting, budget, and other appropriate standards.

There are two types of security assessments that must be conducted periodically in computer facilities: risk assessments and security reviews. A risk assessment is a formal, systematic approach to assessing the vulnerability of computer assets, identifying threats, quantifying the potential losses from threat realization, and developing countermeasures to eliminate or reduce the threat or reduce the amount of potential loss. Risk assessments are to be conducted whenever significant modifications are made to the system.

There are three major IT security controls: management controls, operational controls, and technical controls. The term *management controls* is used to address those controls that are deemed to be managerial in nature. The *technical controls* are security controls that should be implemented on systems that transmit, process, and store information. The *operational controls* address security controls that are implemented by people and directly support the technical controls and processing environment.

Management controls are necessary to manage the security program and its associated risks. They are nontechnical techniques, driven by policy and process, and are put in place to meet IT protection requirements. Program security policies and system-specific policies are developed to protect sensitive information transmitted, stored, and processed within system components. Program security policies are broad and are developed to establish the security program and enforce security at the program management level. System-specific security policies are detailed and are developed to enforce security at the system level. The information, applications, systems, networks, and resources must be protected from loss, misuse, and unauthorized modification, access, or compromise. All organizations that process, store, or transmit information must develop, implement, and maintain an IT security program to ensure the protection of the information. The program security policy establishes the security program, assigns the appropriate personnel, and outlines the security duties and responsibilities for all individuals in the program.

Operational controls focus on controls implemented and executed by people to improve the security of a particular system. Media controls address the storage, retrieval, and disposal of sensitive materials that should be protected from unauthorized disclosure, modification, or destruction. Media protection is composed of two security requirements: computer output controls and electronic media controls. Computer output controls apply to all printout copies of sensitive information and state that all printout copies of sensitive information should be clearly marked. Electronic media controls should encompass all the controls of printout materials; however, procedures need to be established to ensure that data cannot be accessed without authorization and authentication from electronic media that contain sensitive information.

All personnel with responsibilities for the management, maintenance, operations, or use of system resources and access to sensitive information should have the appropriate management approval. Organizations should have personnel security procedures to specify responsibilities of the security personnel and system users involved in management, use, and operation of the system. The IT staff must be alert and trained in offensive and defensive methods to protect the organization's information assets. Adequate staffing and key position backup are essential to running and maintaining a secure environment. Personnel security also includes establishing and maintaining procedures for enforcing personnel controls, including the following:

1. Determining appropriate access levels (logically and physically)
2. Ensuring separation of duties (logically and physically) to not compromise system data or thwart technical controls
3. Conducting security training and providing awareness tools for all staff
4. Issuing and revoking user identifications (IDs) and passwords

Technical controls focus on security controls that the computer system executes. These controls depend on the proper configuration and functionality of the system. The implementation of technical controls, however, always requires significant operational considerations. These controls should be consistent with the management of security within the organization.

Table 10.1   Internet Security Issues Checklist

Security issues/information to be addressed
1. Describe the functions (data transfer, forms-based data entry, or browser-based interactive applications, etc.) you are using the Internet to perform
2. Describe your application category(ies) and how they are integrated with your production systems. (information access = hypertext, multimedia, soft content and data; collaboration = newsgroups, shared documents and videoconferencing; transaction processing = Internet commerce and links to IT applications)
3. What communication protocols are in use? (FTP, HTTP, telnet, or a combination?)
4. How do you control access, Identification & Authorization (I&A), sensitive or private information, no repudiation, and data integrity?
5. Are firewalls and/or proxy servers present? If so, describe the software used.
6. Is data encryption used? Is it hardware or software based?
7. What application languages are being used? (HTML, XML, JavaScript, etc.) Are these static, semidynamic, or dynamic?
8. What database connectivity or application program interfaces (API) are in place?
9. Do you have separate web servers? Describe hardware and software.
10. Describe what controls are in effect for shared resources, including any of the following: password protection, user groups, smartcards, biometrics, data encryption, callback systems, virus scanners, vulnerability scanners, and intelligent agents.
11. Are user logons/passwords challenged frequently and under a multilevel protection scheme? Do you allow synchronization of passwords for a single sign-on?
12. Are passwords changed on a regular basis? How often? Is this system controlled or manual?
13. How many people have administrative rights to the application, telecommunications, and web servers? Are these rights separated by function, or can a single person access all of these?
14. Are backups performed of Internet application files and data files? How often?
15. Is a contingency plan in place? Has it been tested? How often is it updated?

When updating the security plan, the organization should refer to the security issues and questions in Table 10.1 to help ensure that their plan is current.

Web Server Security

Securing the OS that the web server runs on is the initial step in providing security for the web server. The web server software only differs in functionality from other applications that reside on a computer. However, since the web server may provide public access to the computer as well as organization-wide access, it should be securely configured to prevent the web server and the host computer from being compromised by intruders.

One of the precautions to take when configuring a web server is to never run the web service as a root or administrative user (super user). Web services or applications should never be located at the root of a directory structure but in a component-specific subdirectory to provide optimum access management. The web service should be run with the permissions of a normal user. This would prevent the escalation of privilege if the web server were ever compromised. Also, the file system of the web server (directories and files) should not be configured to have write access for any users other than those internal users that require such access. Other precautions and secure configuration issues to consider when configuring a public web server are as follows:

1. The web server should be on a separate local area network with a firewall configuration or demilitarized zone (DMZ) from other production systems.
2. The web server should never have a trust relationship with any other server that is not also an Internet-facing server or server on the same local network.
3. The web server should be treated as an untrusted host.
4. The web server should be dedicated to providing web services only.
5. Compilers should not be installed on the web server.
6. All services not required by the web server should be disabled.
7. The latest vendor software should be used for the web server, including all the latest hot fixes and patches.

The web browser is usually a commercial client application that is used to display information requested from a web server. There should be a standard browser that has been approved for use within the system environment. Because of the security holes in scripting languages, such as JavaScript and ActiveX (Microsoft), it is recommended that all scripting languages not required for official systems operation be disabled within the web browsers.

Network security addresses requirements for protecting sensitive data from unauthorized disclosure, modification, and deletion. Requirements include protecting critical network services and resources from unauthorized use and security-relevant denial-of-service conditions.

Firewalls provide greater security by enforcing access control rules before connections are made. These systems can be configured to control access to or from the protected networks and are most often used to shield access from the Internet. A firewall can be a router, a personal computer, or a host appliance that provides additional access control to the site. The following firewall requirements should be implemented:

1. Firewalls that are accessible from the Internet are configured to detect intrusion attempts and issue an alert when an attack or attempt to bypass system security occurs.
2. Firewalls are configured to maintain audit records of all security-relevant events. The audit logs are archived and maintained in accordance with applicable records retention requirements and security directives.
3. Firewall software is kept current with the installation of all security-related updates, fixes, or modifications as soon as they are tested and approved.
4. Firewalls should be configured under the "default deny" concept. This means that, for a service or port to be activated, it must be approved specifically for use. By default, the use of any service or communications port without specific approval is denied.
5. Only the minimum set of firewall services necessary for business operations is enabled, and only with the approval of IT management.
6. All unused firewall ports and services are disabled.
7. All publicly accessible servers are located in the firewall DMZ or in an area specifically configured to isolate these servers from the rest of the infrastructure.
8. Firewalls filter incoming packets on the basis of Internet addresses to ensure that any packets with an internal source address, received from an external connection, are rejected.
9. Firewalls are located in controlled access areas.

Routers and switches provide communication services that are essential to the correct and secure transmission of data on local and wide area networks. The compromise of a router or switch can result in denial of service to the network and exposure of sensitive data that can lead to attacks against other networks from a particular location. The following best practice solutions should be applied to all routers and switches throughout an application environment:

1. Access to routers and switches is password protected in accordance with policy guidance.
2. Only the minimum set of router and switch services necessary for business operations is enabled and only with the approval of IT management.
3. All unused switch or router ports are disabled.
4. Routers and switches are configured to maintain audit records of all security-relevant events.
5. Router and switch software is kept current by installing all security-related updates, fixes, or modifications as soon as they are tested and approved for installation.
6. Any dial-up connection through routers must be made in a way that is approved by the IT management.

All systems should use antivirus (AV) utilities or programs to detect and remove viruses or other malicious code. The AV software must be kept current with the latest available virus signature files installed. AV programs should be installed on workstations to detect and remove viruses in incoming and outgoing e-mail messages and attachments, as well as actively scanning downloaded files from the Internet. Workstation and server disk drives should be routinely scanned for viruses. The specific restrictions outlined below should be implemented to reduce the threat of viruses on systems:

1. Traffic destined to inappropriate websites should not be allowed.
2. Only authorized software should be introduced on systems.
3. All media should be scanned for viruses before introduction to the system. This includes software and data from other activities and programs downloaded from the Internet.
4. Original software should not be issued to users but should be copied for use in copyright agreements. At least one copy of the original software should be stored according to Configuration Management controls.

Table 10.2 provides an outline of topics of a Systems Security Plan.

As the security plan is being develop, ask the following reflective questions:

1. Does the plan address logical and physical security of the system?
2. Does the logical security include password protection, data encryption (if applicable), and access profiles to preclude access to the data by unauthorized personnel?
3. Does the logical security provide for supervisory intervention if needed (determined case by case)?
4. Are negotiable documents or authorizations stored securely?
5. Does the physical security address not only the security of the physical devices but also the building security?
6. Does the physical security address safety and environment issues?
7. Does the security plan address data and application backup procedures?
8. Does the security plan include recovery procedures?
9. Does the security plan include disaster preparedness and recovery procedures? (These may be in a separate plan.)
10. If a department or organization-wide security plan exists, is there a clear delineation of where the system security plan leaves off and the organization plan takes over or vice versa?
11. Does the logical security include separation of duties between functions to prevent potential fraud situations?

Protecting Mobile Devices

Many folks seem to ignore security policies pertaining to their smartphones. They seem not to realize how they could be exposing themselves, their companies, and

Table 10.2 Systems Security Plan Outline

Contents of the Systems Security Plan	
Outline of topics	1. Scope—Describe the site, giving location, configuration, operations, and processing supported, and identification of IT units and applications covered by the plan
	2. Definitions—Explain any terms that might not be familiar to all readers
	3. Overall security assessment—Discuss policies and practices, addressing assignment of security responsibilities, personnel security clearance policies, audit reports, and training; also assess current and planned activities for the next year
	4. Site plan and equipment schematic
	5. Sensitive application systems (obtain the following information for each system): date of last system evaluation, date of last system certification or recertification, date of next evaluation or recertification
	6. Summary of the risk analysis reports
	7. Continuity plan(s)
	8. Summary of the security reviews for all types of processing platforms in use
	9. Training needs with action schedule
	10. Other supporting documents (terminal security rules, local security procedures, user handbooks, etc.)
Policies and procedures	1. Physical security of resources
	2. Equipment security to protect equipment from theft and unauthorized use
	3. Software and data security
	4. Telecommunications security
	5. Personnel security
	6. Continuity plans to meet critical processing needs in the event of short- or long-term interruption of service
	7. Emergency preparedness
	8. Designation of a IT security officer/manager

their companies' stakeholders to harm. While mobile devices cannot be totally secured, there are some measures that can be taken to afford a measure of security:

1. Do not use hotel wireless networks to access sensitive information.
2. Hotel wired networks are often wide open to eavesdropping. All packets for a set of rooms, a floor or several floors, or even the whole hotel, can be seen by all other systems on the network. Unprotected packets are prime targets capture, analysis, and data extraction. It is best to invest in wireless broadband for employee who must travel and bring their work with them.
3. Encrypt all data on a device in case it is stolen or lost, seemingly a common occurrence. Better yet, do not store any information at all on the device. Store it on the server or in the cloud.
4. Configure devices to block external snooping. Firewalls are a must. Firewalls are also available for many handheld devices.
5. Back up critical information. Sounds obvious, but those on the road might neglect to do this. If the organization does not have its own mobile accessible backup server, then using a cloud service such as Microsoft Skydrive (skydrive.login.com).
6. Do not start a laptop with a USB device attached. This can result in malware loaded directly to the computer ahead of some antivirus software.
7. Secure all wireless access points. Strong, mixed passwords should be used and changed on a frequent basis.

Key Point

Social enterprising may not always be done before the organization's firewall. Thus, security policies need to be created and rigorously enforced. Even if social enterprising is done behind a firewall, there are a host of legal issues that should be addressed.

Appendix A—Social Networking Tools

Blogs

Blogs permit team members the ability to create stream of consciousness notes on any subject.

Qumana Inc.

URL: www.qumana.com/about.php

E-mail Address: info@qumana.com

Qumana Software, Inc., is a leading developer of tools and services for bloggers. Qumana's industry recognized tools include Qumana, a blog editor for online publishing; Q Reader (Lektora), an RSS Reader; and Q Ads, an advertising network for bloggers integrated into the Qumana tool.

Qumana Software develops tools for every blogger: PC & Mac, experienced & novice, and multi-lingual. Qumana Software is headquartered in Vancouver, BC.

Zoundry LLC

URL: www.zoundry.com/

E-mail Address: contact@zoundry.com

Whether you are a beginner or active blogger, Zoundry helps you do more with your weblog: Recommend products. Drop in pictures. Tag your posts. Earn cash rewards for yourself or charities when readers buy from your recommendations.

Brainstorming

Brainstorming is a method used to create new ideas by suspending judgment.

Axon Research

URL: web.singnet.com.sg/~axon2000
E-mail Address: axon2000@singnet.com.sg
The Axon Idea Processor is a sketchpad for visualizing and organizing ideas. The Idea Processor exploits visual attributes such as color, shape, size, scale, position, depth, shadow, link, icon, etc. Visual cues facilitate recall, association, and discovery. Diagrams help you to model and solve complex problems. Visualization reinforces your short term memory.

Banxia Software Ltd.

URL: www.banxia.com
E-mail Address: info@banxia.com
Decision Explorer is a proven tool for managing "soft" issues—the qualitative information that surrounds complex or uncertain situations. It allows you to capture in detail thoughts and ideas, to explore them, and gain new understanding and insight. The result is a fresh perspective, and time saved through increased productivity, release of creativity and a better focus.

The Bosley Group

URL: www.mindmapper.com
E-mail Address: info@mindmapper.com
MindMapper is mind mapping software that lets you perform mind mapping on your personal computer. Mind Mapping is an effective and proven technique for note taking, and more, this mind mapping software is easy to learn and use. MindMapper was specifically designed to be used by anyone from beginners to experts utilizing mind mapping techniques. Thick manuals are not necessary due to a intuitive menu system.

CoCo Systems Ltd.

URL: www.visimap.com
E-mail Address: enquiries@visimap.com
VisiMap supports the way you work. It allows you to quickly and efficiently enter, visualize, restructure, and print, transfer, present, and communicate information using a simple, yet powerful, graphical metaphor that we call a "visual map." A visual map is an essentially hierarchical two-dimensional graphical representation that is similar to other common representations variously called idea maps or brain maps.

VisiMap is an easy-to-use creativity-enhancement and productivity-boosting tool for visual organization, brainstorming, problem-solving, document outlining and management, meeting facilitation, planning, HTML, and website generation, personal organization, and many other day-to-day tasks.

Innovation House

URLs: www.brainstorming.co.uk
E-mail Address: info@brainstorming.co.uk
Brainstorming Toolbox is a dedicated piece of software for brainstorming sessions, and it is designed to complement and enhance the free training given in this site. It gives instant access to the techniques described and brings them to life interactively. To brainstorm more effectively, try Brainstorming Toolbox free for 30 days and we are sure you will discover what an excellent tool it is for the generation of new ideas.

Mindjet LLC

URL: www.mindjet.com
E-mail Address: info@mindjet.com
MindManager is award-winning software that boosts team dynamics and increases productivity, visually! All the power of MindManager Standard Edition plus powerful features to boost team dynamics for increased productivity

- Communicate visually and make decisions faster
- Collaborate on projects via Internet conferencing
- Brainstorm online "real time"—quickly, efficiently, and visually

ParaMind Software

URL: www.paramind.net
E-mail Address: paramind@paramind.net
ParaMind works differently than any other writer's helper on the market. ParaMind was built on the new idea of brainstorming by getting every idea that can be expressed in language by "meaningfully exhausting the interactions of words" in any given subject area. Unlike other brainstorming programs, you can configure ParaMind to suit your individual needs

Concept Mapping is a structured process, focused on a topic or construct of interest, involving input from one or more participants, that produces an interpretable pictorial view (concept map) of their ideas and concepts and how these are interrelated.

Classification

Classification employs a set of preclassified examples to develop a model that can classify the population of stored information.

Attrasoft

URL: attrasoft.com/decision
E-mail Address: webmaster@attrasoft.com

DecisionMaker is Attrasoft's application of neural network technology. Decision-Maker analyze tremendous amounts of information available through a database or a spreadsheet, learning relationships, and patterns. This enables DecisionMaker to detect subtle changes and predict results.

DecisionMaker learn by observation. They must observe enough example behavior to identify the underlying patterns. Through this ongoing, self-learning process, DecisionMaker can acquire far more knowledge than any expert in the field. For example, DecisionMaker can become a medical expert in any medical field in minutes.

Entrieva

URL: www.entrieva.com/entrieva/index.htm
E-mail Address: info@entrieva.com
Semio Taxonomy combines the automation benefits of keyword searching with the superior functionality of browsing document collections by automatically building customized browseable taxonomies, that is, hierarchical structures of categories.

But Semio Taxonomy goes beyond simply placing documents within categories. Semio's unique lexical extraction technology allows the entire content within a document to participate in the browseable categories. So what you get is not an overpopulated document list posing as a category, but a full breakdown of concepts found within the source text collection. The level of granularity this gives to the browsing user provides valuable insight that remains unavailable to those using other technologies.

With the proliferation of web portals and intranets, the number and variety of unfamiliar text collections has never been greater. Like a good city map, SemioMap gives you a high-level visual perspective on the information available to you. With SemioMap, you can navigate through key concepts and drill down to find the specific content that matters most to you.

At the same time, SemioMap provides a sense of context that gives you the ability to quickly observe trends, connections, and weak signals from within the text. Analyses of patents, competitive intelligence data, as well as web portal and intranet content are all facilitated by SemioMap.

The graphical web-based interface displays the interrelationships between concepts in the underlying documents. Even users who are completely unfamiliar with a subject can explore intelligently using the SemioMap interface.

Wincite Systems

URL: www.wincite.com
E-mail Address: ljanocia@wincitesystems.com.
WINCITE is a flexible, Windows-based, multidimensional database application designed to capture, organize, manage, and distribute actionable intelligence. WINCITE's powerful user interface, reporting, and searching tools make it easy

for business development, competitive intelligence, marketing, and strategic planning professionals to utilize mission critical information. Information can then be leveraged by distributing it throughout the organization via the World Wide Web, corporate intranets, Lotus Notes, or e-mail.

WisdomBuilder, LLC

URL: www.wisdombuilder.com
E-mail Address: info@wisdombuilder.com
Wisdom Builder™ is the first in a family of software products that tremendously improves the effectiveness of any organization by reducing time spent in collection and managing information, freeing more time for the critical activities of analysis. Building on 25 years of experience in designing and developing intelligence processing solutions for the government and private sectors, Wisdom Builder™ provides a solution to the problem of how to effectively analyze, collect, and manage the glut of raw data that is currently available.

Collaboration and Social Media

Collaborative software, also known as *groupware*, is an application software that integrates work on a single project by several concurrent users at separated workstations (see also Computer supported cooperative work). In its modern form, it was pioneered by Lotus Software with the popular Lotus Notes. Social Media tools expand upon this to provide collaboration with employees, partners, and customers.

37 Signals

URL: basecamphq.com
E-mail Address: email@37signals.com
Millions of people use Basecamp to collaborate and manage projects online.

Caucus Systems, Inc.

URL: www.caucus.com
E-mail Address: sales@caucus.com
Caucus is an open source, web-based eLearning and discussion platform. It is used in universities, nonprofits, and companies wherever learning, conversation, and coordination must happen together.

Collaboration Fabricators

URL: collabfab.com

E-mail Address: info@collabfab.com
CollabFab is a free web-based collaboration tool designed for small workgroups. CollabFab is easily customizable, and it is designed to run on inexpensive, low powered servers using free server software. When using CollabFab, you can manage and share information about multiple projects with your clients, coworkers, customers, suppliers... with anyone!

Communispace Communications

URL: www.communispace.com/
E-mail Address: sales@comunispace.com
Communispace provides a unique combination of software and services that connect customers, employees, and other key stakeholders. It captures their knowledge, experiences, creative ideas, best practices, and feedback. Problems are addressed quickly, new ideas surface in record time, new products ideas are implemented with greater certainty, and learning takes place around real business issues.

Correlate Technologies

URL: www.correlate.com/products/
E-mail Address: info@correlate.com
Correlate K-Map for Lotus Domino.Doc
    Correlate is a completely integrated product into your Domino.Doc environment, hence leveraging your investment in Domino.Doc. This means that a Correlate K-Map, which may hold multiple documents, supports all key document management features including check-in/check-out, versioning, audit trails, profiling, change notification, and much more.
Correlate K-Map for Microsoft SharePoint Portal Server
    Organize your SharePoint content into meaningful KnowledgeMaps. K-Map your projects, policies and procedures, sales kits, product plans, compliance reporting, and more. The Correlate K-Map Web Part also enables Notebook users to "grab" SharePoint content and make it available offline—for either viewing or editing.

Forum One Communications

URL: www.projectspaces.com
E-mail Address: sales@ProjectSpaces.com
ProjectSpaces is a simple, secure, and powerful online workspace and extranet tool to help your project teams, workgroups, committees, partners, and others easily connect, share, and collaborate. It provides a flexible set of online project management and community features to help busy groups of people manage documents, coordinate projects and activities, and share knowledge and information.

Group Tweet

URL: www.longest.com/group
E-mail Address: support@grouptweet.com
GroupTweet turns a standard Twitter account into a group communication hub where members can post updates to everyone in the group using direct messages. When the group account receives a direct message from a group member, GroupTweet converts it into a tweet that all followers can see.

IBM

URL: www-01.ibm.com/software/lotus/products/connections/features.html
E-mail Address: https://www14.software.ibm.com/webapp/iwm/web/signup.do?source=swgmail&S_TACT=109HD06W&lang=en_US
IBM Lotus Connections is a social software for business. It empowers business professionals to develop, nurture, and remain in contact with a network of their colleagues; respond quickly to business opportunities by calling upon the expertise in their network; and discuss and refine new creative ideas with communities of coworkers, partners, and customers.

KickApps

URL: www.kickapps.com
Contact: www.kickapps.com/contact-us/index.php
A complete social networking application including profiles, groups, direct messaging, videos, photos, activity feeds, widgets, etc.

Moxie Software

URL: www.moxiesoft.com/
E-mail Address: www.moxiesoft.com/tal_about/contact_form.aspx
Enterprise social software connecting people, groups, and teams globally and across enterprises to get work done better and faster than ever before.

Mzinga

URL: www.mzinga.com/home.asp
E-mail Address: LearnMore@Mzinga.com
OmniSocial contains hundreds of features to make community, collaboration, and knowledge sharing pervasive across your business—from one single platform. Learn how OmniSocial's modules give you the tools you need to help your employees, customers, and partners network, interact, collaborate, and learn.

Ning

URL: www.ning.com
Contact: hc.ning.com/ning_contact_us.php
Ning is the world's largest platform for creating social websites. Top organizers, marketers, influencers, and activists use Ning to create an online destination that weaves social conversations in content.

Open Text Corporation

URL: www.opentext.com/livelink/index.html
E-mail Address: info@opentext.com
Livelink is a collaborative application that brings together the best minds in your company and connects them to your business partners, suppliers, and customers, to streamline efficiencies, gain first mover advantage, and save you money.

As a highly scalable collaborative commerce application, Livelink delivers web-based intranet, extranet, and e-business solutions. Livelink removes boundaries and connects you to what matters most. People.

Pluck

URL: www.pluck.com
Contact: www.pluck.com/resources/contact.html
Pluck's Social Application Server provides a host of services and components that relieve web developers of everything except the business-level features and operations of their online social experience. Pluck's Social Application Server provides an extensible, template-based mechanism for adding functionality to Pluck's off-the-shelf product, while allowing enterprises to take advantage of all of the existing functionality of the Pluck applications.

Salesforce.com

URL: www.salesforce.com
E-mail Address: https://www.salesforce.com/form/contact/contactme_cloudcomputing.jsp?
With Chatter, it is easy to work together and know everything that is happening in your company. Updates on people, groups, documents, and your application data come straight to you in real-time feeds.

SiteScape

URL: www.sitescape.com
E-mail Address: info@sitescape.com

SiteScape Enterprise Forum 6.0 is a robust collaboration platform that provides the administrative flexibility and performance required by Fortune Global 2000 organizations. It offers an effective and easy way to communicate, share, and build knowledge, and collaborate with employees, customers, or an extended business network.

Users can host online discussions; share and revise documents and files; chat; schedule meetings using shared calendars; and messaging. The powerful, integrated workflow makes collaboration significantly faster, easier, and more efficient by automating repetitive processes.

Forum managers can quickly and easily customize Forum directly or modify the following sample applications to meet their needs: Contact Manager, Sales Lead Manager, Resume Tracker, Help Desk, and Filtered Discussion Forums.

Forum 6.0 optionally supports CAD and other engineering files, real-time web conferencing, as well as a variety of portals, including Oracle Corporation's 9i Application Server™, Plumtree Software's Corporate Portal™, and Viador Inc.'s E-Portal Suite™.

SiteScape Forum is inherently flexible and fits into any environment. It is totally web-based and can be accessed by any device—desktop, laptop, or PDA—that uses an HTML-based browser.

SocialGo

URL: www.socialgo.com/
E-mail Address: support@socialgo.com
Build a social networking website in minutes with drag and drop tools. Developer skills optional!

Socialtext

URL: www.socialtext.com/
E-mail Address: www.socialtext.com/products/freetrial.php
With Socialtext, everyone knows what is going on. People and teams are synchronized, engaged, and informed. Socialtext provides a broad social software platform that has the ease of SaaS and the security of an on-site appliance. Features include social networking, wikis, microblogging, groups, social spreadsheets, dashboard, internal blogs, mobile, etc.

ThoughtWeb, Inc.

URL: www.thoughtweb.com
E-mail Address: info@thoughtweb.com
ThoughtWeb is a unique web-based capability and a breakthrough in the use of intelligent agent and analytical technology.

ThoughtWeb's purpose is to create and share knowledge and information through the use of free-thinking, proactive personal agents (Success Buddies) that provide individuals with intelligent, personalized advice, and guidance on the web. ThoughtWeb solutions are used to share knowledge, diffuse innovation, and enable proactive collaboration.

ThoughtWeb, Inc., has focused on developing intelligent personal agents that are capable of understanding people's personal goals and visions and providing advice, coaching, and knowledge to help them achieve these goals.

By enabling advanced collaboration between humans and computer-based intelligent agents, ThoughtWeb, Inc., has developed technology with enormous benefits in the fields of consumer marketing and corporate knowledge management.

Content Management

Document Management (also called Content Management) is the process of managing documents through their life cycle—from inception through creation, review, storage, and dissemination all the way to their destruction.

Documentum

URL: www.documentum.com
E-mail Address: info@documentum.com
Documentum eBusiness Platform is the industry standard for managing and distributing large volumes of content within and beyond the enterprise. Based on long-standing expertise for managing electronic content, Documentum provides an open, scalable, and completely reliable platform for building and deploying e-business solutions, enabling collaborative portals, meeting regulatory requirements, and powering global websites. From creation through delivery, Documentum manages the content your business depends on.

HiSoftware

URL: www.hisoftware.com/products/prodoverview.htm
E-mail Address: info@ highsoftware.com
HiSoftware Content Quality and Integrity Management Solutions are enterprise web content testing and test management systems that enable companies to quickly and efficiently build, deploy, and maintain highly dynamic, accessible, usable, and searchable Internet, intranet, and extranet websites regardless of content, type, format, or location.

Hummingbird Ltd.

URL: www.hummingbird.com/solutions/cm/
E-mail Address: getinfo@hummingbird.com

Hummingbird's Document Management and Content Management Solutions Control, organize, access, and share vital corporate information quickly, easily, and accurately. Because enterprises around the world are recognizing that information is the currency of their business, there is tremendous value in ensuring that all corporate information, whether in structured or unstructured formats, is captured, managed, and put to work in a meaningful and efficient way. Document and Content Management Solutions ensure that organizations get the most out of their unstructured data—information stored in text files, e-mails, multimedia, etc.—and use the corporate knowledge contained in the data to gain competitive advantage.

IBM

URL: www-306.ibm.com/software/awdtools/suite/cstudio/support/
E-mail Address: info@ibm.com
Rational Suite ContentStudio integrates a winning combination of market-leading software development tools from Rational with best-in-class web content management software from Vignette. Rational Suite ContentStudio unifies code and content for e-business and accelerates web development. By integrating common tools and processes in one powerful solution, Rational Suite ContentStudio unifies the activities of everyone who contributes to your website—including project managers, analysts, software developers, content managers, web designers, and other business contributors. This comprehensive end-to-end solution unites your team around the Rational Suite Team Unifying Platform, and enables the fast and reliable deployment of your changes at Internet speeds.

Mediasurface plc

URL: www.mediasurface.com
E-mail Address: info@mediasurface.com
Mediasurface 5 is the advanced content management solution that enables people, inside and outside of the organization to interactively create content, whilst adhering to business processes through its flexible workflow capabilities. Mediasurface has blended the best of knowledge and content management into Mediasurface, enabling the user community to be able to intelligently store and retrieve content as and when required.

Microsoft

URL: www.microsoft.com/servers/sharepoint
E-mail Address: info@microsoft.com
Microsoft SharePoint Portal Server 2003 extends the capabilities of Microsoft Windows and Microsoft Office by offering knowledge workers a powerful new way

to easily organize, find, and share information. SharePoint Portal Server delivers dramatic new value as a single solution that combines the ability to easily create corporate web portals with document management, content searching, and team collaboration features.

Opentext

URL: www.opentext.com/
Email Address: info@opentext.com
Web-based, enterprise-scalable, and easy to deploy, Livelink for Document Management provides a single authoritative repository for storing and organizing electronic documents. In addition, Livelink for Document Management delivers a set of sophisticated services for managing and controlling documents, including access control, version control, compound documents, audit trails, workflows for automating document change request, review, and approval processes, extensive indexing and search capabilities, and much more.

Stellent, Inc.

URL: www.stellent.com
E-mail Address: info@stellent.com
Stellent° Universal Content Management offers a flexible, robust, and scalable content management solution that allows employees, customers, and partners to collaborate, contribute, and access business content anywhere worldwide. Stellent helps companies fully maximize the value of their information and intellectual assets by bringing content, such as spreadsheets, contracts, marketing materials, CAD drawings, digital assets, records, and catalogs, to the web where it can be efficiently managed.

Talisma

URL: www.talisma.com
E-mail Address: info@talisma.com
Talisma Knowledgebase enables prospects, customers, partners, and employees to find fast, accurate, consistent answers to their specific questions via the web, 24 hours a day, 7 days a week. Talisma Knowledgebase leverages corporate information stored in the structured Talisma Knowledgebase or other unstructured knowledge sources, including customer support, help desk, FAQs, product, and project documentation.

Vivisimo

URL: www.vivisimo.com

E-mail Address: usinfo@vivisimo.com

The Vivísimo Content Integrator brings federated search, or meta-search, capabilities to public and private organizations. Federated search allows users to perform multiple searches at the same time through as many diverse informational sources as needed, whether they are internal documents, intranets, partner extranets, web sources, subscription services and databases, syndicated news feeds, or intelligence portals such as Hoover's. A user enters a search query through a single search interface that acts as an intermediary to various informational repositories. The query is sent simultaneously to all designated search sources, and results are returned to the user in a single list.

Common Sense Reasoning Engine

OpenCyc

URL: www.cyc.com/cyc/opencyc/overview

E-mail Address: info@cyc.com

OpenCyc is the open source version of the Cyc technology, the world's largest and most complete general knowledge-base and commonsense reasoning engine. Cycorp set up an independent organization, OpenCyc.org, to disseminate and administer OpenCyc, and have committed to a pipeline through which all current and future Cyc technology will flow into ResearchCyc (available for R&D in academia and industry) and then OpenCyc.

Data Mining

Data mining, also known as knowledge discovery in databases (KDD), is the practice of automatically searching large stores of data for patterns. To do this, data mining uses computational techniques from statistics and pattern recognition.

Alterian, Inc

URL: www.alterian.com

E-mail Address: info@alterian.com

Alterian's technology is designed to help companies derive the maximum value from even the largest corporate databases.

The Alterian suite—comprising Alterian Engine, Alterian Developer, and Alterian Distributor—is able to perform in-depth analysis of huge volumes of data, producing detailed reports in a variety of formats. Because, even the most complex analysis can be completed in seconds, Alterian supports "train of thought" analysis to drive improved business performance.

This product can be tailored to lead users through complex processes step-by-step. Multitasking facilities allow you to undertake train of thought analyses, while long processes are running in the background.

ANGOSS Software Corporation

URL: www.angoss.com
E-mail Address: info@angoss.com
KnowledgeSTUDIO is a data mining tool that includes the power of decision trees, cluster analysis, and several predictive models to allow users to mine and understand their data from many different perspectives. It includes powerful data visualization tools to support and explain the discoveries.

Attar Software

URL: www.attar.com
E-mail Address: info@attar.co.uk
XpertRule Miner is Attar Software's next generation product evolved from the established Profiler scalable client-server data mining software. Using ActiveX technology, the Miner client can be deployed in a variety of ways. Solutions can now be built as stand-alone mining systems or embedded in other vertical applications under MS-Windows. Deployment can also be over intranets or the Internet. The ActiveX Miner client works with Attar's high-performance data mining servers to provide multitier client-server data mining against very large data bases. Mining can be performed either directly against the data in situ, or by high-performance mining against tokenized cache data tables.

Attrasoft

URL: attrasoft.com
E-mail Address: webmaster@attrasoft.com
Predictor is Attrasoft's application of neural network technology. Predictor analyze tremendous amounts of information available through your database or spreadsheets, learning relationships and patterns. This enables Predictor to detect subtle changes and predict results.

Crygon DataScope

URL: www.cygron.com
E-mail Address: info@cygron.com
Cygron DataScope is a powerful, easy-to-use data mining and decision support tool. It utilizes innovative data visualization technology that leverages the natural

human ability to see patterns in pictures rather than numbers. The result is decision-provoking database graphics easily understandable by both specialist and non-specialist users.

By seamlessly integrating state-of-the art data mining and decision support algorithms with its data visualization, it offers an analysis environment powerful enough to meet the needs of the most demanding desktop users.

Dynamic Information Systems Corp

URL: www.disc.com/home
E-mail Address: info@disc.com
OMNIDEX is state-of-the-art information access technology that unlocks the door to corporate data. OMNIDEX advanced indexing delivers high-performance applications for Database Marketing, Data Warehousing, Decision Support, Client/Server, E-commerce, and other web applications.

It is an enterprise-wide data access solution that enhances existing databases, flat files, and document files, including relational databases such as Oracle on Open Systems platforms.

Google

URL: www.google.com/enterprise/gsa/index.html
E-mail Address: info@google.com
The Google Search Appliance is a hardware and software product designed to offer large businesses the productivity-enhancing power of Google search. It is a corporate search solution as simple and powerful as Google itself.

The Google Search Appliance makes the sea of lost data on your web servers, file systems, and relational databases instantly available with one mouse click. Just point it toward your content, add a search box to your site, and in a matter of hours, your users will be able to search through more than 220 different file formats in any language. The Google Search Appliance indexes up to 15 million documents, and its security features ensure that users only see the documents to which they have proper access.

InterLeap Inc

URL: www.interleap.com
E-mail Address: sales@interleap.com
InterLeap system for Windows is a new tool for data miners that allows you to take your multidimensional data structures and generate dynamically linked tables. Tables can be drilled down, inserted as objects in other software, linked to scatter plots, and saved for use with different data.

Megaputer Intelligence Inc.

URL: www.megaputer.com
E-mail Address: info@megaputer.com
PolyAnalyst is a complete data mining workspace. It provides the analyst with all the tools they need to find new patterns in data, enabling business intelligence. Unlike OLAP tools, which only reveal patterns that are known in advance, data mining software uses the latest machine learning techniques to find hidden relationships within data. PolyAnalyst provides more machine learning techniques than any other data mining package, making it the most flexible business intelligence solution on the market.

Script Software

URL: www.knowledgeminer.net
E-mail Address: info@knowledgeminer.net
KnowledgeMiner is a data mining tool that enables anyone to use its unique form of modeling to quickly visualize new possibilities. It is an Artificial Intelligence tool designed to extract hidden knowledge from data easily. It was built on the cybernetic principles of self-organization: Learning a completely unknown relationship between output and input of any given system in an evolutionary way from a very simple organization to an optimally complex one.

Spotfire

URL: www.spotfire.com
E-mail Address: info@spotfire.com
Spotfire DecisionSite is a highly configurable eAnalytic application that allows interactive visualization and information analysis, enabling decision makers to make great decisions in eTime. The world's leading research companies have integrated Spotfire's highly graphical environment, along with interactive displays for visualizing, querying, and analyzing information from any source, into their mission-critical work processes.

SPSS Inc.

URL: www.spss.com/clementine
E-mail Address: info@spss.com
It takes in-depth business understanding to find effective solutions to business problems. Clementine's interactive data mining process incorporates your valuable business expertise at every step to create powerful predictive models that address your specific business issues.

Veritas

URL: www.veritas.com/Products/www?c=product&refId=322
E-mail Address: info@veritas.com
Veritas Enterprise Vault™ software provides a flexible archiving framework to enable the discovery of content held within e-mail, file system, and collaborative environments, while helping to reduce storage costs and simplifying management.

Mashups

Mashups are a new emerging paradigm of Web 2.0 that enables developers, and even more talented end users, to create new web-based applications and services that address specific needs and interests.

JackBe

URL: www.jackbe.com
Contact: www.jackbe.com/about/contact_form.php
JackBe's flagship software product, Presto, is an Enterprise Mashup Platform that includes functionality for creating and syndicating enterprise mashups. JackBe launched a cloud-based version of its Presto product in March 2010. It is hosted on Amazon EC2.

Yahoo! Pipes

URL: pipes.yahoo.com/pipes/
Pipes is a powerful composition tool to aggregate, manipulate, and mashup content from around the web.

Text Mining

Text Mining is about looking for patterns in natural language text, and may be defined as the process of analyzing text to extract information from it for particular purposes. Text mining recognizes that complete understanding of natural language text, a long-standing goal of computer science, is not immediately attainable and focuses on extracting a small amount of information from text with high reliability. The information extracted might be the author, title and date of publication of an article, the acronyms defined in a text or the articles mentioned in the bibliography.

Leximancer

URL: www.leximancer.com
E-mail Address: enquiries@leximancer.com
Leximancer makes automatic concept maps of text data collections. You can use this system for knowledge discovery, subscription services, and document organization.

Megaputer Intelligence Inc.

URL: www.megaputer.com/products/tm.php3
E-mail Address: info@megaputer.com
Making correct decisions often requires analyzing large volumes of textual information.

Social Web Browsers

A few web browsers include extensions for social networking applications.

Flock

URL: www.flock.com
E-mail Address: shawn@flock.com
People use the web today in extremely different ways than they did a decade ago. However, web browsers—the application at the center of all that we do online— has not kept pace with these changes in online behavior.

Flock was founded on the vision that the web browser can and should enable the richest user experience possible across information-gathering, sharing, communication, self-expression, and interaction.

Rock Melt

URL: www.rockmelt.com
E-mail Address: questions@rockmelt.com
RockMelt is a browser built on Chromium, with extensions for Facebook and Twitter.

Appendix B—Community of Practice Practitioner's Guide

1. Introduction

The CoP Practitioner's Guide presents information in the same order that you should follow as you roll out Communities of Practice.

2. Getting Started—How to Create A Community

Purpose	OK—so how do you start? How do you translate this concept of "community" into a functioning body that provides value to its members and the enterprise? How do you facilitate a group of individuals, possibly from different organizations, backgrounds, and locations, into a viable, living source of relevant knowledge that members can tap into? This transformation—from concept to a working reality—is the goal of this section.
Expected Outcomes	• A clear understanding of the roles and responsibilities involved in a community • A community identity • A foundation for community activities
Products	• An established collaborative work environment (instant messenger, chat, e-mail, Corporate Document Management System [CDMS] work space, facilities, community experience locator, etc.) • An orientation workshop for community members • An assessment of community viability
Key Tasks	1. Conduct core planning 2. Prepare for initial community workshop 3. Host initial community workshop 4. Check community progress 5. Build Community Experience Locator
Key Task 1: Conduct Core Planning	The Core Group (working group of key community members) needs to conduct a meeting to determine what building blocks must be in place to launch a community. This section addresses the following building blocks as agenda items for a Core Group planning meeting: • Community Identity • Community Type • Community Roles and Responsibilities • Community Membership • Collaborative Work Environment

Each of these areas is discussed in detail. Additionally, a sample core planning agenda is provided as a tool at the end of this section.

It is essential that those individuals who participated in the community's originating sessions—sessions that identified the community's critical knowledge needs, attend this planning meeting as well. The community's Functional Sponsor, Community Leader, and Facilitator should also be in attendance (if not included in the originating group). (See Community and Corporate Roles and Responsibilities located at the end of this section for a detailed description of the Functional Sponsor, and Community Leader).

Agenda Item: Create Community Identity

Lay the groundwork

One building block for working together is a collective understanding, or identity, for the community. The identity should address the community's purpose, how the community supports the company's Mission and Goals, how the community determines whether or not it is adding value, what members need from the community, and what cultural norms or conventions will be honored.

To save community member time, the Core Group may choose to develop a strawman model that addresses community identity and purpose. By investing some time upfront the Core Group develops the community identity, which will be used during the initial community workshop. Conversely, the community may best be served by fleshing out these ideas itself—the exercise of "thinking collaboratively" may begin to form a shared sense of community among members.

In either approach, the collective identity will be a useful tool when trying to generate interest and membership in the community.

Tip: If the Core Group chooses a strawman model approach, it must be open to a change in direction once presented to the community—try to avoid "pride of ownership."

Agenda Item: Types of Communities

Understanding the intent of the community

A collective understanding of the intent of the community is useful in further clarifying the identity and purpose of the community. There are four types of communities:

1. **Helping Communities** provide a forum for community members to help each other solve everyday work problems.
2. **Best Practice Communities** develop and disseminate best practices, guidelines, and procedures for their members use.
3. **Knowledge Stewarding Communities** organize, manage, and steward a body of knowledge from which community members can draw.
4. **Innovation Communities** create breakthrough ideas, knowledge, and practices.

Determining the primary intent for a community will help to determine how the community will be organized in terms of key activities that it will undertake, community structure, and leadership roles. Although communities may serve more than one of these purposes, most communities focus on one type and develop their structure with that specific intent in mind.

Agenda Item: Clarify Roles and Responsibilities

What roles are played in a community?

Communities may be supported by "corporate" roles that provide resources and infrastructure support, or the community may provide these roles internal to its own community. Useful community roles include a Functional Sponsor, a Core Group, a Community Leader, a Facilitator, and a Logistics Coordinator. These roles are useful when getting a community up and running, creating and maintaining tools to foster collaboration, planning community events, creating or capturing knowledge, sharing knowledge, and providing continued focus and support. Typical community and "corporate" roles and responsibilities are provided at the end of this section.

Agenda Item: Identify Community Members

Who should be included in the community?

Anyone who wants to participate should be welcome at community events. Notwithstanding, it is recommended that prospective community members—individuals who could learn from each other and have a stake in the community's success—be identified and cultivated. Consider positions in the organization who could contribute and benefit from sharing knowledge about their roles.

Without members, there is no community

The essence of a community is its members. Membership is voluntary rather than prescribed. Members are self-organizing and participate because *they get value* from their participation.

Participation should not be mandated

The Core Group and the Community Leader should personally invite prospective members to the initial community workshop and subsequent forums until the community takes on momentum. When encouraging participation, emphasize that this is not another task force or project team. Communities do not have task plans or deliverables. Stress that membership is voluntary and individuals are encouraged to participate only if they see the community purpose to be meaningful and believe they could gain from or contribute to the community.

What makes a good member?

Good members embrace and appreciate diversity of thought and perspective and are key thought leaders.

Tip: A technique for identifying those individuals in your organization that "connect" the informal networks already operating in your organization is social networking and knowledge flow diagramming. Looking at a network of relationships can help you to identify the integrators, or the employees who are seen by many as experts or who are trusted as an information source. Recruiting such individuals [for your community] will make your communication effort easier, as these people have a wide reach in the informal communication network of the organization.

Tip: An alternative technique would be to use the Knowledge Needs Supply Mapping [technique] to identify thought and opinion leaders in your organization. A discussion of this technique is provided as a tool at the end of this section.

Publicize commencement of new communities— stress benefits for members

Tip: The Core Group could "write a short article for publication in internal magazines or bulletins, describing the outcomes of community interaction and what the community sees as the next milestone in its development. This public declaration can set up a creative tension that will help motivate the community to advance."

Agenda Item: Define Collaborative Work Environment

The community will need an operational environment in which to collaborate. The Core Group will need to identify what mechanisms are available and can be put in place.

How will members work together?	Some companies use a Corporate Document Management System (CDMS) as the standard for document management, workflow, and shared workspace.
	Another possibility is the use of chat room and instant messaging capabilities.
	The Community Leader will also need to arrange for meeting rooms. Depending on membership, video conferencing may also be required.
Key Task 2: Prepare for Initial Community Workshop	First and foremost, the goal of the initial community workshop should be to engage member interests and stimulate continued involvement—not increase workload for the members. The first workshop should also serve to begin building relationships among members. Careful planning can help ensure the success of the initial community workshop.

Develop Agenda for Orientation Workshop

The agenda for the initial workshop should include at least the following. A sample agenda is provided as a tool at the end of this section.

- Solidify community identity
- Clarify community intent
- Begin building relationships (exercise)
- Clarify roles
- Provide overview of methods to create, capture, and share knowledge
- Provide overview of how selected tools, e.g., CDMS, may be used to further community goals
- Identify highest priority knowledge needs
- Identify next steps to satisfy specific knowledge needs

The Functional Sponsor should join the workshop to welcome members, encourage participation, and spark dialogue.

Let Core Group establish themselves as members—not directors	*Tip: Consider facilitator services for at least the initial community workshop—the Facilitator should be involved in planning this community orientation and should assist in developing the agenda.*

An e-mail invitation could easily be lost in the shuffle	*Tip: Just sending an e-mail invitation to prospective members is not enough. The Core Group and the Community Leader must reach out, in person, or by telephone, to begin building personal relationships. Personal invitations provide an opportunity to distinguish the community from other requests for time—to stress what the individual can gain from the experience.*
Don't burden members with "administrivia"	*Tip: The community should be free to focus on its purpose— building its knowledge base. This can't be overstated. What you don't want is for the community to get "turned off" by procedural or administrative duties before it even starts.*
Give them a reason to keep coming	*Tip: To jump-start the community, invite a guest speaker to share a best practice/innovation in an area of particular interest to the community.*

Optimum location is critical The optimum location for a workshop is off-site so that interruptions can be controlled. The most successful arrangements for the room include a U-shaped table for participant seating with a Facilitator table in the front for projection equipment and Facilitator supplies.

The room size should reflect the number of team members. If a room is too small, people will feel cramped and trapped. If a room is too large, intimacy will be difficult to establish.

If using flip charts, solid, smooth walls are required for posting and maintaining the *group memory*—discussions and decisions made by the group and documented on flip chart paper. Electronic means, e.g., electronic whiteboards, to capture group memory would also be useful.

What supplies will you need? Three or four easel boards with extra pads of papers (one for each possible subgroup).

- Markers
- Masking tape
- Name tents
- Access to a copier/printer
- Laptop

Key Task 3: Host Initial Community Workshop The initial community workshop presents a *one-time opportunity* to engage member interest. As they say, "first impressions are the most lasting." This orientation should convince members that leadership is ready to invest in the community.

A sample agenda is provided as a tool at the end of this section. The following tips for a successful workshop are cross-referenced to the appropriate agenda item.

Agenda Item: Provide a Guest Speaker

An interview may generate more interest than a canned briefing

Consider conducting an interview with your guest speaker rather than having them deliver a formal briefing. Not only will this approach to knowledge exchange more closely resemble the desired "give and take" of community interactions, it will also demonstrate a useful community technique for gathering knowledge.

Members of the Core Group should serve as provocateurs. Interview questions designed to stimulate interesting dialogue should be prepared.

Tip: Have some questions on hand to spark dialogue during the question and answer period.

Tip: A good learning technique is for the group to collectively list the key or salient points surfaced during the guest speaker's presentation or interview. This serves to reinforce concepts. Key points should be posted on a flip chart and recorded as a possible new knowledge nugget for posting in the shared workspace. A variation might be to hold this exercise until the end of the workshop and summarize key points learned throughout the workshop.

Agenda Item: Solidify Community Identity

Community identity has several components and each needs to be clarified and agreed upon, including common purpose, relationships, success criteria, and norms for interacting.

A community is a network of relationships

The first workshop is a good opportunity to begin the process of building person-to-person relationships among members. It is the human relationships that will sustain the community over time and provide a sense of reciprocity and obligation among each other. To foster this, it is suggested that a relationship-building exercise be included in the initial and subsequent workshops. A sample exercise is provided as a tool at the end of this section. Additional exercises can be found as tools in Section 3, Creating Knowledge.

A common purpose unifies and creates a sense of urgency The best way to unify a community is for its members to share a common purpose. A community's purpose should be centered around knowledge areas that carry a sense of urgency and incite people's passion ... the purpose should be directly connected to the challenges its members face in their work.

Success criteria guide community evolution It is essential that the community realize that it is responsible for determining its success—not enterprise leaders. Members must set their own success criteria for two reasons: it raises the sense of ownership in the CoP and when individuals develop their own performance measures, more demanding targets are set.

Some general success criteria include:

- Sustained mutual relationships
- Quick mobilization for discussion
- Shared methodology
- Rapid flow of information and fostering of innovation
- Acknowledged participant base
- Knowledge of what others know, what they do, and how they contribute
- Mutually defined identities
- Ability to assess appropriateness of actions and products
- CoP developed (or sustained) tools, language, and definitions
- Open communication channels

Here are some other possible success criteria:

- Satisfaction of specific knowledge goals
- Reduction in hours needed to solve problems
- Drop in rework
- Number of innovative/breakthrough ideas
- Member satisfaction survey results
- Transfer of best practices from one member to another
- Adoption of best practices or innovations that were "not invented here"
- Less redundancy of effort among members
- Avoidance of costly mistakes
- Quantitative measures
- Success stories

A word on quantitative measures	Quantitative measures are most valuable when they are tracked over time and compared against a baseline recorded at the start of the initiative. For this reason, it is advisable to try to leverage existing measures if possible. Metrics are particularly important to KM because a KM return on investment often takes significant time to appear. Putting a KM program in effect will impact other business processes as the organization learns to use and leverage the new KM capabilities. This "acculturation" to KM can take 18 to 36 months in some cases. In no case should a KM program be expected to show a return on investment in less than 12 months.
Leverage existing metrics—use available baseline data	For example, if one of the organizational goals is to improve customer satisfaction, there should already be an existing baseline metric for customer satisfaction. The KM initiative should leverage the process already in place to track customer satisfaction in order to track and observe progress towards the goal.
Anecdotes, or stories, can be more powerful than numbers	A story about how knowledge was leveraged in the organization to achieve value does two things. First, it creates an interesting context around which to remember the measure being described. Second, it educates the reader or listener about alternative methods that they themselves might employ to achieve similar results, thus helping to "spread the word" about the KM program and speed up the cultural change. Qualitative measures such as stories, anecdotes, and lessons learned often fulfill one of the primary benefits of KM measurement: allocation of resources and support to your KM pilot project.
Link to business objectives	It is critical that a community be able to link its purpose to specific business drivers or objectives of the organization. By establishing this link, the community can demonstrate direct value to the organization.
Norms help keep a community connected	When people work together or sit close enough to interact daily, they naturally build a connection—they find commonality in the problems they face, see the value of each other's ideas, build trust, and create a common etiquette or set of norms on how to interact. It simply emerges from their regular contact. When building more "intentional" communities, it is tempting to jump right to

"official community business" before the community has had time to form. During community events, allow some time for "technical schmoozing" allowing members to share immediate work problems and to begin helping each other.

Although norms will evolve over time, some initial conventions can easily be discussed and possibly adopted by the community in the initial workshop. Here are some examples.

- Relevant information will be shared as soon as possible
- One conversation at a time during discussions
- Member preferences for regular meeting times, places, etc.
- Frequency of events (schedule or standard—2nd Wednesday of every month)
- An "open meeting" policy—with few exceptions, anyone can attend any meeting
- All planned workshops should have an agenda—each agenda should provide for standard points of discussion, e.g., action item assignment, and tracking
- How to identify areas of interest for evolving agenda items
- Use of facilitators
- When documentation is desired and how the community will ensure its preparation; perhaps a role that rotates amongst members

Tip: Once the community agrees to its "identity," this message should be posted in the workspace as a "welcome" to prospective members.

Tip: Attendees at the workshop should be polled to identify individuals who could benefit from and contribute to the community's knowledge base.

Agenda Item: Prioritize Knowledge Needs

Member agreement on knowledge needs is key to continued involvement

The community must have a shared understanding about what knowledge it needs. Although the proceeding analyses identified needed knowledge, skills, and information (KSIs), it is wise to build consensus around which KSIs are most critical to community members. The *community* should prioritize its knowledge needs.

Tip: In a large group, an effective prioritization method is multi-voting. Allow each member to cast five votes based on what they believe to be the five highest priorities (not allowed to cast more than one vote on any one item). This will quickly identify where there is the most energy and urgency.

Tip: Another prioritization technique is to build consensus on decision criteria, e.g., mission need, safety, cost, and risk. Once consensus is reached on the criteria, the prioritization of knowledge against mutually agreed to criteria will foster commitment and build ownership of the community process.

How will we transform a knowledge need into a knowledge nugget?

Agenda Item: Plan of Action

Once the top knowledge needs have been agreed to, the community should decide how it wishes to approach satisfying these needs. For example, "will the community conduct a search to acquire needed knowledge? Would a "problem solving session" produce the needed knowledge?" (See Section 3, Creating Knowledge, for suggested techniques.) A plan of action should address the "who, what, and when" of how the knowledge need will be satisfied.

Open members' minds to the possibilities of collaborative work tools

Agenda Item: Collaborative Environment

This agenda item is intended to provide members with an overview of available collaborative technology. The goal is not to provide hands-on training,; but rather, to explore collaborative tools and how they can be used to promote member interactions with each other and the knowledgebase.

Schedule the next community forum before you wrap for the day

Agenda Item: Wrap-Up

To close the session, the community should agree to some next steps—at least enough to confirm a date for the next session and suggested agenda items.

Tip: If action items are identified, the Core Group should volunteer for as many as possible—the Core Group should be seen as a resource for the community, not the other way around.

Tip: In closing, conduct a roundtable (where each participant shares their thoughts—whatever is on their minds) to solicit gut reaction, initial reservations, enthusiasm, etc. Be sure to listen rather than defend.

Key Task 4: Check Community Progress

The Community Leader and Core Group should do a quick progress check after the community's first event to ensure the community is on the road to success. The answer to each of the following questions should be "yes." Questions where the answer is "no" present a potential barrier to the community's success. For each identified barrier, a solution should be developed and implemented.

1. Does the community have a common purpose–is the purpose compelling to leadership, prospective members, and their functional managers?
2. Is the common purpose aligned with the organizational strategy?
3. Is the right sponsorship in place—a respected leader who is willing to contribute to the community?
4. Does the Functional Sponsor agree with the community's scope, purpose, and membership?
5. Are Core Group members and the Community Leader strong, content experts, enthusiastic, and able to develop the community?
6. Do members' functional managers agree that "time away from the job" is valuable?
7. Do we have the right content experts to provide perspective and meaning in our membership?
8. Is there a shared space and context for dialogue, advice, and work?
9. Do we have enough members to keep the community alive?
10. Are collaborative tools in place? Are members "set" to use them?
11. Are needed resources, e.g., meeting rooms, VTC, participation in conferences, travel dollars, conference fees, etc., available?

The list is provided as a tool at the end of this section.

Lessons learned provide valuable insight

A second valuable exercise for the Core Group and Community Leader would be to have a "lessons learned" discussion to evaluate how well the initial workshop went. This information will be useful to improving the community's next event, but also, will be beneficial to the next time a new community is initiated. A sample form for collecting lessons learned is provided as a tool at the end of this section.

Tip: A variation might be for the community to complete this exercise in lieu of a roundtable.

Key Task 5: Build Community Experience Locator	Another useful tool for rapidly getting the "right" information to the "right" person at the "right" time is to create a community "experience locator." The locator could be resident on a community's shared workspace and could include key information about members' experience, e.g., top three jobs held and significant experience. A key word search capability might be a feature of this tool. A sample CoP/Experience Locator template is provided as a tool at the end of this section.

Tip: Consider developing your experience locator and hosting it in CDMS.

Tools	• Sample Core Group Planning Meeting Agenda • Community and Corporate Roles and Responsibilities • Social Networks and Knowledge Flow Technique • Knowledge Needs/Supply Map • Sample Community Workshop Agenda (Orientation) • Suggested Exercise: Building Relationships • Community of Practice Early Progress Checklist • Lessons Learned Report Template • Community of Practice/Experience Locator Template

Sample Core Group Planning Meeting Agenda

1. Set Up
    1.1 Welcome
    1.2 Introductions (if applicable)
    1.3 Review objectives/agenda
2. Create Community Identity
    2.1 Clarify purpose
    2.2 Review prioritized knowledge needs
    2.3 Consider success criteria
    2.4 Consider community norms
3. Clarify Community Intent
    3.1 Review types of communities
    3.2 Determine the intent and focus of the community
4. Clarify Roles and Responsibilities
    4.1 Review Functional Sponsor role
    4.2 Review Community Leader role
    4.3 Review Core Group role
    4.4 Review Logistics Coordinator role
    4.5 Review Facilitator role
5. Identify Community Members
    5.1 Review personnel identified in proceeding analysis
    5.2 Brainstorm additional prospective contributors
    5.3 Devise methods to "get the word out"
6. Define Collaborative Work Environment
    6.1 Explore capability for shared workspace (electronic)
    6.2 Evaluate chat room/discussion tools
    6.3 Identify meeting rooms (VTC capabilities)
7. Wrap Up
    7.1 Review next steps/action items
    7.2 Review meeting objectives

Objectives

■ Clarify community origination and purpose
■ Identify prospective community members
■ Determine best methods for community collaboration

Community and Corporate Roles and Responsibilities

Within the context of knowledge management (KM) there are two categories of roles: (1) those associated with a specific community of practice, and (2) those that support and link multiple Communities of Practices and other KM initiatives, e.g., building infrastructure for knowledge transfer. Corporate roles are not specific to a particular community. As the KM strategy evolves and communities are rolled out, corporate roles, for example, Infomediaries, may gain more prominence. It is recognized that some communities will form as a grassroots movement and will not use any corporate resources—some may already be in place and successful. Roles, in this context, do not equate to job positions; they can be viewed as the different hats people wear to accomplish a task. These role descriptions are provided as a guide and should be tailored to suit your community's needs and resources.

Community of Practice Roles and Responsibilities

Functional Sponsors pave the way for community success

Every community must have a Functional Sponsor. The functional sponsor is typically someone who can pave the way for community success. A community's sponsor believes in the value of knowledge sharing and commends participation in community activities. Further, sponsors promote the value of membership across an organization thereby encouraging community growth and commitment of organizational resources. Sponsorship may be shared by more than one person; this may be important if community membership spans multiple organizations.

- Makes community participation a priority for its members
- Builds support for community with Commanding Officers, functional managers, and opinion leaders
- Bolsters community membership—spreads the word
- Plans and coordinates allocation of resources (ensures funding is in place for awards, etc.)
- Acts as champion for the community
- Sets direction and provides guidance
- Resolves issues
- Works with Community Leader to track progress of community

A Core Group is instrumental in establishing effective work methods for the community

The Core Group, a subset of the community, is a working group that initially performs start-up activities, e.g., planning. The Core Group is made up of knowledgeable and experienced members of the community—members who are super subject matter experts. Once the community is established, the Core Group will continue to provide ongoing organizational support.

For example, Core Group members may use their knowledge of the discipline to judge what is important, groundbreaking, and useful and to enrich information by summarizing, combining, contrasting, and integrating it into the existing knowledge base.

- Participates in community
- Gains support of functional managers
- Ensures the infrastructure is in place to meet the knowledge objectives of the community
- Builds community experience locator
- Creates collaborative environment
- Harvests/creates new knowledge
- Establishes taxonomy
- Prescribes tool usage/functionality

Community Leaders provide day-to-day support while serving as a contributing member

The Community Leader, an active member of the community, serves an integral role in the community's success. The Leader energizes the process and provides continuous nourishment for the community. The Leader must continuously strive to further the community's goals.

- Serves as a subject matter expert on the focus of the community
- Plans and schedules community activities
- Connects members with each other
- Brings in new ideas when the community starts to lose energy
- Interfaces with the Functional Sponsor
- Bolsters community membership—spreads the word
- Represents community at briefings
- Acts as liaison with other communities
- Recognizes contributions
- Manages day-to-day activities of the community (collateral duty)
- Tracks budget expenditures (if applicable)

Without members, there is no community

The essence of a community is its members. Membership is voluntary rather than prescribed. Members are self-organizing and participate because they get value from their participation.

- Enjoys continuous learning as a result of participation
- Bolsters community membership—spreads the word
- Populates community experience locator, if applicable
- Works in relevant business process; acts as a subject matter expert on data, process, or both
- Looks outside community to identify relevant information
- Conducts interviews to capture knowledge
- Presents new information to community to determine value added
- Acts as content owner by updating, creating, replenishing, and owning data in repository
- Scans best practice materials
- Performs benchmarking
- Develops rules governing assets; assures documentation consistency
- Participates in face-to-face knowledge sharing experiences
- May be a Core Group member
- May document community proceedings

A Facilitator can serve as a resource for a community

A Facilitator can ensure community forums are productive for all members by acting as an independent CoP process expert.

- Helps create and foster collaborative environment
- Provides process analysis expertise
- Provides tool expertise
- Provides expertise about group dynamics and techniques to help community solve problems and evolve over time

Functional Support provides the backbone

The role of Functional Support provides the backbone for storing knowledge in the collaborative environment.

- Provides on-the-spot expertise on the CoP building process
- Provides help desk services on CoP building process and specific tool support
- May document community proceedings

Corporate Knowledge Management Infrastructure Roles

Logistics Coordinator	The role of Logistics Coordinator provides the administrative workload for a community.

- Coordinates calendars/schedules meetings/events
- Coordinates facilities
- Arranges for equipment

Infomediary	The Infomediary acts as an information broker.

- Gleans data across communities for relevance
- Possibly "connects" data across communities
- Acts as liaison to related projects and Communities of Practice

Project Historian	The Project Historian is not part of a community of practice. The role of the Project Historian is to document project decisions and events so that this information is not lost and can be reused by corporation.

- Provided by individual Project Teams, Business Process Reengineering, or Enterprise Resource Planning effort, or other types of teams or activities
- Captures project history: main events, major discussions/ decisions, sources of information, contacts, etc.

Sample Community Orientation Workshop Agenda

1. Set Up
   1.1 Welcome (from Functional Sponsor)
   1.2 Introductions
   1.3 Review objectives/agenda
2. Guest Speaker
   2.1 Presentation
   2.2 Questions and answers
3. Relationship Building (exercise)
4. Community Identity
   4.1 Clarify purpose
   4.2 Consider success criteria
   4.3 Consider community norms
   4.4 Identify additional prospective members
5. Clarify Community Intent
   5.1 Review types of communities
   5.2 Determine the intent and focus of the community
6. Knowledge Needs
   6.1 Review prioritized knowledge needs
   6.2 Build consensus on prioritization technique
   6.3 Determine top knowledge needs
7. Plan of Action
8. Collaborative Environment
   8.1 Describe tools available for community use
   8.2 Determine member needs for installation, training, or access
9. Wrap Up
   9.1 Review action items/next steps
   9.2 Review meeting objectives
   9.3 Plan next get together

Objectives

■ Solidify community identity
■ Prioritize knowledge needs
■ Develop plan to satisfy highest priority knowledge need

Relationship Building Exercise

Title: Connect with Community Members

Purpose: This exercise is designed to help build personal relationships between members and to begin to answer the questions, "What *do we* know, what *do we need* to know, and *who knows* it?"

Group Size: 5-40

Estimated Time: 20–60 minutes depending on group size

Props: A set of blank, individual, member index cards strung together on a loose ring—perhaps a community key ring! Each member should have a blank set.

1. **Instructions:** Organize participants into groups of four to six (adjust according to group size).
2. Explain that the goal of this activity is to learn about each other's unique backgrounds and perspectives as well as "getting to know" each other better.
3. Give each participant a set of blank index cards.
4. Explain the directions:
   - Each subgroup should convene for 10 minutes to complete your index card.
   - For each member, complete the factoid card.
   - After 10 minutes, disperse subgroup members and regroup into new subgroups—be sure that everyone speaks with each member in one of the subgroup sessions. (Note: Rotations should last just long enough for members to gather information, but still want more time—whet their appetite!)
5. Repeat subgroup formation until each member has completed a card for each member.
6. **Tips:** Provide complete set of blank cards to new members as they join and encourage them to complete them, one-on-one, with each member.
7. As new members join, provide new index cards to existing members and encourage them to complete new cards informally and add them to their rings.

Community of Practice

Early Progress Checklist

1. Does the community have a common purpose—is the purpose compelling to leadership, prospective members, and their functional managers?
2. Is the common purpose aligned with the enterprise strategy?
3. Is the right sponsorship in place—a respected leader who is willing to contribute to the community?
4. Does the Functional Sponsor agree with the community's scope, purpose, and membership?
5. Are Core Group members and the Community Leader strong, content experts, enthusiastic, and able to develop the community?
6. Do members' functional managers agree that "time away from the job" is valuable?
7. Do we have the right content experts to provide perspective and meaning in our membership?
8. Is there a shared space and context for dialogue, advice, and work?
9. Do we have enough members to keep the community alive?
10. Are collaborative tools in place and easily accessible? Are members "set" to use them?
11. Are needed resources, for example, meeting rooms, VTC, participation in conferences, travel dollars, conference fees, etc., available?

Lessons Learned Report	
Situation	
Observer	
Date	
What Went Right?	
What Went Wrong?	
Suggestions	

Community of Practice/Experience Locator Template

With today's technologies, for example, e-mail and the Internet, knowledge can be rapidly transferred. Only how does someone know whom to contact if they want to learn more about a specific topic? Consider the following true anecdote:

I joined the organization on March 16, 1998, without previous experience. After one week of training, I joined a project team. After one day of training on the project, I was assigned a task to learn a particular technology that was new to everyone on the team. I was given a bunch of books and told that I had three days to learn how to create a project using this technology.

In my first week of training, I remembered learning about the company's expertise database. I sent an e-mail to four people I found in the database asking for their help. One of them sent me a document containing exactly what I wanted. Instead of three days, my task was completed in half a day.

So how do you connect knowledge seekers with knowledge holders and facilitate knowledge exchange? One method seen in industry today is the use of experience locators or "corporate yellow pages." Each community should post a CoP descriptor on the corporate website. The descriptor should be easily accessible by employees and should provide the following types of information.

- Name of community
- Purpose of community (purpose and scope)
- Name of Functional Sponsor (organization, location, phone number, e-mail)
- Name of Community Leader (organization, location, phone number, e-mail)
- Name of Core Group members (organization, location, phone number, e-mail)
- Membership contact information (organization, location, phone number, e-mail) (or direct link to members)
- Membership profiles (could include key information about members' experience, for example, top three jobs held, fields of expertise, project experience, education, training, certifications, and publications)
- A listing (or link to) of community knowledge assets

Some interactive play could enhance the usefulness of a CoP/Experience Locator including key word search capabilities and the ability to conduct an instant messaging session with a community member identified as a subject matter expert or alternatively contact experts via e-mail if that person is not online at that moment.

3. Creating Knowledge

PURPOSE

The purpose of this section is to provide your community with suggested tools to help it create, capture, and share its knowledge. This section consists primarily of tools. A tool, in this instance, does not refer to automated systems for transferring information. Rather, these tools are techniques or forums for thinking, for example, techniques for generating ideas and building relationships, or forums that promote knowledge flow and transfer. The following is a list of tools discussed in this section.

- Ad-hoc sessions
- Roadmap to generating new knowledge (problem solving and brainstorming)
- Learning history
- Interviews
- Action learning
- Learn from others
- Guest speakers
- Relationship building
- Systems Thinking

The inventory, storage, and migration of explicit knowledge, for example, publications, documents, and patents, are addressed in Section 4.

Though resource intensive, efforts to create and transfer knowledge can't be neglected

Converting tacit knowledge to commonly held community knowledge can be resource intensive, but the gains can be extraordinary. To cite some industry examples: Companies have saved millions by transferring knowledge from one part of the organization to another. Ford claims $34 million was saved in just one year by transferring ideas between Vehicle Operations plants; Texas Instruments saved enough from transferring knowledge between wafer fabrication plants to pay for building a whole new facility; Chevron reduced its costs on capital projects alone by $186 million. In fact, neither transferring common knowledge nor creating new knowledge can be neglected; the first is critical for current viability, the second for future viability.

Communities offer a mechanism to continuously grow and transfer knowledge as illustrated in Figure A2.1.

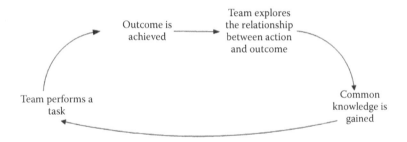

Figure A2.1   Common knowledge.

Once common knowledge is gained, a second cycle would be to leverage this knowledge across an organization: take gained knowledge, translate it into usable forms, and transfer it to others who can adapt it for their own use.

EXPECTED OUTCOMES	• Designs for community forums for critical thinking and knowledge flow • Practical techniques for knowledge creation, capture, and transfer
What technique should I use?	This section introduces each tool and provides a brief description. Where noted, supplemental information or templates are provided as tools at the end of this section. As an introduction to the Tool Section (end of this section), a matrix is presented with possible learning need scenarios. For example, a community member would like to learn how to perform a particular task. The matrix would suggest two techniques: conducting interviews or an action learning set.
Ad-hoc Sessions	A possible success criterion discussed earlier was the ability of the community to rapidly mobilize in response to a member's "call for help." Being able to quickly pull together a group for a 30-minute brainstorm or just as a sounding board is a priceless resource. Instant messaging is a great device for calling together a quick session. Instant messaging, e-mail, conference calls, VTC, or chat rooms can also be used in lieu of a face-to-face session for rapid input. In general, any or all of these technologies can be used inside a single network security domain without any problem. However if, for example, the instant messaging

or chat room protocols must traverse one or more firewalls to include all desired participants, this situation needs to be investigated ahead of time to ensure that the firewall is already configured to pass the required protocols. If the firewall blocks these signals, further analysis is required to ensure that opening a firewall port will not create unacceptable security vulnerabilities in the network. Under such circumstances a *prior* consultation with the local Information System Security Manager (ISSM) is strongly recommended.

Tip: the community's experience locator would serve as a useful tool when a member needs to quickly reach out to someone who "has done this before."

Roadmap to generating new knowledge

An excellent approach to creating and sharing knowledge about best practices is to host facilitated, collaborative problem-solving meetings. These forums serve many purposes: (1) solving relevant, day-to-day problems, (2) building trust among community members by actually helping each other, and (3) solving problems in a public forum, thereby creating a common understanding of tools, approaches, and solutions.

Often during problem-solving discussions, communities will discover areas where they need to create common standards or guidelines. These discoveries may splinter to smaller, more focused work groups to develop detailed standards for incorporation into best practice recommendations. This is an example of how communities naturally trigger continuous process improvement.

A five-step roadmap for problem solving as a means to generate new knowledge is provided as a tool at the end of this section. This roadmap works well for best practices that can easily be reused, e.g., methodologies, analytical models, diagnostic approaches, case studies, and benchmark data.

Learning History

A learning history is a very useful tool to capture tacit knowledge resident in the minds of individuals. A learning history is a retrospective history of significant events in an organization's recent past; described in the voices of people who took part in them. Researched through a series of reflective interviews, the learning history uses feedback from employees at all levels to help an organization evaluate its progress.

A technique to capture tacit knowledge resident in individual minds

Organizations can learn by reviewing their successes and their failures, assessing them systematically, and recording the lessons in a form that employees find open and accessible. To quote the famous philosopher, George Santanya, "Those who cannot remember the past are condemned to repeat it." Learning from our mistakes can lead to subsequent success—failure is the ultimate teacher.

Recording staff members' experience with technical projects, war time operations, change programs, technical conferences or symposia, leadership conferences, workshops, site visits, etc., can help to ensure that useful knowledge is shared and that mistakes are not repeated. In debriefings, interviewees recall their experience, in their own words, in a way that reflects their collective learning experience.

The interview can be transcribed into a question/answer format, a standardized document format, or preserved as a video. Regardless of the medium, what is important is to ensure that a record is made while events are still fresh in the mind, and, ideally, before a project's conclusion. In effect, this allows access to accumulate hindsight, as opposed to hindsight that has been tempered by poor memory recall and defensive reasoning.

At Ford, learning histories are used by a car parts division, an assembly plant, and in product design and development. In the assembly plant, Ford attributes quality improvements of 25% per year since 1995, compared with less than 10% achieved for the two comparable factories.

A six-step approach to creating a learning history is provided as a tool at the end of this section.

Storytelling

Storytelling, the construction of fictional examples to illustrate a point, can be used to effectively transfer knowledge. An organizational story is a detailed narrative of management actions, employee interactions, or other intra-organizational events that are communicated informally within the organization.

Conveying information in a story provides a rich context, remaining in the conscious memory longer and creating more memory traces than information not in context. Therefore, a story is more likely to be acted upon than normal means of communications. Storytelling, whether in a personal or organizational setting, connects people, develops creativity, and increases confidence. The use of stories in organizations can build descriptive capabilities, increase organizational learning, convey complex meaning, and communicate common values and rule sets.

Conduct Interviews

Conducting interviews with subject matter experts, stakeholders, process performers, customers—anybody that can shed new light on a topic or issue—is an excellent method to gather knowledge for the community and its knowledge base. These guidelines are provided as a tool at the end of this section.

Action Learning

Action learning is a new way of approaching learning. It is a very simple concept revolving around the fact that people learn by doing. Put simply, action learning involves the formation of a small group of people who share common issues, goals or learning needs. This group, called an action learning set, works to resolve issues and achieve these goals together, meeting regularly, about once a month, to reflect on progress, issues and solutions and refine the way forward. The team is able to brainstorm on alternative approaches or offer advice to an individual on how to proceed in achieving specific goals. The emphasis is on trying new things and evaluating the results. A methodology for action learning is provided as a tool at the end of this section.

Action Learning is task oriented and may be useful for approaching narrowly focused issues. However, a community is not expected nor encouraged to undertake large, task-oriented projects, e.g., reengineering, systems requirements definition, or policy overhauls. When the community recognizes the need for a major project, it should route the candidate project to leadership for direction. The community may wish to volunteer its subject expertise to a subsequent project team, if appropriate.

Learn from others—share relentlessly

Not all learning is derived from reflection and analysis. Sometimes the most powerful insights come from looking outside your realm or industry to get a new perspective. Organizations stop changing when people stop learning and get stuck in the knowing.

Consider benchmarking to identify better ways of doing business; site visits or tours to "see" how a practice is applied in a specific environment; and interactions with customers to better understand their problems, preferences, and feedback on service/products.

Tip: The American Productivity and Quality Center offers a benchmarking methodology as well as a wealth of information about best practices on its website (http://www.apqc.org).

Not only should your community learn from external sources, it should leverage existing knowledge resident in the organization. Seek out existing sources of knowledge, e.g., work products from other departments and communities, exhibitors at knowledge fairs, or commissioned studies. One of the objectives of KM is to make these resources easily available to both the individual and the community.

Guest speakers

Inviting guest speakers to community forums is an opportunity to bring a fresh perspective or point of view into the community. Speakers should be selected based upon relevance to community purpose or targeted areas of interest.

- Solicit ideas for speakers or topic areas from community members.
- Consider internal *and* external sources for relevant speakers. Possible sources include professional associations, sister organizations, supplier/partner organizations, project historians, etc.
- When appropriate, consider inviting representatives from other communities to speak and to begin building links across communities.

Relationship-building exercises

The strongest communities are built upon strong relationships. Relationships typically form naturally from working together over a period of time. It wouldn't hurt to occasionally work a relationship-building exercise into community forums. Several exercises are provided as tools at the end of this section.

Systems Thinking

Systems Thinking provides an approach for managing complexity. It is a tool to help decision-makers understand the cause-and-effect relationships among data, information, and people. It identifies archetypes (or patterns) that occur over and over again in decision making. In short, it expands individual thinking skills and improves both individual and group/team decision making. Additional information on systems thinking is provided at the end of this section.

TOOLS	• Suggested Techniques for Scenarios
	• A Roadmap to Generating New Knowledge
	• Learning History—Overview
	• Storytelling—White Paper
	• Interview Guidelines
	• Action Learning
	• Relationship-Building Exercises
	• Systems Thinking

Scenario	Ad Hoc Sessions	Roadmap	Learning History	Story-telling	Interviews	Action Learning	Learn from Others	Guest Speakers	Relationship Building	Systems Thinking
Suggested Techniques for Scenarios										
No information is available on a subject					✓	✓	✓	✓		
A practice performed differently by many with varying levels of success—seeking a best practice for adoption by all		✓	✓		✓		✓	✓		
A common problem with many alternatives—seeking a best practice		✓	✓	✓	✓					✓
You want to energize the community with new ideas				✓				✓		✓
A method to test or prototype alternatives to determine a best practice		✓				✓				
One or more members need to learn how to perform a specific task					✓	✓				
A new tasking from Command leadership—how best to implement?		✓				✓				✓
A problem has been identified but is not yet clearly understood—root cause?		✓	✓		✓					✓
You need an answer in a hurry or you need to bounce an idea off colleagues	✓				✓					
An exercise or event has occurred—was it successful?			✓	✓	✓			✓		
Build consensus on a topic with high levels of conflict or controversy		✓							Brain Writing	✓
Need to generate and evaluate ideas									Brain Writing	
To prepare a group to derive lessons learned—think beyond the obvious		✓		✓					"What's the Moral of the Story?"	
Think creatively—see the same thing in a new light		✓		✓			✓		"New Product Offering"	✓

A Roadmap to Generating New Knowledge

This roadmap is a variation on an approach commonly used for problem solving. It may be useful to a community if it is trying to solve a problem shared by many members or to develop a best practice that can be adopted by members. The roadmap leads the community through a series of steps: define a problem, conduct analysis, generate ideas, select a best practice, or solution, and capture the knowledge in an explicit form. A group or an individual can use this approach. The steps remain the same.

Problem Exploration and Definition

Explore the problem and determine if additional information is needed. For example, members may decide to observe specific practices or research existing information on a topic. Other methods to collect more information might be to conduct interviews with impacted individuals or subject matter experts.

Jumping to a conclusion without understanding a problem can save time, but it could also waste time if you solve the wrong problem. Before jumping to the wrong conclusion, consider the following:

- Examine the problem from all angles—try to see it from the perspective of an employee, a customer, or a supplier
- Separate fact from fiction—perception is important but it must be distinguished from fact
- Identify key players—who is affected by the problem, who is responsible for solving the problem, and who has the authority to accept a solution
- Dissect or decompose the situation—break the problem down into pieces
- Determine plan for gathering information—survey, interviews, observations, brainstorm sessions, and benchmark reviews if needed

Clearly defining a problem, using clear, plain English, is like having your finger on its pulse. A clear definition builds a strong foundation for subsequent fact finding, communication, and analysis. A good definition:

- Distills the situation into a brief, concise statement
- Use key words to "get to the bottom" of the situation
- States what a problem is rather than what it isn't
- States a problem in terms of needs—not solutions

Analysis

Typically, what you "see" is only the tip of the iceberg—or the symptoms of a problem rather than its root cause. It is important to distinguish cause from effect to ensure that you are actually solving the source of the problem, not just addressing its symptoms. Consider a medical analogy. You have many symptoms of the common cold, but in fact, you have a sinus infection that can only be cured with an antibiotic. While using over-the-counter cold medicines to alleviate your symptoms, your original infection continues to worsen. This is also true in an organization. By addressing only the symptoms, you miss the root cause and the condition persists and may even worsen.

Discovering the root cause of a problem can be tricky. Sound questioning techniques are a good start. Using your problem definition statement, answer the following questions.

- Why does the problem persist?
- Where did it start and where did it come from?
- Why doesn't it resolve itself or just go away?
- What caused it in the first place?
- What changed right before it started?
- Why do we keep getting sucked back into the situation?
- Why won't things improve no matter what we try?

Still not sure? Don't move to the solution phase until you are sure you have found the root cause. Test your tentative conclusion using the following questions. The proposed root cause must pass the entire test to be the true root cause. If the results of these evaluations aren't conclusive, continue analysis until you can answer yes to each question.

How to Know When You've Found the Root Cause		
Desired Response	*Test Question*	*Yes/No*
Dead end	You ran into a dead end when you asked, "What caused the proposed root cause?"	_____
Conversation ends	All conversation has come to a positive end.	_____
Feels good	Everyone involved feels good, is motivated and uplifted emotionally.	_____
Agreement	All agree it is the root cause that keeps the problem from resolving.	_____
Explains	The root cause fully explains why the problem exists from all points of view.	_____
Beginnings	The earliest beginnings of the situation have been explored and are understood.	_____
Logical	The root cause is logical, makes sense, and dispels all confusion.	_____
Control	The root cause is something you can influence, control, and deal with realistically.	_____
Hope	Finding the root cause has returned hope that something constructive can be done about the situation.	_____
Workable solution	Suddenly workable solutions, not outrageous demands, begin to appear.	_____
Stable resolution	A stable, long-term, once-and-for-all resolution of the situation now appears feasible.	_____

Use of analytic techniques, for example, diagramming and process modeling, can also be applied during the analysis stage. A few additional techniques for analyzing a problem:

- Napoleon—imagine you are someone else to gain new perspectives
- Morphological analysis—systematically examine each attribute of the problem
- Create a deadline
- Sleep on it

Idea Generation

Once the root cause is identified, it is time to generate possible solutions. This is the time to be creative. One useful way to generate a storm of ideas with a group is a facilitation technique called brainstorming. The brainstorming process is useful in two ways: it enhances the flow of ideas and innovations, and it builds consensus and commitment via a participative process. There are four rules that must be followed for a truly effective brainstorm session.

- Quantity versus quality—the more ideas, the greater the likelihood of a useful one
- Freewheeling—open the gate and allow ideas to freely flow; build on the ideas of others even if they seem wild or outrageous
- Defer judgment—the surest way to shut down creative thinking is to judge each idea as it occurs. You are not deciding on ideas at this point, simply thinking imaginatively
- Hitchhike—if there is a lull in the flow, try making more out of what has already been said, changing it a little, adding to it. For example, if a client meeting was suggested, add ideas for how to structure the meeting. Voila, a new idea!

A useful process for brainstorming is presented below:

- Frame a session with an idea-seeking question, for example, "what are all the ways ..." or a general topic—write the question or topic where everyone can see it
- Clearly state purpose (to generate a storm of ideas) and brainstorming rules
- Establish a time limit—20–30 minutes
- Try a round robin to encourage participation, allowing members to pass or "green light" participants to speak out in any order that naturally occurs
- Encourage participants to build on others' ideas
- Post all ideas
- Allow no evaluation, criticism, or discussion while ideas are being generated—look out for "killing phrases."
- Allow participants time to think—don't let a lull in the storm stop the session
- After all ideas have been generated, reduce the list by questioning, categorizing, and consolidating

Remember, the goal is to think creatively and view the problem from a new perspective. To quote Nobel Prize–winning physician, Albert Szent-Gyorgyi, "Discovery consists of looking at the same thing as everyone else and thinking something different." Another creative genius, Albert Einstein, once said, "Problems cannot be solved at the same level of consciousness that created them." Before generating ideas, try some creativity exercises.

When generating ideas, avoid mental locks, for example, "I already have the answer." The following table provides a listing of common mental locks and possible techniques to overcome them.

Mental Locks	*Consider*
The right answer	There is often more than one right answer.
That's not logical	Excessive logical thinking can short-circuit your creative process—be curious, look for surprises.
Follow the rules	Challenge the rules. "Slaying sacred cows makes great steaks"—Dick Nicolosi, philosopher.
Be practical	Ask "what if" questions. Use them as stepping stones.
Play is frivolous	Use play to fertilize your thinking. Make a game of it.
That's not my idea	Specialization limits you. Develop an explorer's attitude. Leave your own turf.
Don't be foolish	Foolish thinking can get you out of a rut.
Avoid ambiguity	Too much specificity can stifle your imagination.
To err is wrong	Don't be afraid to fail. "A ship in port is safe, but that's not what ships are built for"—Grace Hopper, Inventor.
I'm not creative	Believe in the worth of your ideas.
I don't have time	You don't have time not to.

Solution Selection

The goal at this point is to narrow the list of ideas into feasible, creative, and win-win alternatives. By using an objective, criterion-based method to select ideas, you will coincidentally make the decision-making process much easier in that you have defined the terms for reaching consensus. The process therefore becomes fact-based and less emotionally charged.

Establishing objective criteria is similar to judging a sporting event. Olympic judges use consistent, objective criteria to evaluate the performance of athletes to select winners. In addition to establishing criteria, you may want to prioritize criteria. For example, some criteria may be mandatory, while others are optional. Another technique might be to set acceptable ranges. For example, if an idea meets less than 80% of the criteria, it will be removed from the running.

If a clear winner does not emerge, identify the best and worst outcomes for each idea and/or the pros and cons of each idea. Another step might be to validate the practice with stakeholders or peers. For a final check, ask yourself the following questions:

- Is the best practice, or alternative, based upon good, sound reasoning and data?
- Were the right people involved in the problem-solving process?

Following this roadmap will serve to create new knowledge that can improve not only your own job but also the overall performance of your organization as well as the jobs of sailors and peers in other organizations.

Knowledge Capture

It is recommended that all new knowledge, or best practices, generated by the community, be presented with at least the following pieces of information. Readers should be encouraged to call either the point of contact (originator) or members to gain more understanding of the topic.

- Date Prepared
- Point of Contact—include name, organization, and contact information
- Members who participated in development of best practice and contact information
- Problem Statement
- Background—note any research that was conducted during the exploration phase and a summary of significant findings. Include findings from root cause analysis.
- Alternatives Considered—list significant ideas that were considered and explain reasons for nonselection.
- Best Practice—provide sufficient information to clearly express best practice. If additional materials, for example, models, business rules, etc., were developed, include them. Consider how graphics could be used to enhance knowledge transfer.

Learning History—Overview

A learning history is a retrospective history of significant events in an organization's recent past; described in the voices of people who took part in them. Researched through a series of reflective interviews, the learning history uses feedback from employees at all levels to help an organization evaluate its progress.

A learning history goes beyond simply gathering best practices and other lessons learned. A learning history

- Provides the time and space for participants to openly reflect on the learning from the initiative or exercise,
- Enhances the reflection process so that team members begin to make new connections and see how their actions ultimately produce final outcomes,
- Gathers information from a variety of perspectives to reduce bias,
- Analyzes data to draw out key themes,
- Contains accurate, validated information,
- Is written in the words of those involved, not paraphrased in the words of consultants, and
- Provides a vehicle to promote discussion among participants in the initiative

Approach

A learning history is a structured process for gathering information related to a project, mission, or initiative. The steps to create a learning history are depicted in Figure A2.2.

Figure A2.2   The processing of gathering information for a learning history.

Step 1. Select Interview Candidates
Interview candidates are selected to give a variety of perspectives on the process. The selection of interview candidates in a thorough learning history should include those who initiated, participated in, or were affected by the project in any way.

Step 2. Conduct Interviews
Interviews can be conducted in person, or by telephone when in-person interviews are not possible. The interviews generally average about 45 minutes in length and are conducted by the same interviewers whenever possible to maintain consistency. The interviews are designed to be reflective, to allow the interview candidate to speak freely without the constraints of a structured interview. No more than six general questions are prepared in advance. Additional questions are asked during the interview based on the responses of the interview candidates to gather more specific information. General interview questions might include

- What was your role in the exercise/initiative?
- How would you judge the success of the initiative?
- What would you do differently if you could?
- What recommendations do you have for other people who might go through a similar process?
- What innovative things were done or could have been done?

Step 3. Record and Transcribe Interviews

Interviews are recorded to ensure that the quotes used in the learning history are accurate. The recorded interviews are transcribed to enable analysis of interview data.

Step 4. Analyze Data

The interview data is analyzed and sorted to identify like themes and subthemes. Quotes are identified to support the major themes from a balance of perspectives.

Step 5. Document Key Themes and Supporting Quotes

In this step, assemble and record the themes and supporting quotes into the right-hand column of the document (see section entitled Format of Document). The quotes should be in no particular order but are designed to provide a picture of the theme from the different perspectives of the interview candidates.

Now develop the left-hand column of each section, which includes commentary and potential questions for consideration that relate to the adjacent quotes. The left-hand column commentary does not reflect the questions asked during the interview process but rather comments, questions, and conclusions posed by the author to the reader for further reflection.

Step 6. Validate Quotes

In the final step in the process, validate the quotes that are used in the learning history document with the interview candidates. Although interviews were recorded and quotes are anonymous, quotes are validated to ensure they were not taken out of context and truly represent the intent of the speaker. Quotes are sent to each interview candidate for correction and a signature of approval.

Format of Document

Part 1: In this section, describe the theme and any related practices of successful organizations.

Part 2: In this section, present the quotes that describe the theme in the right column. The quotes presented in the learning history are not inclusive of all the quotes received; rather, the quotes selected are designed to be representative of the various perspectives of interview candidates and representative of the information gathered throughout the interview process.

The left column of the document *does not* list questions asked during the interview, but records commentary and questions posed to the reader by the author for further consideration when reading the document. The commentary on the left relates to the adjacent quote or quotes. The commentary is presented to provide the reader with ideas for reflection. The reader is encouraged to record their own thoughts and questions as they read.

Part 3: The final section of the theme is a summary of the key points from the quotes in Part 2. Questions for further consideration relating to the theme are presented at the end of this section.

The format of each section is depicted below.

Theme Title

Part 1
Overview of the theme.

Part 2

| *Commentary, conclusions, and potential questions to be asked that relate to the adjacent quotes.* | Quotes from interviewing process. The quotes represent key responses to questions posed by the learning consultant during the interview process. |

Part 3
Brief summary of quotes, as heard by the learning consultant. Additional questions for the purpose of providing more clarity to the theme.

The Use of Storytelling

Storytelling, the construction of fictional examples to illustrate a point, can be used to effectively transfer knowledge. An organizational story is a detailed narrative of management actions, employee interactions, or other intra-organizational events that are communicated informally within the organization.

A variety of story forms exist naturally throughout organizations, including scenarios and anecdotes. Scenarios are the articulation of possible future states, constructed within the imaginative limits of the author. While scenarios provide an awareness of alternatives—of value in and of itself—they are often used as planning tools for possible future situations. The plan becomes a vehicle to respond to recognized objectives in each scenario. An anecdote is a brief sequence captured in the field or arising from a brainstorming session. To reinforce positive behavior, sensitive managers can seek out and disseminate true anecdotes that embody the value desired in the organization. The capture and distribution of anecdotes across organizations carries high value. Once a critical number of anecdotes is captured from a community, the value set or rules underlying the behavior of that community can be determined. Understanding these values has allowed the utilization of informal as well as formal aspects of the organization.

Conveying information in a story provides a rich context, remaining in the conscious memory longer and creating more memory traces than information not in context. Therefore, a story is more likely to be acted upon than normal means of communications. Storytelling, whether in a personal or organizational setting, connects people, develops creativity, and increases confidence. The use of stories in organizations can build descriptive capabilities, increase organizational learning, convey complex meaning, and communicate common values and rule sets.

First, stories have the ability to increase our descriptive capabilities, a strength in this age of uncertainty where we must be able to describe our environment and have the self-awareness to describe our individual capabilities. Description capabilities are essential in strategic thinking and planning, and create a greater awareness of what we could achieve. Fictional stories can be powerful because they provide a mechanism by which an organization can learn from failure without attributing blame. Some organizations actually create characters from archetypes taken from a large number of organizational anecdotes. These characters are used over and over again. Once established, they become a natural vehicle for organizational learning and a repository for organizational memory.

When well constructed, stories can convey a high level of complex meaning. The use of subtext can convey this meaning without making it obvious. Subtext is a term that refers to an unstated message not explicit in the dialogue of the story. Analogies are often used to aid in the transfer of particularly complex information and knowledge to give the human mind something to relate to. This form of learning has been used throughout human history to transfer complex concepts and core values.

Finally, because stories communicate common values and rule systems, they provide a mechanism to build organic organizational response to emerging requirements. This means that as new situations and new challenges arise in response to an ever-changing world, a common set of values will drive that response at every level of the organization. Snowden explains that to operate in a highly uncertain environment, we must have common values and rule systems that support networks of communities self-organizing around a common purpose. Stories provide just such a catalyst. Snowden states that in this world, old skills, such as story and other models drawn from organic rather than mechanical thinking are survival skills, not nice to haves.

The World Bank has used what they call a Springboard Story over the past several years to move that organization to a knowledge organization. The Springboard Story, a powerful method of communicating knowledge about norms and values, is a transformational story that enables the listener to take a personal leap in understanding how an organization or community or complex system may change. The intent of this type of story is not to transfer information, but to serve as a catalyst for creating understanding within the listener. These stories enable listeners to easily and quickly grasp the ideas as a whole in a nonthreatening way. In effect, they invite the listener to see analogies from their own histories, their own contexts, and their own fields of expertise.

These Springboard Stories were told from the perspective of a single protagonist who was known to the audience and actually in the predicament being told in the story; there was an element of strangeness or incongruity to the listeners which could capture their attention and imagination; the story had a degree of plausibility and a premonition of what the future might be like; and there was a happy ending. Happy endings make it easier for listeners to take the imaginative leap from the explicit story to the implicit meaning.

With the advent of the Internet and intranet, there is a larger opportunity to use stories to bring about change. Electronic media adds moving images and sound as context setters. Hypertext capabilities and collaboration software invites groups, teams and communities to co-create their stories. New multiprocessing skills are required to navigate this new world, skills that include the quick and sure assimilation of and response to fast-flowing images and sounds and sensory assaults.

Interview Guidelines

The Interview Guidelines are a reference for conducting interviews to gather information.

Steps in Conducting Effective Interviews

Prepare for Interview

1. Determine the purpose of the interview and the associated types of information that will be collected.
2. Identify the categories of questions to be asked during the interview (e.g., knowledge requirements, knowledge sharing and interaction, knowledge exchange).
3. Specify the areas of data necessary to meet the objectives of the interview.
   - Attempt to conduct interview in their workspace in case you need to access info/data located in their office.
   - You should notify them in advance of the interview of your data requirements.
4. State questions utilizing the following techniques:
   - Ask open-ended questions. (e.g., how can the process be improved?)
   - Ensure clarify of meaning by eliminating ambiguity. (e.g., how would you rate the professionalism of your staff? Professionalism can have various meanings to different people.)
   - Keep questions simple. (e.g., rate agrees or disagree, "Our staff was both fast and friendly.")
   - Watch out for biased questions, which can be difficult to detect and hinders obtaining insight. (e.g., do you wish me to pass on any complements to the CEO?)

During the Interview

5. Introduce yourself, your objective, and the agenda of the interview, specifically:
   - ■ Find out if interviewees have any objectives of their own for either the KCO implementation or the interview. Their objectives are important because you can use this information to motivate or enable the implementation of the KCO in the organization.
   - ■ Ask if they have any general questions pertaining to the project.
   - ■ Explain how information will be used.
6. Put the interviewee at ease about the note taking by explaining that the notes are to be used as reference of what is discussed. Try to capture their exact words, particularly if you think they may be of high importance. Ensure understanding throughout the interview and paraphrase back to them what you understood that they said.
7. Utilize the Funnel Technique to move from general ideas to detail. For example:
   - ■ Initially broad ("Tell me about...," "Describe...")
   - ■ More detail ("Who? What? When? Where? How?")
   - ■ Very detailed ("Yes"/"No" to verify information)

After the Interview

8. Document your finding as soon as possible and follow up on areas of uncertainty with interviewees.
9. Send them a summary of their comments (if relevant) to confirm what you heard and how you interpreted their statements.

Ladder of Inference

The ladder of inference is a model that describes an individual's mental process of observing situations, drawing conclusions, and taking action. When we say the fact is ... What we are actually saying is the fact, as I understand it based upon my data selection process, cultural and personal background, judgments, beliefs and assumptions is ... Why is this important? This is important as there are a lot of steps in between the data and the actions we take based upon that data. By allowing others to explore our thinking process, we may reveal more effective and higher leverage solutions.

After an event takes place our mental processing immediately screens out a certain percentage of the data. In other words, our vision is naturally blurred and only absorbs a certain amount of the data that represents the life events.

When we look at the data we have collected, we attach our own personal meaning and cultural biases to the data that we observe. No data, therefore, is pure–it is influenced by whoever analyzes the data. Based on the meaning we attach to the data collected, we make inferences or judgments and arrive at conclusions which influence our behavior. Therefore, one piece of data could lead to as many different conclusions as there are people analyzing that particular piece of data. Over time, the conclusions we reach from an event or pattern of events develop our belief system. We become fixated on certain ways of viewing how the world works, creating our own mental models that are invoked each time an event takes place.

All too often, people fall into what may be termed "competency traps"—a routine of problem solving that provided initial success and is used over and over with little regard for how accurately it fits with the current problem. The ladder of inference helps us break out of that trap by providing us an easy tool to ask, "What assumptions am I making about this particular situation that may limit my deeper understanding of the problem?" As we work to more clearly understand the problem, we may actually be able to reframe the problem.

The ladder of inference helps us understand why it is important to make our reasoning steps explicit. By consciously reviewing the data which supports our conclusions, we can improve our ability to explore complex problems and reduce those instances where we "jump" to conclusions based upon data that is incomplete.

People often employ defensive behaviors such as trying to control situations that we have little control over, always acting as if we're in control, and never saying "I don't know." By having a tool which provides us an opportunity to say, "As I understand what you're saying, x leads to y which results in z … am I on track with your thinking?" we don't have to resort to trying to defuse complex issues on our own or end up attempting to cover up the fact that we don't have a clue.

When people in organizations jointly practice skilled incompetence, the result is the formation of defensive routines. By having a mutually acceptable tool, we can inquire into each other's thinking without resorting to rudeness.

A very powerful application of the ladder of inference is to introduce it at the beginning of a project. When team members commit to individually and collectively examining their beliefs and assumptions and making them explicit, a great deal of time spent arguing and going around in circles can be eliminated.

Left-Hand Column

The left-hand column is the basic premise that during conversations there are actually two conversations taking place. One conversation is explicit. This conversation consists of the words that are actually spoken throughout the exchange between two or more persons. The other conversation consists of what the individuals are thinking and feeling but not saying. The term "left-hand column" is derived from an exercise designed to explore what is not said, but thought about, during the course of a conversation. This "tool" offers a way to actually study our conversations so that we can redesign them to be more effective at creating the results that we wish to create.

People need an introduction to this tool before you can begin using it as a team effectively. Here is an exercise you can use to introduce the team to it.

Step 1: Choosing a Problem

Select a difficult problem you've been involved with during the last month or two. Write a brief paragraph describing the situation. What are you trying to accomplish? Who or what is blocking you? What might happen? Examples include:

■ The rest of the organization is resisting, or you believe they will resist, a change you want to implement

■ You believe your team is not paying much attention to the most crucial problem

Step 2: The Right-Hand Column (What was said)

Now recall a frustrating conversation you had over this. Take several pieces of paper, and draw a line down the center. In the right-hand column, write out the conversation that actually occurred. Or write the conversation you're pretty sure *would* occur if you were to raise this issue. The discussion may go on for several pages. Leave the left-hand column blank until you've finished.

Step 3: The Left-Hand Column (What you were thinking)

Now in the left-hand column, write out what you were thinking and feeling, but not saying.

Step 4: Individual Reflection: Using your left-hand column as a resource

You can learn a great deal just from the act of writing out a case, putting it away for a week, and then looking at it again. As you reflect, ask yourself:

■ What has really led me to think and feel this way?

■ How might my comments have contributed to the difficulties?

■ Why didn't I say what was in my left-hand column?

■ What assumptions am I making about the other person or people?

■ How can I use my left-hand column as a resource to improve our communications?

Step 5: Discuss in pairs or a small group

The pairs or small groups review one or more of the left-hand columns written in step 3. The conversation should focus on exploring the assumptions behind both speakers' words, discussing alternative ways in which the participant could have conducted the conversation so that he or she would have been more satisfied with the outcome.

Action Learning

Overview

Action Learning is a new way of approaching learning. It is a very simple concept revolving around the fact that people learn by doing. Put simply, action learning involves the formation of a small group of people who share common issues, goals, or learning needs. This group, called an action learning set, works to resolve issues and achieve these goals together, meeting regularly, about once a month, to reflect on progress, issues, and solutions and refine the way forward. The team is able to brainstorm on alternative approaches or offer advice to an individual on how to proceed in achieving specific goals. Emphasis is on trying new things and evaluating the results.

Method

Action Learning is cyclical. It consists of the following steps:

1. Identify task and learning opportunity
2. Planning together
3. Doing
4. Reflecting
5. Sharing the learning
6. Closing out

Identify Task and Learning Opportunity

Determine the objectives of the action learning program. Form the Action Learning set: Discuss with the team the development needs and job challenges that might be addressed by action learning. Not all of the members of the set will necessarily have the same development need, but these should be similar. It is important for the group to understand the development needs of the individuals within the group and any development needs of the group as a whole. An Action Learning set is ideally 5–8 people in size to allow for good discussion within the sessions. Assign somebody to facilitate the group meeting sessions, asking questions of the participants to draw out the key learning points. Define how often the group will meet and some ground rules for the meetings. Identify any subject matter experts who might be able to come and talk to the group.

Planning Together

The official start of an Action Learning program should be in the form of a start-up workshop. Ideally the workshop should be held off-site to allow the participants to spend time away from the usual distractions of the workplace. Included in the agenda for the workshop should be time for the following activities:

- Developing personal learning plans and a common view of the purpose of the action learning set.
- Declaring individual objectives for membership of this action learning set and identifying medium-and short-term actions that can be taken to progress toward these objectives. In addition, set members should be asked how they will know when objectives have been reached or how they will be able to measure their progress.

- Identifying opportunities to apply new ideas and learning points in the workplace.
- Introduction to the practice of reflection and keeping a learning log to capture key learning and progress
- Reviewing at the end of the section, what went well, and what could be done to improve the format for future sessions

Doing

This is time spent working on a task on the job. The members of the action learning set spend time experimenting with new approaches and testing new ideas developed during the action learning set meetings, all with the aim of making progress on a problem, project, or issue of importance to them. The following should be referred to as instructions during this phase:

- Refer back to the action plans developed during the planning workshop.
- Before taking action, reflect on what you think the outcome of the action will be. If possible, record this in the learning log.
- Take action. Try out the approach as planned. This is where you do the work you do every day, but with the benefit of advanced planning and documenting your expectations before you act.
- Look for evidence of how effective you have been. What did you observe?
- Write down your observations in the learning log. This is where you create the opportunities to learn, by reflecting on your observations both by yourself and with the benefit of the perspective of others at the next set meeting.

Reflecting

This is a regular session where members of the action learning set come together to reflect on the progress they have made on their work issues. It is a time for challenging assumptions, exploring new ways of thinking about problems, and planning what to do next in the workplace. It is also an opportunity for set members to bring up specific issues of their work that they would like others to think through with them, as well as offer their thinking support to explore the issues and problems raised by others.

- Plan reflection sessions on a regular basis and as far in advance as possible, ensure maximum attendance.
- Book enough time to allow the thorough exploration of issues of importance. Try 30 minutes per person plus an extra 30 minutes as an estimate when planning reflection sessions.
- Make sure that participants have prepared for the reflection session by updating learning logs and notifying the facilitator of any key issues they wish to discuss.

■ The facilitator should ensure that each individual declares what actions they intend to take once they leave the reflection session and what outcomes they expect from these actions.

Sharing

This is where new knowledge, skills, and experiences can be shared outside of the action learning set to allow other individuals and teams to benefit from the experiences. Capturing the knowledge that grows out of the action learning experience contributes to the intellectual capital of the organization. As new knowledge is added to the KCO website over time, users will find more and more content that is timely and applicable to their current learning needs.

■ Newsgroup and threaded discussion features can be included on the KCO website to allow action learning set members to collaborate online. This can open up the set so that others can see what is being achieved.
■ The KCO website should keep a running list of all action learning sets. Each entry should list basic information about the members, the set's objectives, and the timing of the set's meetings as well as the contact details of the set facilitator.
■ Some action learning sets may decide to create a learning history, a document that describes the day-to-day work of the team and also attempts to capture how the set's learning evolved and changed during the project.
■ At the conclusion of the action learning set, the team members, with the help of their facilitator, can select the information from their experience that others would probably find valuable, and post it to the KCO website. Suggested topics would include objectives, conclusions, recommendations, etc., as well as experts that were consulted and planning documents such as agendas.

Closing Out

The purpose of a close-out event is to ensure that the action learning set reflects on the time spent together and reviews the progress made against the original objectives. The close-out session is facilitated in the same way as the regular reflection sessions and includes the administrative tasks associated with disbanding of the set. The most important of these tasks is to decide which resources and learning points are to be shared with the rest of the organization.

■ Plan the event to allow time to reflect on both the task that the set has been working on between sessions as well as the individual and team learning that has occurred through the process
■ In advance of the close-out session, all set members should be asked to prepare their reflections. The facilitator may choose to issue a structured form to focus this preparation. Suggested questions include: What has become

clearer to you since the start of the action learning program? How has your perspective of the task or problem changed during the time you have spent as a member of this action learning set? What were the defining moments of the set—at what points did major breakthroughs take place?

Relationship Building Exercises

Title: Brain Writing

Purpose: Collaborate on an idea or issue when sensitivities or conflict are anticipated; gather ideas and opinions in a nonthreatening manner

Group Size: 4–8 people for focused issue or idea and wording is important

Up to 20 people if intent is to gather ideas and opinions

Estimated Time: 4–8 people, 10 minutes

Up to 20 people—20 minutes to write and 10 minutes to discuss

Props: Blank paper and writing utensil for each participant

Instructions:
1. Pose or frame the question, issue, or problem facing the group. Ask each person to write on the top of the paper:
   - An answer (if a question is posed)
   - A resolution (if an issue is presented)
   - An idea (if a problem is confronted)
   - Proposed wording (if a statement is being crafted, e.g., a mission)
2. Ask each person to pass their paper to the person on their left.
3. Each person should then comment on the paper in front of him or her by either rewording the suggestion below the original or commenting on his or her opinion of the suggestion. When complete, pass the paper on.
4. This should continue until the papers return to their originator.
5. Discuss the findings. Most often, consensus will have built around a small number of suggestions, narrowing the discussion field.

Variations: If ideas have already been generated, post each one on a sheet of flip chart paper and post them around the room. Give people a marker and have them travel around the room commenting on as many items as desired, as many times. When the activity dies down, review each chart to determine if the comments lead to a common conclusion.

Tips: Suggest people use a check mark to indicate agreement.

This technique may be used to assess group opinion and to narrow the field prior to voting.

Title: What's the Moral of the Story?

Purpose: To practice sifting through information and deriving lessons learned.

Group Size: 8–20

Estimated Time: 8–10 Minutes

Props: Fables

Instructions:

1. Ask participants to pair up.
2. Distribute fables.
3. Explain that fables and folk tales are short fictional narratives that illustrate a moral, or a lesson. They are an indirect means of telling truths about life. Thus, they have a level of meaning beyond the surface story.
4. Tell pairs they have 5 minutes to read two fables and add a humorous moral to it.
5. After 5 minutes, ask members to discuss possible morals to the story.

Variation: Use fables without known morals and ask the group to develop some.

Suggested Fables from Aesop

THE COCK AND THE JEWEL

A cock, scratching for food for himself and his hens, found a precious stone and exclaimed: "If your owner had found thee, and not I, he would have taken thee up, and have set thee in thy first estate; but I have found thee for no purpose. I would rather have one barleycorn than all the jewels in the world."

Moral: The ignorant despise what is precious only because they cannot understand it.

THE CROW AND THE PITCHER

A crow perishing with thirst saw a pitcher, and hoping to find water, flew to it with delight. When he reached it, he discovered to his grief that it contained so little water that he could not possibly get at it. He tried everything he could think of to reach the water, but all his efforts were in vain. At last he collected as many stones as he could carry and dropped them one by one with his beak into the pitcher, until he brought the water within his reach and thus saved his life.

Moral: Necessity is the mother of invention.

The Ass and His Shadow

A traveler hired an ass to convey him to a distant place. The day being intensely hot, and the sun shining in its strength, the traveler stopped to rest, and sought shelter from the heat under the shadow of the ass. As this afforded only protection for one, and as the traveler and the owner of the ass both claimed it, a violent dispute arose between them as to which of them had the right to the shadow. The owner maintained that he had let the ass only, and not his shadow. The traveler asserted that he had, with the hire of the ass, hired his shadow also. The quarrel proceeded from words to blows, and while the men fought, the ass galloped off.

Moral: In quarreling about the shadow we often lose the substance.

Title: New Product Offering

Purpose: To get members to "see things differently" and better understand the varying perspectives members bring to the community.

Group Size: 8–24

Estimated Time: 30 minutes (will vary with number of subgroups)

Props: A common object, e.g., a feather duster, a stapler, or a yo-yo.

Instructions:

1. Explain to the group that the object they see before them can be anything—anything that is except what it is. Their job is to name the product, describe its uses, create a marketing strategy including price, and present their new product offering to the community.
2. Organize participants into subgroups of 3 to 5 members.
3. Allow the subgroups to develop their ideas and practice their presentation (about 20 minutes).
4. Each subgroup introduces its new product offering to the group.

Tips: Lead the group in clapping after each performance.

Purpose of Systems Thinking

As a tool for collective inquiry and coordinated action, the purposes of Systems Thinking are:

- Foster team learning and collaboration.
- Tell compelling stories that describe how the system works.
- Discover the system structure behind problems.
- Describe our own mental models and those of others about why the system performs as it does.
- Test possible strategies against intended results and for unintended consequences.
- Identify higher-leverage interventions.

As a result, Systems Thinking enables us to:

- Understand how organizations and other complex systems really function.
- Change our own thinking to match the way such systems operate.
- Change our behavior so that we are working with these complex forces instead of against them to create what we want.
  - Develop greater appreciation for the impact of our strategies on others in the system.
  - Be aware of the impacts of time delays and the need to balance short-term and long-term objectives and strategies.
  - Anticipate unintended consequences of well-intentioned strategies.

Steps in Systems Thinking

1. State the Issue & Tell the Story: Begin your inquiry with the evidence. What are some of the facts that make you or others think that there is an issue?
2. Graph Performance Patterns Over Time: What are the trends?
3. Establish Creative Tension & Draft a Focusing Question: When the trends are visible, we can state how this reality differs from our vision. A good focusing question describes the patterns in the context of what we want. For example: Why, despite our efforts to improve quality, do we continue to miss deadlines?
4. Identify Structural Explanations: What are key causes and consequences of the trends we observe? How do the consequences, particularly our own responses to the situation, become the cause of more problems?
5. Apply the Going Deeper Questions: What are the deeper structures that keep this set of causes and consequences in place? Is this system successfully accomplishing a purpose other than the stated one? Are beliefs and values causing the situation to persist?

6. Plan an Intervention: Based on our understanding of the structure, what is our hypothesis about how to change it? What general approaches are needed? What specific actions?

7. Assess the Results: Since our intervention is based on a theory of the situation, the results of our attempts to improve things provide new data, allowing us to continue through the steps again, if necessary.

Systems Thinking usually adds value when situations are:

■ Problematic
■ Long-standing
■ Resistant to change interventions

Systems Thinking is often helpful as a planning resource. In particular, a systems view can help you plan for growth, anticipate limits to growth, predict and avoid actions that can undermine partnerships, and avoid shooting yourself in the foot (by producing a worse situation than you already have).

In general, Systems Thinking rarely helps us find the single right answer; other problem-solving tools are more efficient in cases where there truly is an answer. Systems Thinking provides the most value when it illuminates the possible choices embedded in complex, divergent problems, and their likely consequences. The final choice is ours.

DO Use Systems Thinking to:

■ Identify or clarify a problem.
■ Increase creative discussion.
■ Promote inquiry and challenge pre-conceived ideas.
■ Bring out the validity of multiple perspectives.
■ Make assumptions explicit.
■ Sift out major issues and factors.
■ Find the systemic causes of stubborn problems.
■ Test the viability of previously proposed solutions.
■ Explore short and long term impacts of alternative or newly proposed solutions or actions.

DON'T Use Systems Thinking to:

■ Impress people or win an argument.
■ Validate prior views.
■ Hide uncertainties.
■ Blame individuals.

Systems Thinking vs. Traditional Approaches

Traditional Thinking	Systems Thinking
The connection between problems and their causes is obvious and easy to trace.	The relationship between problems and their causes is indirect and not obvious.
Others (either within or outside our organization) are to blame for our problems, and must be the ones to change.	We unwittingly create our own problems and have significant control or influence in solving them by changing our behavior.
A policy designed to achieve short-term success will also assure long-term success.	Most quick fixes either make no long-term difference or actually make matters worse in the long run.
In order to optimize the whole, we must optimize the parts.	Focus on policies that optimize the whole rather than each of the parts.
Aggressively tackle many independent initiatives simultaneously.	Target and orchestrate a few key changes over time.

4. Building the Knowledgebase

PURPOSE	Provide a framework for building your community's knowledgebase.
EXPECTED OUTCOMES	• Establish knowledge inventory and folder structure • A process for capturing documents for content management systems • A framework to continually improve business processes leveraging lessons learned and reusing best practices • Identified target efficiencies in mission related measures such as: cycle time, customer service, and total ownership cost
ROLES/RESPONSIBILITIES	A CoP's knowledgebase requires several roles in order for business process owners to successfully implement. These roles include:

- Community Sponsor
- Community Leader
- Community members
- Facilitator
- Logistics Coordinator

These roles were mentioned and discussed in detail in Section 2.

PRODUCT(S)

- Requirements Traceability Matrix (RTM); matrix of groupware functions that the community will focus on for its first release of the knowledgebase
- List of identified community media (documents, presentations, spreadsheets, etc.) that includes specific documents
- List of folders used for organizing community media
- Graphical model and supporting narrative of "AS-IS" media flow between the community and stakeholder organizations
- List of community members and the folders that they have been assigned to for life-cycle development
- Groupware electronic repository that features all of the functions listed in the RTM, all identified media, and a completed folder structure. Media will have been migrated to the groupware application under the given folder structure
- List of asset rules that ensures all groupware transactions are done in a manner consistent across the community
- Graphical model and supporting narrative of "TO-BE" media flow between the community and stakeholder organizations. Includes list of business performance measures and expected efficiencies (e.g., cycle time = 8 weeks; goal 4 week reduction)

KEY TASKS

- **Requirements**; Map identified collaborative tool functions to business requirements to simplify deployment, narrow training scope, and ensure more efficient use of the groupware.
- **Inventory**; Define knowledge assets in a business process context and identify whether created by the community or borrowed from other business owners.
- **Taxonomy**; Develop a business context classification structure for organizing inventory. It should provide an intuitive navigation scheme for members and other interested communities
- **Flow Model**; Model AS-IS business processes based on the flow of inventory assets to and from customers. Focus on how assets are created and disseminated.
- **Migrate**; Provide necessary technical support to migrate inventory assets that exist in legacy repositories. Inventory should be organized, classified as relevant, and mapped to a classification owner. Owners are typically subject mater experts from within the community.
- **Map**; Identify owners of the Inventory folders and designate life-cycle responsibility at a folders structure level.
- **Asset Rules**; Establish business rules for the use of the groupware to maintain consistency while performing business transactions. Designate which groupware functionality will be used to process specific transactions.
- **Transformation**; Identify, in priority order, High Value—Low Risk business processes that provides the group with the highest value in terms of Customer Service, Cycle Time Reduction, and Total Ownership Cost. Members should focus on measures that correlate to related business performance measures.
- **Training;** Secure computer-training facilities to allow "hands-on" training for members. Transformed business processes will be simulated in a training environment for user testing and acceptance.
- **Help Desk**; Enable a functional help desk specifically for community members.

Key Task 1: Requirements	This task is aimed at narrowing the functional scope of the selected groupware application to only those functions that enable the achieving of mission related measures (e.g., reduction in cycle time).
Narrow the functional scope of your groupware application	Given a groupware application, conduct a functional analysis of the application. At minimum the analysis should include: • Function Name • Description • Release List all of the functions that the groupware application is capable of performing (e.g., Add a new document). This list should not include any extended or custom functionality. Focus on the base functionality of the groupware. Once a list has been prepared, convene the community members to review the list. Leaders should aim at obtaining consensus over which functions meet the general requirements of the community's needs within the first release of the knowledgebase. Enter 1 for Release if the community requires the function in the first release. Enter 2 or 3 respectively if the community feels as though the particular function can be postponed to a later release.
Base your assessment on past experience and lessons learned	The community is expected to base its function decisions on lessons learned and past experiences. **Work Product: Requirements Traceability Matrix**—Excel spreadsheet containing the following elements: REQ ID, REQUIREMENT (or Function Name), DESCRIPTION, RELEASE (version of the implementation that will contain the corresponding function), NEW or EXISTING, FULL/PARTIAL, COMMENTS, DOCUMENTS
Key Task 2: Inventory	Inventory offers community members the opportunity of identifying all media associated with established business processes.
Take an inventory of all community media	With the help of a facilitator or community leader, convene a session of community members and conduct a brainstorming session on media that are either inputs to or outputs of the community's business processes.

Conduct both group and individual inventory	Once the list has been developed, assign each member the responsibility of reviewing the baseline list and adding media not captured during the community session. Compile the baseline list along with the individual input from community members. This will become the baseline inventory for the community. **Work Products: Inventory List**—Excel spreadsheet containing the following elements: ASSET ID#, NAME, DESCRIPTION, BEST PRACTICE, RECORDS MANAGEMENT META DATA
Key Task 3: Taxonomy	The objective of Taxonomy building is to provide an intuitive structure for users who are interested in obtaining information from or contributing to a community's practice.
Build group and individual lists	Convene the community to brainstorm a list of categories based on the prepared inventory list. The objective of the brainstorming session is to develop as complete list as possible. Disregard the length of the list. The actual list can be finalized during a separate community session.
Consolidate lists and assign inventory items to categorie ***Tip: Limit consolidated list to ~9 categories*** ***Tip: Limit sub categories to 3 levels***	Once the group has developed a list, distribute the list to group members and have them conduct a personal assessment of the list. Community members add, consolidate, or recommend deletions to the list. Community leaders will consolidate the group and individual lists into a single group list. Once completed, begin assigning inventory items to their respective categories. **Work Product: Taxonomy List**—Excel spreadsheet consisting of the following elements: *FOLDER ID #, CATEGORY, LEVEL, OWNERS, STATUS, DESCRIPTION, and REVISION NOTES.*
Key Task 4: Flow Model	The purpose of flow modeling is to graphically illustrate how inventory items are transferred between organizations as business transactions are conducted. The model will present a view that allows for easy identification of AS-IS business processes.
Easy way to identify business processes	To begin, model the organizations involved in the inventory exchange as depicted in Figure A2.3.

Using the baseline inventory list, illustrate how each item travels between community and organization. In some cases, an inventory item may traverse several paths between organization and community until the business process cycle is completed.

Layout stakeholder organizations	The "AS-IS" flow model is complete when each of the inventory items has been illustrated on the model.
Illustrate the inventory path between community and stakeholder	Once the graphical model has been completed, the leader will write a narrative that describes the path of community inventory items. The general community member should write the narrative in terms that are easily comprehensible. Within the narrative, incorporate details that are not readily apparent within the model.
Model all core processes and associated inventory	**Work Product:** *AS-IS model and narrative of the business process and the knowledge assets transacted during the identified processes. Illustration of community, stakeholders or customers and the direction flow of assets between services and customer.*

Key Task 5: Map *Community members share the responsibility of maintaining its workspace*	Mapping provides a means for the community to maintain its data. Community members will be designated as the point of contact for a particular category of data within the knowledgebase. As with any community, all members must participate in the maintenance and upkeep of its locale. Likewise, the groupware community will also share the responsibility of maintaining its community.
Assign primary and alternate members to folders	Mapping is a relatively quick and informal process. Convene a meeting of community members. Using the established Taxonomy list, have community members volunteer for folders that fall within their area of responsibility. Record these assignments in the ASSIGNED OWNER column of the taxonomy list. Additionally, have members volunteer for folders as an alternate point of contact. Therefore, each folder will have two community members who are familiar with the folder structure, content, and access privileges granted the folder.
	***Work Product*: See Taxonomy List**—Excel spreadsheet of ASSET CLASSIFICATIONS and ASSIGNED ONWER

Key Task 6: **Migration**	Migration of data is important to demonstrating the capabilities of the groupware application. It also provides a means of validating what has been accomplished in terms of data organizations. Finally, it provides a context for discussing how Inventory and Taxonomy contribute to the community's business processes
	Migration begins with validation of both Inventory and Taxonomy lists. This ensures what has been gathered thus far accurately reflects the needs of the community. Convene the community and conduct a quick review of both lists. Pay particular attention to those Inventory items that a) are not associated to a business process and b) are not products of the community. Items that are not associated to a business process may be considered for removal. Items that are not a product of the community may exist as parts of an adjacent community. If so, eliminate redundancy by cutting out "borrowed" items. Once the lists have been validated, begin populating the project workspace according to the Taxonomy. Data can be populated manually or in batch. Tools are available for large scale conversions.
	Work Product: Tool user accounts for all Core Group members and operational prototype of current release of the collaborative workspace.
Key Task 7: **Asset Rules**	Asset Rules provide members with groupware guidelines for moving data in and out of the knowledgebase. It also designates which groupware function will be used to support specific transactions in a business processes.
	An example of an asset rule is using a compound document instead of a folder to collect and present periodic volume releases of a newsletter. In this case, two different groupware functions could be used to achieve similar results. Establishing asset rules provides a consistent means for interacting with the knowledgebase.
	Sets of asset rules exist for each business process supported. Regardless of the size, rules must be put in place to avoid difference in practitioner usage. Asset rules will most commonly be identified with a business process. However, in some cases, specific documents may have an asset rule associated to it specifically.

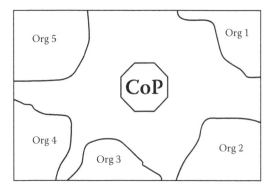

Figure A2.3   Sample flow model.

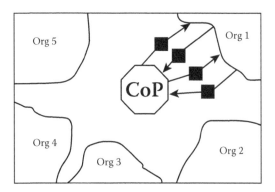

Figure A2.4   Sample flow model with path example.

Begin with listing the different processes or documents that will require an asset rule. Remember, all transactions conducted within the groupware application will require a set of asset rules that provide guidance to the community members.

For example, a particular community maintains a community calendar within its groupware application. The document format of the calendar is a Microsoft Word file. To provide guidance to the community on the use of this document, the following asset rules have been created:

- Calendar only maintained by assigned owner
- Community members who need to add a date to the calendar will use the groupware's document Check-in/Check-out function
- The community will maintain three months of its calendar. One month of past events and two months of future events
- All community members will create a change notification on the community calendar thus allowing them to receive e-mail notification upon calendar update

Again, a set of asset rules should be developed for each process or document involved in a community business transaction. Asset rules should be reviewed periodically to ensure applicability and effectiveness.

Work Product: ***Asset Rules***—Excel spreadsheet including BUSINESS RULE NUMBER, BUSINESS RULE, DESCRIPTION, REVISION, STATUS, and COMMENTS

Key Task 8: Transformation	Transformation is key to achieving value from the knowledgebase. The use of the knowledgebase process implies communities will undergo a transformation in how they do business. If transformation is not achieved, the community has done nothing more then increase its burden and develop another data repository.

To transform, begin by selecting "High Value–Low Risk" flows of inventory identified in the flow model stage. The flow selection should be based on that which the community believes would bring the highest value at the lowest risk to the community's mission. List and prioritize which flows will be transformed into the groupware application such that all future transactions relating to the selected process will be conducted via the groupware.

Once processes have been listed and prioritized in terms of value and risk, prepare an assessment or "gap analysis" of the "AS-IS" process and the "TO-BE" process. The analysis should include: |

- List of stakeholders who will be affected by the process change
- Changes to the process in terms of steps required to complete the process—Are there any changes to the process? If so, document the changes.
- Measures and metrics for assessing the value achieved by transforming the "AS-IS" process to the groupware application environment
- Document asset rules associated to conducting the process in the "TO-BE" environment

Work Product: TO-BE model and narrative of the business processes transacted. Includes a Gap Analysis identifying changes to AS-IS model and documented asset rules.

Key Task 9: Training	Training ensures that all community members possess the necessary skill to function within the collaborative work environment. Community leaders should not assume that its members understand and can operate within the knowledgebase without training and support.

Training in this context includes more than just application training. It includes context-based training that is rooted in business process. That is, members are trained in both the use of the groupware application and the business processes it supports. This way, training has relevance to the community member and has immediate application.

Training can be accomplished within the community by identifying a training lead for the community. Typically, this person will possess an above average aptitude for Information Technology and has a good grasp of the business processes.

The trainer will use the Requirements Traceability Matrix (RTM) developed earlier in the process to design a course for community members. The RTM provides the basis for the training. That is, it lists what groupware topics the trainer will cover. It is up to the trainer to select the business context of the functional topics. The trainer should develop a group of use cases or scenarios that illustrates to community members how the groupware will be utilized within the community's business environment. An example of a use case is:

Update group calendar

- Login to groupware
- Check-out calendar
- Add new calendar entry
- Check-in calendar

There is no replacement for hands-on training. Where possible, utilize a training center to deliver training to community members.

Training should be designed to be brief and specifically geared towards business processes. Long training session greater than 1.5 hours has proven to be ineffective. If training seems to long, scale back on the coverage areas. Keep it manageable, applicable, short, and enjoyable for your community members.

Tools	
	• Sample Requirements Traceability Matrix
	• Sample Inventory Template
	• Sample Taxonomy and Mapping Template
	• Sample Asset Rule Template

5. Sustaining Communities

Purpose Congratulations—your community has met and begun to form. The community is working together to develop and share best practices. How do you keep the community moving in a forward direction? How do you keep members coming back for more?

This section is designed to help community leadership assess progress, recognize the natural evolution of community interactions, recognize and reward both individual and community contributions, and continuously foster innovation and growth.

Expected Outcomes
- Process adjustments
- Continuous infusion of new knowledge

KEY TASKS	1. Assess community progress
	2. Understand community evolution
	3. Recognize community contribution
	4. Spark new knowledge creation and sharing

Key Task 1: Assess Community Progress

Once your community is up and running, community leadership should periodically check progress. In Section 2, a Community of Practice Early Progress Checklist was introduced as a tool. In this section, that tool has been expanded to assess ongoing community effectiveness. This expanded tool, Community of Practice Regular Progress Checklist, is provided at the end of this section.

As the community evolves, so may the strategic objectives of its members' organizations. A community should ask itself, "have we satisfied our highest priority knowledge needs? Do remaining needs still reflect strategic objectives? Have our knowledge needs changed?"

Community members should be polled periodically to gain insights on how they believe the community is performing. In other words, is it serving its members, the organization, and the enterprise?

One relatively simple method to gather member feedback is to facilitate occasional "lessons learned" discussions with the group. A template to capture this information was provided in Section 2. A second way would be to collect written responses using a survey instrument. A generic Community Member Satisfaction Survey is provided as a Tool at the end of this section. The survey should be tailored to your community's purpose and success criteria.

Key Task 2: Understand Community Evolution

Similar to the stages of group development, forming, norming, storming, and performing, communities will also undergo evolutionary stages. As Communities of Practice evolve, they go through stages of development characterized by different levels of interaction among members and different kinds of activities.

Key Task 3: Recognize Community Contribution	When you reward people for certain behaviors, e.g., sharing knowledge, they will want to do more of it. Therefore, developing meaningful rewards is essential to sustaining community goals and achieving a knowledge centric organization.
If you use it, say so	Meaningful recognition can come from peers as well as leadership. Community members should be encouraged to acknowledge individual and organizational contributions on a personal level. If knowledge culled from the knowledgebase is useful to an individual's work, that individual should reach out to the contributor and personally acknowledge the contribution. It doesn't need to be formal—a simple phone call or e-mail expressing appreciation could suffice.

Sample Requirements Traceability Matrix

Req ID	Requirement	Description	Release	(N)ew/ (E)xisting	(F)ull/ (P)artial	Source	Comments	Documents
1.0	**SECURITY**							
1.1	Login	Used to verify that a user is authorized. Also helps keep track of who added, modified, viewed and otherwise accessed content.	1					
1.2	Change Password	Allow users to change secure encrypted password.	1					
1.3	Logout	To prevent others from gaining unauthorized access, users are encouraged to logout when finished	1					
2.0	**SITE SEGMENTS**							
2.1	Enterprise Workspace	Central repository of your organization's knowledge. Stores documents and other information that is meant to be generally available to all users.	1					
2.2	Project or Workgroup Workspace	Team collaborative environment for projects to share and exchange specific project related information.	1					

Sample Requirements Traceability Matrix *(Continued)*

Req ID	Requirement	Description	Release	(N)ew/ (E)xisting	(F)ull/ (P)artial	Source	Comments	Documents
2.3	Personal Workspace	Allow users to create a customized view of their own personal data, project data, and enterprise data. Allow persons to share their workspace with other designated users.	2					
3.0	**NAVIGATION**							
3.1	Standard navigational controls on workspaces	Provide a consistent means of navigating site and "quick links" to specific site content.	1					
3.2	Provide consistent access to context sensitive help	Make a help link available in every view.	1					

Sample Taxonomy and Mapping Template

Folder ID #	Category	Level	Owner(s)—Mapping	Status	Description	Revision Notes

Sample Asset Rule Template

BR#	Business Rule	Description	Revision	Status	Comments
1.0	Update	Classification owners who have been designated as first point of contact, have final approval authority over all content posted to the assigned area.	1.0	A	
2.0	Event Expiration	Dated assets such as event or training schedule items will be scheduled for expiration one day after the item date.	1.0	A	
3.0	Periodicity	Update periodicity for an asset will be determined by the First and Second points of contact assigned to the classification area.	1.0	A	
		If an asset requires updating, First point of contact will perform the update or reset the asset periodicity.			
4.0	Gatekeeper	Gatekeeper will have access to all classification areas. Access includes the ability to update, delete, restrict access, and renew assets update periodicities.	1.0	A	

Peer nomination for rewards can be especially valued	People, if properly motivated and encouraged, will freely contribute if they know they are truly adding value to the Enterprise. Peer nomination for rewards can be especially valued. An example might be a team of individuals contributing lessons learned on a particular assignment to the knowledgebase. A second team utilizes these lessons on a similar assignment, resulting in improved decision-making capability and improved results. They nominate the first team for some kind of reward and recognition based on these results.
Blow your own horn	The Community Leader and Core Group should continuously promote and publicize individual and community contributions to organizational goals. Contributors could be recognized in newsletters, websites, staff meetings, luncheons, etc. Consider hosting or participating in knowledge fairs to "show off" your successes.
Employees receive personal acknowledgments from senior leadership	Another mechanism for community leadership to recognize contributors is to inform senior leadership of success stories. The information should be accompanied with a request for a personal note of appreciation from senior leadership to individuals and/or communities commending their work and acknowledging how their contribution has contributed to the bottom line.
	Incorporate knowledge management expectations into formal performance evaluations and incentive compensation systems. For example, Ernst & Young evaluates its consultants along several dimensions, one of which is their contribution to and utilization of the knowledge asset of the firm. At Bain, a consulting firm, the partners are evaluated each year on a variety of dimensions, including how much direct help they have given colleagues. The degree of high-quality person-to-person dialogue a partner has had with others can account for as much as one-quarter of his or her annual compensation.

Not invented here but I did it anyway!	Create a new award that promotes desired behaviors. For example, "Texas Instruments created the NIHBIDIA Award: Not Invented Here But I Did It Anyway". Starting in 1996, TI's annual Best Practices celebration and Sharing Day (where all the Best Practice teams staff booths to publicize and answer questions about their practices) culminates in an award ceremony for those organizations that have most successfully shared best practices and knowledge—and produced great results. The organizations involved (and sometimes there are more than two involved) receive an award from the senior executives at TI for collaborating on the exchange of best practices. This is a highly prestigious award in TI, because it reinforces both the process and the results. Rewards and recognition may be healthy and useful in the early stages of building enthusiasm for transfer. However, in the long run and for a sustainable effort, employees have to find the work itself rewarding.
Key Task 4: Spark New Knowledge Creation and Sharing	Members should be continuously polled to identify new areas of interest or challenge. As needs evolve, the Core Group should seek interesting ways to bring knowledge to the community. Be creative—reach outside the organization for relevant seminars, training opportunities, tours and site visits to relevant industry and government operations, and guest speakers.
If only we knew what we know	Consider sponsoring cross-community forums to gain additional insights. Understanding the purpose and inventory of knowledge assets owned by other communities could essentially expand your community's knowledgebase.
Look outside for innovations	In most professional disciplines, there is a plethora of relevant publications, websites, associations, etc. Who has time to read all of the available information? Perhaps your community would be interested in assigning members to scan specific information sources on a routine basis and cull interesting knowledge nuggets for the benefit of the entire community. If available, don't forget to use the Corporate KM Infomediary who can scan across knowledgebases to identify potentially relevant information.

Don't just stockpile new knowledge in a database To counter the "if I build it, they will come" mentality, consider other vehicles to "push" knowledge gains throughout the enterprise. As best practices are identified, have them written up by professional writers, and have them embedded in all kinds of places—in training programs, possibly in policies and procedures—in as many different dimensions of the organization as possible.

Get to work and start talking Try to create informal settings for member interactions. For example, coordinate Bring Your Own Lunch (BYOL) sessions. Simply put, a BYOL means you get together over lunch, typically in a meeting room. Since everyone has to eat anyway, it takes little time away from busy schedules, members can come and go as they please, and prospective members can visit and check out the group, etc.

The emphasis is open dialogue—informal, agenda-less weekly meetings with no pressure to come to resolution. Attendees can get input on any topic. The only structure is the time and place.

Your community may decide to adopt this easy approach to informal networking and knowledge sharing. If so, have the community select a regular BYOL (bring your own lunch) day and time, e.g., every other Wednesday at noon. To foster the process, the Core Group or the Community Leader should find a room that can always be used for BYOL day. Until the forum becomes habit, the Leader should personally invite members and prospective members to drop in on a regular basis.

Tools • Community of Practice Regular Progress Checklist
• Community Member Satisfaction Survey

Community of Practice

Regular Progress Checklist

1. Has the community revisited its purpose—is the purpose still compelling to leadership, active and prospective members, and their functional managers? Is the common purpose aligned with the Command/Enterprise strategy?
2. Is the community in agreement on the top priority knowledge needs to tackle?
3. Has the community assessed its performance against its success criteria?

4. Are the Functional Sponsor and senior leadership kept abreast of community progress and issues?
5. Are Core Group members and the Community Leader strong, content experts, enthusiastic, and able to sustain the community?
6. Do members' functional managers agree that "time away from the job" is valuable?
7. Do we have the right content experts to provide perspective and meaning in our membership?
8. Is there a shared space and context for dialogue, advice, and work?
9. Do we have enough members to keep the community alive?
10. How are attendance trends?
11. Are collaborative tools, e.g., discussion threads or a website, in place? Are members "set" to use them?
12. What are usage trends for collaborative work tools?
13. Are needed resources, e.g., meeting rooms, VTC, participation in conferences, travel dollars, conference fees, etc., available?
14. Has a process been established for creating, organizing, publishing, storing, and sharing knowledge? Are common templates in place? Is there a process for distributing explicit knowledge and alerting others that it is available?
15. Can bottom line improvements (cycle time, customer service, TOC reduction) be demonstrated?

Community Member Satisfaction Survey		
Community name:		
	Yes	No
Is there a common purpose that galvanizes community members to contribute to the knowledgebase?		
Are you likely to recommend the community to your professional colleagues?		
Does your manager recognize and value your involvement in the community?		
Are community activities part of your job?		
Is there an acknowledged member base?		
Does the community share a mutual understanding of its identity?		
Does the community sustain a common methodology, process, and language?		
Does the community scan external sources for new ideas and innovations?		
Is the community free of the "not invented here" syndrome?		

	Rating				
	5	4	3	2	1
Technology is leveraged to support collaboration.					
The community serves as a reliable source for workable solutions and/or best practices.					
Needed information is quickly accessed and easy to apply.					
Community members enjoy open channels of communication.					
Community participation contributes to your individual success.					
Members enjoy continuous learning.					
Resources and effort are invested in developing a supporting infrastructure for the community.					
The community quickly mobilizes for ad hoc discussions.					
Ranking: 5 = exceeds expectations, 1 = does not meet expectations					

- What do you like best about the community?
- What do you like least about the community?
- How would you improve the community?

Note: This appendix was adapted from the NAVSEA Community of Practice Practitioner's Guide. May 2001. Retrieved from http://knowledge.usaid.gov/documents/cop_practicioners_guide.pdf.

Appendix C—Knowledge Discovery Techniques

Knowledge can be transmitted between or among people, but this does not mean that it can only be copied. People learn rather than are taught, and knowledge transferred is recreated by the recipient. So it can change as it replicates and will not always take the same form. The key concept in this regard is to understand the extent to which useful knowledge can actually be codified. One of the simpler concepts to grasp is the difference between "explicit" and "tacit" knowledge.

A large number of organizations have seized on this concept as a way of capturing knowledge that resides inside their organizations and that they hope will prove to be a valuable asset. Sometimes, this is limited to programs of managing the firm's Intellectual Property. This form of knowledge management has been characterized as "defensive"—that is, concerned with protecting some aspect of the organization's activity.

There are, however, other forms of knowledge that are not so easily amenable to being codified. Typically, these are skills or abilities, sometime physical in nature, that resist easy replication. Sports stars are the example most often cited to explain this difference, but the concept can also be illustrated by examples from what are often referred to as "creative" occupations or even in design and engineering work. At the root of this is an understanding that some forms of knowledge do not exist outside their context and that some forms of knowledge are created socially.

Since some forms of knowledge or experience cannot easily be codified, then the experience of one person—or a group of people—cannot always be written down and passed on in book form for another group to replicate. Learning from the experience of others may require additional approaches and other skills. Table C.1 lists some of the techniques discussed in this appendix.

Innovation is one of the key drivers of knowledge management and other collaborative activities in commercial organizations. It is very strongly marked in research-based industries—such as pharmaceuticals—particularly where new developments can be converted into major financial assets such as patents. However, there are other forms of innovation, such as improved internal processes or new services to offer.

Table C.1 Knowledge Discovery Techniques

Technique	Basic/advanced	Requires cultural change?
Exit interviews	B	N
Speed dating	B	N
Mind mapping	B	N
After action reviews	B	N
Project reviews	B	N
Baton passing	B	Y
Virtual teams	B	Y
Coaching and mentoring	B	N
Intellectual capital	B	Y
Communities of Practice	B	Y
Social network analysis	A	N
Complex adaptive systems	A	Y
Knowledge audits	A	N
Design of space	A	Y
Knowledge harvesting	A	Y
Domain knowledge mapping	A	Y
Storytelling	A	Y

Knowledge management is a collection of approaches designed to answer two questions

How do we know what we know?
How do we get to know what we need to know?

Although understanding the sources of existing knowledge is not the only component of a successful knowledge management strategy—creating new knowledge is, in the longer term, even more important—understanding the sources of knowledge to support service improvement activities is nevertheless a vital one.

There are a wide and diverse set of sources that can be categorized into three main areas: your customers, your own organization, and others.

Learning from customers: Customers are a major source of knowledge of areas of service improvement. The skill, however, lies in understanding what to ask and in interpreting the answer. Many organizations have put in place customer complaints systems, but it is not always clear how these are used to derive lessons that can feed service improvement.

This is where the technology of customer relationship management can fit in. However, it is not just the recording of the customer interactions that is important. It is also the mining of the data. This is the knowledge management dimension—the need to combine insights from a number of sources in order to gain a better understanding of the sources of innovation.

Learning from your organization: In almost all organizations, the chief source of expertise and the wellspring of innovation come from within the organization itself. Although every organization produces some of its "organizational capital" in the form of manuals and procedure documents, most of its actual capital is contained in the minds and the behaviors of its employees. The chief issues in trying to liberate this capital are: getting buy-in from the staff that control access to this learning. They may need to get some value from this in terms of material reward or recognition. Understanding that this expertise may be contained in parts of the organization other than the ones that provide the specific service.

The management of the organization may be the biggest problem in opening up this source either because of a distrust on the part of the individuals or groups with access to this capability or because new ways of working may threaten existing power structures. Actually knowing where the expertise lies in your organization is the other major inhibitor to effective organizational learning. The ways of addressing this are to adopt some of the methods identified as being useful ways of capturing tacit knowledge.

Learning from other organizations: This is easily the largest, most complex, and most diffuse source of knowledge. Organizations can usually learn a considerable amount from other comparable organizations. These other organizations do not need to be the same type of organization. Sometimes, very dissimilar organizations can be the greatest source of learning. However, in order to take advantage of this learning, organizations must be able to learn from the experience of others.

Knowledge Management Techniques

An important area for sharing knowledge and expertise is in solving specific problems. A number of basic techniques have been developed for this.

Exit interviews: This is normally seen as a basic HR activity. Its specific relevance to knowledge sharing and collaboration is the link to retaining specialist knowledge within the organization. In a number of commercial organizations, this is linked to retaining the intellectual property of the company. Exit interviews are a long-standing and well-known technique in the human resources field. From the HR perspective, they are a way of gaining insights into how employees see the organization and identifying potential areas for improvement.

Interest has grown more recently, however, in the potential of exit interviews as a knowledge management tool. Put simply, a number of organizations have begun to realize that much valuable information and knowledge about the way jobs are done or customer expectations are locked inside the heads of employees (i.e., tacit rather than explicit knowledge) and can easily be lost if they leave the organization without recording or passing on their understanding and expertise.

The traditional, HR-focused exit interviews can be conducted in a number of ways, including by telephone, by questionnaire, or even via the Internet. However, for knowledge management objectives, a face-to-face interview is the only realistic approach.

There is no single agreed approach to conducting knowledge-focused exit interviews. Each organization can develop its own approach that fits its own particular circumstances.

The principal value of exit interviews lies in their simplicity. However, their successful use depends on how well the process is integrated with other knowledge-sharing activities. The results from the interviews need to be fed back into other developmental processes, to ensure that the value of any knowledge or information gained is immediately accessible by other parts of the organization.

Exit interviews are, therefore, a spectrum that includes other forms of "knowledge elicitation." These include support for "blogging" and more elaborate forms of "knowledge harvesting," discussed later in this chapter.

Speed dating: The purpose of "speed dating" is to elicit the largest number of potential solutions to a problem. The person with the problem will then be able to sift the responses to see if any offer potential solutions. It is possible to organize the speed dating in any way that is convenient, but one basic approach is as follows:

1. A range of people from different backgrounds are arranged into groups.
2. Those people with a problem and who are looking for a potential solution then go around each group in turn.
3. The person with the problem has a short period (say, 5–10 min) to explain the problem.
4. The group offering solutions then has a short period (say, 10–15 min) to suggest as many solutions as they can.

The chief benefit of this technique is that, apart from the cost of bringing people together, it is comparatively cheap. It does allow a range of different people to contribute to identifying potential solutions.

At its simplest, it involves someone with a specific problem presenting it briefly to a group of individuals from different backgrounds. The group listening then has a short period of time to suggest possible answers. To be effective, the process needs to be repeated several times with other groups.

Mind mapping: Mind mapping is a well-established technique that was developed in the 1960s by Tony Buzan. It is a graphic technique that allows one individual—or a group—to visualize the relationships among a range of related topics and to represent them in the form of a diagram. Its primary purpose is to clarify thinking and understanding. Tony Buzan (http://www.mind-map.com/EN/mindmaps/how_to.htm) has written extensively on mind mapping, and there are various printed guides available that document the processes.

Successful mind maps help visualize the relationship between different components of an issue. They can be very personal, but they can also be used to reveal and discuss differences in understanding between people who need to collaborate on a specific issue.

The potential application of mind mapping to organizational improvement activities is in the structure it offers to allow groups of people to explore or clarify thinking—and thus access or share knowledge—particularly in identifying linkages across different components. In this regard, it offers some interesting links to Ishikawa (or "Fishbone") diagrams used in quality improvement activities. And the linking of corporate objectives to detailed performance measures which are at the heart of the use of the Balanced Scorecard to support strategic management.

Organizational Learning Approaches

Organizational learning is a key component of any knowledge management strategy or any attempt to harness the experience of an organization to improve its performance.

There is a major area of overlap between organizational learning approaches and collaboration. A number of the techniques developed to support organizational learning are, therefore, of direct interest or use to knowledge management approaches.

After Action Reviews: This is one of the simplest approaches to learning from doing. It was originally developed by the US military to learn the lessons from combat. An After Action Review (AAR) is a professional discussion of an event, focused on performance standards, that enables soldiers to discover for themselves what happened, why it happened, and how to sustain strengths and improve on weaknesses. There are several important features of his definition. First of all, the emphasis is on a professional discussion. The discussion is structured and is based on the expectation that there was a plan to be followed and preexisting standards that were to have been observed in carrying out the tasks. Finally, and most importantly, the use of AARs needs to feed into performance management and service improvement activities. It is not a stand-alone activity.

An AAR is both an art and science. The art of an AAR is in obtaining mutual trust so that people will speak freely. Innovative behavior should be the norm. Problem solving should be pragmatic, and employees should not be preoccupied with status, territory, or second guessing "what the leader will think." There is a fine line between keeping the meeting from falling into chaos where nothing real gets accomplished, to people treating each other in a formal and polite manner that masks issues (especially with the boss) where again, nothing real gets accomplished.

It consists of several basic questions:

1. What was supposed to happen?
2. What actually happened?
3. Why was there a difference?
4. What did we learn?

The important thing to notice from this approach is that, to be effective, it needs to be removed from any attempt to assign blame. The major advantage of AAR is its independence of any technology and its ability to be used in a variety of situations form very small reviews to quite large ones.

Project reviews: Project reviews are in some ways a more sophisticated version of the AARs. In general, they are used to review larger areas of work than those for which AARs are employed. They are often linked to more complex methodologies for large-scale project management.

It is a major technique for codifying knowledge, since it attempts to capture learning points from the experience of delivering projects. It can be linked to a number of performance management activities.

Baton passing: "Baton passing" is a more sophisticated approach to passing on the lessons from a recently experienced process to another team that is about to undergo the same process. It is a technique developed by Victor Newman of European Pfizer Research University. It is a more sophisticated technique for passing lessons learned than in the two review methods outlined earlier.

The key elements in baton passing are that the team that has just successfully completed the process should record their experiences immediately after the process is completed. So, the key feature is the "just-in-time" knowledge transfer. The specific requirement that led to its being developed was for project teams which had just successfully completed a project review to pass on the lessons to the next project team about to embark on a similar phase of activity. The reason for adopting a just-in-time approach was to capture the experience of a group that had successfully completed a rarely encountered process. It becomes important then to capture the knowledge and experience before it is lost, because it is unlikely to be of use to the successful team at least for some time.

The key phases in the process are

1. Build, identify, and capture experience
2. Review and exchange experience between outgoing and incoming teams to connect learning and questions
3. Produce an action plan to be able to mobilize the lessons
4. Commit the plan to action

The applicability of this technique to service improvement is to use the learning gained in one area to prepare the next area for the same test.

Organizational Design Approaches

A number of approaches to collaboration and sharing knowledge have a strong component of organizational change and redesign. These are more formal approaches than those in the earlier section.

Virtual teams: The distinguishing characteristic of virtual teams is that they are collections of individuals or groups who are located apart physically but who need to collaborate across physical boundaries. Often this is because they are working on a specific project but there are other circumstances in which this kind of approach is productive. In research-based activities—such as in pharmaceutical companies—it may be important to get research teams to collaborate. This may to be maximize scarce resources or, more usually, to try to generate new areas of knowledge from existing ones.

Virtual teams offer a way of bringing together the distributed resources to work on a number of projects. They offer greater flexibility in the use of resources and the ability produce new expertise from old.

Key issues for the successful use of virtual teams are

1. The need to have occasional physical contact at the outset of the project as some basic degree of physical contact is important for communication and building trust. This has been confirmed by a number of research studies.
2. The need to address cultural differences among the various members of the team. In multinational firms, this is usually a problem of different national cultures.

Direct physical contact and building in a degree of socialization can contribute to breaking down these barriers. The effective use of technology can also be a key determinant of the success or failure of virtual teams. Effective information systems can allow collaboration, while ineffective ones can hinder effective communications. E-mail tends to be the simplest of methods that are employed, but more elaborate technologies include collaboration software or the use of video-conferencing technologies.

The potential contribution of virtual teams to performance improvement is in the direction of resources toward the solution of particular tasks. It is quite a common experience in organizations that experience or expertise is restricted to one organizational unit and cannot easily be released to another one if the only way to do this is to transfer the member of staff.

Virtual teams offer the opportunity for individuals or groups to collaborate without changing organizational boundaries. They also differ from many matrix management structures in that they do not necessitate changes in formal reporting structures. However, creating and maintaining virtual teams are not without their challenges. Several key areas need to be addressed.

1. *Job design.* Team working methods and expectations need to be dealt with explicitly. This also includes designing job accountability and decision-making authority.

2. *Team design.* As virtual teams are meant to overcome the limitations of traditional organization boundaries, they need new criteria. These include identifying the purpose of the team and selecting members who fit. More importantly, the team needs to have a clear identity and a defined statement of purpose.
3. Communication methods are essential to the success of virtual teams because physical contact is kept to a minimum. Communications need to be comprehensive (i.e., keeping each other fully informed), frequent but preferably with short messages. Quality of communication is the most important aspect.
4. Leadership appears to have a key impact on the success of virtual teams. This includes setting clear goals and providing continuous feedback on performance.
5. *Trust.* Trust is at the heart of almost all successful knowledge management practices. It is best established by social interaction, particularly at the start of the project.
6. *Cultural awareness.* The cultural dimension should be tackled at the outset to improve coherence and minimize misunderstanding.
7. *Technology.* Once again, this is a key enabler—not only to ensure frequent contact but relatively advanced technology will be required to support collaboration.

Coaching and mentoring: Coaching and mentoring are well-known techniques from human resources and organizational development work. Their relevance to knowledge-based work is the opportunities they provide for direct person-to-person assimilation. In this regard, they are similar to the way that apprentices have traditionally learned their craft.

Not all useful information can be conveyed by capturing tacit knowledge and codifying it, for example, in the form of guides or handbooks. Certain types of knowledge are best provided by observing someone else at work and, where possible, copying and asking questions. The principal advantages of mentoring and coaching are

1. The personal contact and therefore the opportunities for socialization and internalizing knowledge.
2. It can strongly reinforce cultural aspects of work. It offers opportunities for feedback and development.

However, the corresponding disadvantages are

1. It can be very intensive and time consuming. This may in some cases interfere with normal work activities.
2. Although it is strong at imparting existing knowledge, it can hinder the development of new knowledge or expertise.

For these reasons, coaching and mentoring are often restricted to very highly regarded areas such as senior management development.

Cultural Approaches

Many of the most effective knowledge management approaches have their basis in understanding the cultural aspects of organizational behavior and on concentrating on improving the cultural bias toward sharing knowledge or other information.

Identifying intellectual capital: "Intellectual capital" is a concept that has been gaining in acceptance in commercial organizations but is not yet used much or understood in the public sector—except, perhaps, for people who concentrate on organizational development activities.

The concept can be traced back to work carried out for the Skandia Corporation by Leif Edvinsson. The model developed there was intended to demonstrate the importance of assets other than financial ones to the value and performance of a company.

The nonfinancial forms of capital are for the most part intangible assets, but they represent things of value to the organization. Customer capital represents the value of the customers to the organization and, in particular, their contribution to future income and profits. Customer capital can also be represented in terms of the feedback or ideas that can be obtained from consultations, surveys, or reviews of complaints.

Structural capital represents all the nonhuman, nonfinancial aspects. It includes all the processes and procedures that an organization has developed. In the commercial world, the processes and procedures are often the source of competitive advantage. Human capital is a rather easier concept to explain. In its most basic form, it consists of all those intangible assets contributed by employees—their skills, experience, knowledge, and abilities (current and potential). In service-based organizations, human capital is often the key source of improvement and innovation. It is capable of being increased or renewed—either by staff turnover or by education, development, and the acquisition of new skills. There are a number of issues with the measurement of either the level of human capital in an organization or its financial valuation. Some progress has been made on including valuations for human capital in areas such as transfer fees for sportsmen and women and in the market valuation of companies whose intellectual assets far outweigh their tangible ones. This has long been true of consultancy forms, for instance, or companies such as Microsoft.

Social capital is the name given to a set of processes which attempt to stress the importance of the relationships that are built and developed by individuals who work together to provide goods or services. Most people will recognize this in the strength of working relationships and goodwill that exists among effective teams. Although it is intangible, it is real. Social capital covers the value that is generated by the interaction between people in organizations.

Social capital is essential to exploiting intellectual capital. This is because much of the knowledge created by individual is created in social contexts rather than by them acting alone. Social capital is one of the major contributions made by teams to the efficiency and effectiveness or organizations.

Intellectual capital is less of a technique that can be applied directly than a way of analyzing and interpreting the basic capacity of an organization. It helps identify the assets that an organization has which can be used to improve its effectiveness and its ability to change and to innovate. The key to opening up intellectual capital is, therefore, developing a measurement and reporting system that can account for these assets in a reasonably objective fashion.

Building Communities of Practice: Communities of Practice are a comparatively new but very powerful way of developing links among individuals and groups that can develop links to share experiences across wider groups. A community of practice (CoP) is essentially a social network—a group of individuals who have recognized and expressed a need to share knowledge (and information) or collaborate in a specific and usually work-related area. The term is a relatively recent coining, but the concept is a very old one. It is, however, an idea that has begun to take off.

The strength of CoPs is that they can be formed around any topic of interest or concern. Communities can also be short-lived or long-lived, depending on the nature of the area of interest. Although the typical CoP is formed by people from similar backgrounds, it is also potentially a very powerful approach for bringing together a range of disparate people to share knowledge and experience to tackle a new problem, where the questions have still to be formulated and the answers are not yet clear.

CoPs differ from teams or workgroups in a number of quite significant ways.

Teams tend to have very specific goals with targets or demonstrable objectives. CoPs tend to concentrate on wider areas of interest that can develop over time. Teams are usually a formal part of the organizational structure, while CoPs are more amorphous and are often voluntary.

Although CoPs are not dependent on technology, there is no doubt that the greater availability of IT has offered the opportunity to boost their importance. The key technologies in this area are e-mail, bulletin boards, and collaboration software.

The experience in commercial organizations is that managerial organization of CoPs is unlikely to lead to their being successful. Most successful CoPs tend to be self-organizing, and this offers challenges to organizations, particularly very hierarchical or highly structured ones.

The potential contribution of CoPs to performance improvement is quite easy to see.

CoPs offer the opportunity not only to learn directly from the more experienced individuals but also can provide a space in which ideas can be put forward and explored without being put directly into practice.

Advanced Techniques

Social network analysis: Social network analysis is at the same time a specific academic technique and a useful way of analyzing the way that communications flow through an organization. As an analytical activity, it does help illuminate the way social relationships can improve or impede the flow of knowledge. However, there is no preferred model—the analysis demonstrates the situation.

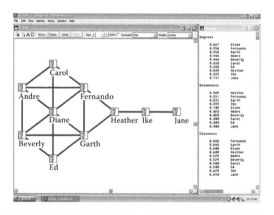

Figure C.1   Social network analysis.

KM staff who wish to design a preferred outcome need to mold the organizational structure. Social network analysis is essentially an analytical technique but one which can be used diagnostically. However, the key skill required for its successful application is in the design of the questionnaires that are required to elicit the basic data. Accurate and relevant data is the key to properly mapping the network. The resulting network map is a strongly visual description, as shown in Figure C.1.

Knowledge audits: Knowledge audits are quite a complex but potentially very effective approach to identifying and describing the way knowledge is created and stored in organizations. The audits cannot be open ended and need to be prepared and, in particular, to be based on a basic analysis of knowledge types and knowledge flows.

Design of space: The design of working space is a very powerful aspect of the use of knowledge management techniques to improve effective working. There is a whole body of research in a range of different settings that demonstrate the impact that the design of working space has on working relationships and collaboration. In general, working space should be created to allow individuals a degree of freedom in meeting so that spontaneous conversations can develop.

This is often referred to as the "water cooler" approach. Key aspects of design include the provision of neutral spaces and wide corridors that enable chance meetings to occur and take place without anyone feeling that they are interrupting someone else's work.

A particular analysis of the approach to designing office space can be found in *The New Office*, by Francis Duffy. Duffy's book divides office space into four sorts:

1. The HIVE—open plan, humming with activity
2. The CLUB—18th-century coffee-house style, for deals and ideas and bonding
3. The DEN—for intense communicative work among a small number of people
4. The CELL—where an individual works in a contemplative sort of way

Knowledge harvesting: Knowledge harvesting covers a range of techniques that aim to recover knowledge assets from many forms of tacit knowledge contained within an organization. Several of the approaches are concerned with capturing tacit knowledge and codifying it—that is, turning it into explicit knowledge. The principal techniques include developing communities of interest, which hare parallel activities to Communities of Practice and encourage activities such as web logging ("blogging"). Another technique is to use resources such as internal directories as guides to likely sources of expertise.

Domain knowledge mapping: This is a rather more complicated approach to identifying knowledge that is recognized as important but not well defined. It is often useful for beginning the recording of knowledge in newly developed fields.

Domain knowledge mapping often concentrates on developing high-level knowledge models. This is often a helpful way of providing an overview of available and missing knowledge in core business areas. Knowledge mapping is a good example of a useful knowledge management activity with existing knowledge acquisition and modeling techniques at its foundations.

It particularly concentrates on the visualization of relationships particularly in newly evolving or complex areas of study.

Storytelling: Storytelling is quite simply the use of stories in organizations as a communication tool to share knowledge. It is a deceptively simple approach, but it has been put in the category of advanced techniques because its effective use is quite a complex matter.

Although virtually all people are attracted to stories, not everyone is good at telling them. Stories have to be well selected for the appropriateness and content as well as their presentation. This is a skill well understood by traditional storytellers, and the skills often require years to acquire and be developed into a useful activity.

A rare example of storytelling in the public sector—the NHS, in this case—is provided on this website: http://www.affinitymc.com/The-Power-of-Storytelling.htm.

Tools for Organizing Knowledge Assets

There is a wide range of software available for organizing knowledge assets.

Tools based on database technologies. These are very heavily influenced by computing theories and rely frequently on relational database models. They are optimized for highly structured data but have more difficulty in dealing with unstructured data. However, newer RDBMS often have support for other structures.

Electronic Document Management systems (EDMS). These are increasingly touted as being the answer to all knowledge management problems, largely because they work with unstructured information as well as highly structured information.

Metadata management systems. Metadata is key component of all comprehensive management systems. However, there is a dearth of metadata schemes that relate to service improvement or performance management. One area, however, where something similar has been developed is in the metadata layer of Business Intelligence or other reporting tools. In addition to allowing the mapping between object names used in the service areas with the usually less meaningful table names and views, these metadata layers also frequently support the creation of new objects derived from underlying values in the base data. This allows the creation of standard approaches for deriving or calculating Performance Indicators or other values in a consistent fashion.

Generalized retrieval systems. These use variety of technologies, but there is an increasing preference for very sophisticated probabilistic searching methods, often based on Bayesian inference.

A popular area for the deployment of the searching tools is in support of CRM systems, to allow multiskilled agents to access organizational information. These developments are managed in a variety of ways. Increasingly, suppliers of CRM and Help Desk software are including software often described as "Knowledge Management" software. This is often used to extend the capability of the basic system by allowing agents to record how new or unusual problems were dealt with and making the resulting knowledge available to colleagues who might face the same problem in future.

Tools for collaboration: The other main category of tools is those for collaboration. This is an area that is less structured and therefore in some ways less highly developed than the tools for organizing knowledge. There are two main categories of collaboration software—systems that have been written for specific groups or for specific purposes. These include a whole range of different software types. They include, for instance, project management software, which has moved on from task recording and scheduling packages that were used primarily to produce Gantt charts and to calculate the critical path, to repository-based collaborative systems.

There are a wide variety of collaborative tools—from development tools such as Lotus Notes/Domino to systems designed to provide Enterprise Information Portals. The recent concentration on portals provides a good example of the issues that need to be addressed in providing generic solutions to knowledge work and collaboration. Portals offer a range of services that are intended to allow information services simply to be "plugged in" to the portal and then can be made available to desktops throughout the organization. In reality, however, portals can be extremely complex software environments that require considerable programming resources to utilize properly. The choice of the basic platform is, therefore, one of the critical success factors for any portal project.

The other significant IT component that relates to both the organization of knowledge assets and collaboration areas is intranets. "Intranet" is an increasingly loose term: its strict meaning applies to the deployment of Internet technologies within a single organization. In practice, however, it is used as a kind of shorthand for a collection of information management and collaboration tools, delivered to a set of desktops.

Many organizations have encountered difficulties with the effective deployment of intranets. The main problems have been:

1. Poor information management, where duplication has been permitted and information has been allowed to get out of date.
2. Like the Internet, intranets are subject to a Gresham's Law of information and knowledge, where the less useful material is all too easy to find, but the genuinely useful material is not in regular circulation.
3. A proliferation of intranets, each based on an organizational unit, thereby reinforcing internal barriers instead of trying to help break them down problems of cultural fit between the opportunities offered by the technology and the wider organizational culture. The latter needs to support a degree of openness in the use of the technology, otherwise effective collaboration is unlikely to result.

Frameworks

The literature on knowledge management is replete with proposed frameworks of varying degrees of complexity. Although there are competing models, there are basically two major approaches:

1. Maturity models
2. Strategy or implementation frameworks

The maturity models—which are common in other areas—purport to describe a journey that it is possible to make from less sophisticated to more sophisticated approaches.

A good example of the maturity model is the Siemens KMMM model (http://w4.siemens.de/ct/en/technologies/ic/beispiele/kmmm.html). Based on the well-known Capability Maturity Model (CMM) from the Software Engineering Institute, KMMM includes an analysis model and a development model.

Implementation frameworks can be simple or complex, often depending on the sophistication of the organization. One well-regarded framework is that devised by British Petroleum, which consists of three steps:

1. Create awareness
2. Build knowledge assets
3. Leverage knowledge assets

When considering the application of knowledge management to process improvement, managers should look to the simplest possible approach that is congruent with organizational goals. That predisposes them to frameworks such as the BP model.

Producing Corporate KM strategies

Knowledge management "strategies" are highly problematic. They tend to imply that there is a well-defined path to achieving knowledge management. That is an arguable concept. A very useful model is that of George von Krogh (2000), who suggests the following "enablers":

1. Instill a knowledge vision
2. Manage conversations
3. Mobilize knowledge activists
4. Create the right context
5. Globalize local knowledge

Theories of knowledge—epistemologies, to give them their formal name—provide a huge area of debate that covers philosophy, psychology and, more recently, areas of information theory. The span of this work also reaches from the ancient world to the present and across a range of different cultures. There are two basic approaches to understanding the nature of knowledge—and of knowledge creation in particular—which may be of use in planning the introduction of knowledge management initiatives.

The *Cognitive* model that regards knowledge as essentially something objective and transferable. This approach stresses the capturing of tact knowledge and its embedding into more explicit forms. The resulting "knowledge" can therefore be shared and reused. This model is very strongly linked to approaches that stress the importance of explicit knowledge as a form of intellectual property. It is also the model that lies behind most of the IT systems which are sold as "knowledge management systems." These are very heavily reliant on regarding knowledge management as being essentially a more complex form of information processing, where cognitive abilities are seen as the major inputs which the technology can transform into the desired outputs.

The *Social* model, which is sometimes called the *Community* or *Connectiveness* model, stresses that knowledge creation is essentially a social process. This model emphasizes the importance of social interaction both to the creation and to the dissemination of knowledge. It is naturally a view held very strongly in the social sciences and to professionals and researchers who concentrate on organizational development and human resources processes. The most important formulation of the theory, however, is probably that of Nonaka and Takeuchi in their book, *The Knowledge Creating Company* (1995). The theoretical basis of this book also relies on far Eastern philosophies as well as modern business practices. The principal idea expounded in that work is the kinds of knowledge that need to be created to drive innovation are essentially social. The Nonaka and Takeuchi model sees knowledge management as an iterative process, whereby tacit knowledge is often shared in social contexts before being made explicit and explicit knowledge is often internalized before being used to help create new forms of tacit knowledge.

The **Autopoietic** model is a more recent development but one that has excited a lot of interest. The word *autopoiesis* ("self-creation") was created by two biologists, Humberto Maturano and Francisco Varela, to explain a theory about the `development of organisms.

They developed these findings toward a theory of knowledge in their book, *The Tree of Knowledge* (1987), which proposed a theory of knowledge creation based on the interaction of individual organisms with their environment. In this model, "knowledge" does not exist independently of the organism (as it does in the cognitive model), and it is created by the individual organism and not by the interaction with other organisms (as in the social model). There are considerable implications in this model for any systematic view of knowledge management. The model has, however, been criticized for a number of things, perhaps the most significant in this context being the assumption that what may hold for simple organisms, may not hold for the complex, self-aware higher organisms.

Knowledge management needs to be undertaken for some practical reason. The two main reasons are

1. To provide some degree of protection for current intellectual property or assets. These approaches tend to concentrate more on turning tacit knowledge into explicit knowledge, or "knowledge harvesting." They have been characterized as a "survival" strategy.
2. To provide a source for future or continuing competitive advantage. This focuses on the creation of new knowledge or on new ways of exploiting existing knowledge. This approach is characterized by emphasis on collaboration. This is sometimes referred to as an *advancement strategy*.

Innovation is a critical issue for commercial organizations. In some industries, such as pharmaceuticals, this is a major reason for investing in knowledge management initiatives. The knowledge proposition is that significant additional stakeholder value, and competitive advantage will be derived if the expertise, information, and ideas of employees, partners, and customers are continually developed and used in all business and decision-making processes.

References

Van Krogh, G., Ichijo, K., and Nonaka, I. (2000). *How to unlock the mystery of tacit knowledge and release the power of innovation.* Oxford: Oxford University Press.

Appendix D—Staff Competency Survey

Directions: Please rate your perception of your abilities on a scale of 1 to 5 with 1 being the lowest and 5 being the highest. In addition, please use the same scale to rate the importance of this trait in your current work environment.

Communications

1. Professionals must communicate in a variety of settings using oral, written, and multimedia techniques.

Your self rating:
Low   High
1   2   3   4   5

Importance of this trait to your organization:
Low   High
1   2   3   4   5

Problem Solving

2. Professionals must be able to choose from a variety of different problem-solving methodologies to analytically formulate a solution.

Your self rating:
Low   High
1   2   3   4   5

Importance of this trait to your organization:
Low   High
1   2   3   4   5

3. Professionals must think creatively in solving problems.

Your self rating:
    Low   High
    1 2 3 4 5

Importance of this trait to your organization:
    Low   High
    1 2 3 4 5

4. Professionals must be able to work on project teams and use group methods to define and solve problems.

Your self rating:
    Low   High
    1 2 3 4 5

Importance of this trait to your organization:
    Low   High
    1 2 3 4 5

Organization

5. Professionals must have sufficient background to understand the functioning of organizations since the product/service must be congruent with, and supportive of the strategy, principles, goals, and objectives of the organization.

Your self rating:
    Low   High
    1 2 3 4 5

Importance of this trait to your organization:
    Low   High
    1 2 3 4 5

6. Professionals must understand and be able to function in the multinational and global context of today's information-dependent organizations.

Your self rating:
    Low   High
    1 2 3 4 5

Importance of this trait to your organization:
    Low   High
    1 2 3 4 5

Quality

7. Professionals must understand quality, planning, steps in the continuous improvement process as it relates to the enterprise, and tools to facilitate quality development.

   Your self rating:
   Low   High
   1 2 3 4 5

   Importance of this trait to your organization:
   Low   High
   1 2 3 4 5

8. Error control, risk management, process measurement, and auditing are areas that professionals must understand and apply.

   Your self rating:
   Low   High
   1 2 3 4 5

   Importance of this trait to your organization:
   Low   High
   1 2 3 4 5

9. Professionals must possess a tolerance for chance and skills for managing the process of change.

   Your self rating:
   Low   High
   1 2 3 4 5

   Importance of this trait to your organization:
   Low   High
   1 2 3 4 5

10. Education must be continuous.

    Your self rating:
    Low   High
    1 2 3 4 5

    Importance of this trait to your organization:
    Low   High
    1 2 3 4 5

11. Professionals must understand mission-directed, principle-centered mechanisms to facilitate aligning group as well as individual missions with organizational missions.

    Your self rating:
    Low   High
    1 2 3 4 5

    Importance of this trait to your organization:
    Low   High
    1 2 3 4 5

Groups

12. Professionals must interact with diverse user groups in team and project activities.

    Your self rating:
    Low   High
    1 2 3 4 5

    Importance of this trait to your organization:
    Low   High
    1 2 3 4 5

13. Professionals must possess communication and facilitation skills with team meetings and other related activities.

    Your self rating:
    Low   High
    1 2 3 4 5

    Importance of this trait to your organization:
    Low   High
    1 2 3 4 5

14. Professionals must understand the concept of empathetic listening and utilize it proactively to solicit synergistic solutions in which all parties to an agreement can benefit.

    Your self rating:
    Low   High
    1 2 3 4 5

    Importance of this trait to your organization:
    Low   High
    1 2 3 4 5

15. Professionals must be able to communicate effectively with a changing work force.

Your self rating:
Low   High
1   2   3   4   5

Importance of this trait to your organization:
Low   High
1   2   3   4   5

Appendix E—Behavioral Competencies

Companies interesting in stimulating learning and growth among employees will be interested in this list of behavioral competencies for employees and managers.

For Employees

Communicates Effectively

1. Listens to others in a patient, empathetic, and nonjudgmental way; acknowledges their ideas in a respectful manner; questions appropriately.
2. Is straightforward and direct; behavior is consistent with words.
3. Discusses concerns and conflict directly and constructively.
4. Communicates in a timely fashion.

Promotes Teamwork

1. Networks with other employees within and outside of one's area; makes internal referrals to connect people with each other.
2. Readily volunteers to be on teams.
3. Is a participating and equal partner on teams; has the same purpose as the team; encourages cohesion and trust.
4. Is receptive to and solicits other team member's advice and ideas.
5. Keeps supervisor/team informed of status of work so that surprises are minimized.
6. Verbally and nonverbally supports established decisions and actions; represents the collective stance.

Presents Effectively

1. Understands the makeup of the audience and is sensitive to their values, backgrounds, and needs.
2. Presents ideas clearly so that others can easily understand their meaning.
3. Delivers presentations with the appropriate level of expression and confidence.
4. Incorporates humor when appropriate and in good taste.

Makes Sound Decisions

1. Knows when a decision is necessary and makes decisions in a timely manner.
2. Connects decisions to strategic plans; separates essential from nonessential information considering all logical alternatives when generating conclusions.
3. Seeks and considers input from others who are close to the situation before establishing a course of action.
4. Considers the relevance and impact of decisions on others prior to making decisions.

Uses Resources Wisely

1. Considers need and cost prior to making resource-related requests and decisions.
2. Makes maximum use of available resources through the efficient and creative use of people, time, material, and equipment.
3. Reduces waste, reuses materials, and recycles appropriate materials.
4. Functions within the budget.

Takes Initiative and Accepts Accountability

1. Is proactive; plans ahead; sees things that need to be done and accomplishes them on own initiative and on time.
2. Accepts responsibility and consequences for one's decisions and actions.
3. Follow through on commitments; does what one says on will do—the first time.
4. Acknowledges, accepts, and learns from mistakes.

Lives Company's Values

1. Demonstrates the organizational and professional code of ethics including honesty, respect, dignity, caring, and confidentiality.
2. Demonstrates and consistently applies organizational principles, policies, and values to all employees and situations.
3. Respects and operates within the boundaries established for one's job and personal boundaries set by others.
4. Promotes a positive work environment.

Demonstrates a Customer First Approach (Internal Partners and External Customers)

1. Anticipates customers' needs; facilitates customers to express their needs; listens to customer and hears what they say.
2. Promptly attends to customers' needs (e.g., answers phone and returns phone calls within a reasonable amount of time).
3. Treats customers with respect, politeness, and dignity while maintaining appropriate boundaries.
4. When appropriate, provides the customer with options for action in response to their needs.

Generates New Ideas

1. Generates imaginative and original ideas that will bring about positive change.
2. Seizes opportunities to expand on other people's ideas to create something new and add value.
3. Encourages others to create new ideas, products, and solutions that will add value to the organization.

Demonstrates Flexibility

1. Adapts to and accepts changing work schedules, priorities, challenges, and unpredictable events in a positive manner.
2. Is visible and accessible; is approachable even when interruptions are inconvenient.
3. Is receptive to new ideas that are different from one's own ideas.
4. Offers to help others when circumstances necessitate sharing the workload.

Demonstrates a Professional Demeanor

1. Demonstrates acceptable hygiene and grooming; dresses appropriately for one's job.
2. Uses proper verbal and nonverbal communications and tone with internal partners and external customers and patients.
3. Places work responsibilities and priorities before personal needs while at work.
4. Maximizes positive and professional communication with internal partners and external customers and patients; minimizes complaining and nonfactual communication.

Stimulates and Adapts to Change

1. Stimulates positive attitudes about change; pushes the change process along.
2. Takes personal responsibility for adapting to and coping with change.

3. Commits quickly when change reshapes one's area of work.
4. Accepts ambiguity and uncertainty; is able to improvise and still add value.

Continually Improves Processes

1. Anticipates and looks for opportunities to improve steps in the development and delivery of one's products or services; takes logical risks that may lead to improvement and change.
2. Examines one's work for conformance to predetermined plans, specifications, and standards.
3. Freely shares and promotes new ideas that may lead to improvement and positive change, even when the idea may be unpopular.
4. Seeks input from others who are closest to the situation in making improvements.

For Managers

Organizational Acumen

1. Demonstrates thorough knowledge of the company model, organizational history, and values.
2. Applies knowledge of services, products, and processes to understand key issues within own division and work unit.
3. Demonstrates understanding of and ability to influence organizational culture, norms, and expectations.
4. Contributes to fosters and supports changes resulting from organizational decisions and initiatives.

Strategic Direction

1. Integrates own work and that of one's work unit with the organization's mission, values, and objectives.
2. Analyzes and utilizes customer, industry, and stakeholder inputs in strategic and operating plan processes.
3. Establishes workgroup priorities to support strategic objectives.
4. Gathers input from internal and external resources to analyze business unit needs.
5. Promotes and embraces innovation and creativity to achieve organizational and work unit goals.
6. Develops work unit plans and measures that are aligned with division and organization strategic objectives.
7. Defines operational goals for work unit.
8. Integrates strategies and plans with other areas.

9. Promotes and supports the use of corporate and cross-functional teams.
10. Ensures customer and employee confidentiality through monitoring access to information to individuals who have need, reason, and permission for such access.

Systems Improvement

1. Demonstrates understanding of the "big picture"—interrelationships of divisions, departments, and work units.
2. Incorporates a broad range of internal and external factors in problem solving and decision making.
3. Solicits and incorporates customer and stakeholder needs and expectations into work unit planning.
4. Applies and encourages the use of process improvement methods and tools.
5. Encourages and supports innovative and creative problem solving by others.
6. Integrates process thinking into management of daily operations to enhance quality, efficiency, and ethical standards.
7. Utilizes data in decision making and managing work units.

Communication

1. Communicates the mission, values, structure, and systems to individuals, groups, and larger audiences.
2. Provides leadership in communicating "up," "down," and "across" the organization.
3. Reinforces organization's key messages.
4. Creates a work environment for and models open expression of ideas and diverse opinions.
5. Routinely includes a communications plan in work and project planning.
6. Applies, communicates, and educates others about organizational policies and procedures.
7. Keeps employees informed of industry trends and implications.
8. Understands, communicates, and administers compensation and benefits to employees.

Employee and Team Direction

1. Anticipates and assesses staffing needs.
2. Maintains and updates staff job descriptions, linking employee job descriptions and projects to unit, division, and corporate strategies.
3. Recruits, selects, and retains high-performing individuals.
4. Provides information, resources, and coaching to support individual/team professional and career development.

5. Applies knowledge of team dynamics to enhance group communication, synergy, creativity, conflict resolution, and decision making.
6. Assures staff has training to fully utilize technological tools necessary for job performance.
7. Delegates responsibilities to coaches, and mentors employees to develop their capabilities.
8. Involves staff in planning and reporting to ensure integration with operational activities and priorities.
9. Coaches employees by providing both positive and constructive feedback and an overall realistic picture of their performance.
10. Ensures that core functions in areas of responsibility can be continued in the absence of staff members—either short term or long term.
11. Recognizes and acknowledges successes and achievements of others.

Financial Literacy

1. Partners with financial specialists in planning and problem solving.
2. Develops and meets financial goals using standard budgeting and reporting processes.
3. Continually finds ways to improve revenue, reduce costs, and leverage assets in keeping with the organization's strategic direction and objectives.
4. Uses financial and quantitative information in work unit management.
5. Communicates unit budget expectations and status to employees.
6. Coaches employees on financial implications of work processes.

Professional Development

1. Keeps up-to-date with external environment through professional associations, conferences, journals, etc.
2. Nurtures and maintains working relationships with colleagues across the organization.
3. Demonstrates commitment to professional development, aligning that development with current and future needs of the organization whenever possible.
4. Models self-development and healthy work/life balance for employees.

Appendix F—Balanced Scorecard Metrics

All metrics are accompanied by targets. For the most part, these are percentages that will be ascertained via a calculation based on data entry of raw data. Some targets have the word "Baseline" encoded. Baseline indicates that the metric is informational—for example, only the raw value will be displayed (i.e., aggregated by the specified period—weekly, monthly, etc.). The targets should be set to default (or 0 in the case of baselined targets). The entirety of metrics provided is greater than the "norm" for a typical Balanced Scorecard, which usually has just a few key metrics per perspective. It should be noted that many of these metrics can be modified to measure systems developed using social software engineering methods. In particular, note the social software engineering metrics listed at the end of the learning and growth perspective.

Financial Objectives	Measures	Targets	KPI
Optimize cost efficiency of purchasing	Cost to spend ratio [1]	<1%	F1
	Negotiated cost savings [2]	≥20%	F2
	Costs avoided/total costs [3]	≥10%	F3
	Percentage of goods and services obtained through competitive procurement practices [4]	≥19%	F4
Control costs	Dollar amount under budget	Baseline	F5
	Dollar amount over budget	Baseline	F6
	Budget as a percentage of revenue	≤30%	F7
	Expenses per employee	≤35,000	F8

Financial Objectives	Measures	Targets	KPI
Control costs	Cost of acquired technology/ technology developed in house	≤50%	F9
	% new products/services where breakeven point is within 1 year	80%	F10
	Total cost of ownership [5]	≤$6,000 per device per year	F11
	Overtime ratio [6]	≤25%	F12
	Cost performance index [7]	≥	F13
	Average breakeven point [8]	≤1.5 years	F14
	Schedule performance index [9]	≥1	F15
	Total cost reductions due to use of technology	≥33%	F16
	Workforce reduction due to use of new products	≥10%	F17
	Contractor utilization [10]	≤35%	F18
Increase business value	Revenue from new products or services [11]	Baseline	F19
	Average ROI [12]	≥1	F20
	% resources devoted to strategic projects	≥55%	F21
	% favorable rating of project management by top management	≥93%	F22
	Average cost/benefit ratio	≥22%	F23
	Net present value [13]	≥1	F24
	Assets per employee	Baseline	F25
	Revenues per employee	Baseline	F26
	Profits per employee	Baseline	F27
Improve technology acquisition process	Total expenditures	Baseline	F28
	Total expenditures/industry average expenditures	≥1	F29
	Amount of new technology acquired through M&A	Baseline	F30

[1] Operational costs/purchasing obligations (goods and services purchased).

[2] Cost savings compared to total costs.

[3] Costs avoided compared to total costs. You can avoid costs by reusing hardware/software, utilizing a partner, etc.

[4] Difference between average qualified bid and the cost of the successful bid. The sum of each calculation is aggregated into a new savings ratio for all transactions.

[5] Additional capital costs—software, IT support software, and network infrastructure.

Technical support costs—hardware and software deployment, help desk staffing, and system maintenance.

Administration costs—financing, procurement, vendor management, user training, and asset management.

End user operations costs—the costs incurred from downtime and, in some cases, end users supporting other end users as opposed to help desk technicians supporting them

[6] Overtime hours/regular hours worked

[7] Ratio of earned value to actual cost. EV, often called the *budgeted cost of work performed*, is an estimate of the value of work actually completed. It is based on the original planned costs of a project.

[8] Breakeven analysis. All projects have associated costs. All projects will also have associated benefits. At the outset of a project, costs will far exceed benefits. However, at some point, the benefits will start outweighing the costs. This is called the *breakeven point*. The analysis that is done to figure out when this breakeven point will occur is called *breakeven analysis*.

[9] SPI is the ratio of earned value to planned value and is used to determine whether or not the project is on target. (See Cost performance Index for a definition of earned value—EV).

[10] Cost of external contractors/cost of internal resources.

[11] Use real dollars if systems are external customer facing. Use internal budget dollars if these are internal customer facing systems.

[12] Return on investment. Most organizations select projects that have a positive return on investment. The return on investment, or ROI as it is most commonly known, is the additional amount earned after costs are earned back.

The formula for ROI is

$$ROI = \frac{Benefit - Cost}{Cost}$$

Organizations want ROI to be positive.

[13] NPV is a method of calculating the expected monetary gain or loss by discounting all expected future cash inflows and outflows to the present point in time. If financial value is a key criterion, organizations should only consider projects with a positive NPV. This is because the positive NPV means the return from the project exceeds the cost of capital—the return available by investing elsewhere. Higher NPVs are more desirable than lower NPVs.

Formula for NPV

$$\text{NPV} = -II + \left(\text{sum of}\right)\left[OCF/\left(1 + R(r)\right)t\right] + \left[TCF/\left(1 + R(r)\right)n\right]$$

where:

II = initial investment
OFC = operating cash flows in year t
t = year
n = life span (in years) of the project
R(r) = project required rate of return

(from http://www.mtholyoke.edu/~aahirsch/howvalueproject.html)

[14] Use research from a company such as http://www.infotech.com/.

Customer Objectives	Measures	Targets	KPI
Increase customer satisfaction	% of customers satisfied with system timeliness (speed)	≥92%	C1
	% of customers satisfied with responsiveness to questions	≥92%	C2
	% of customers satisfied with quality	≥92%	C3
	% of customers satisfied with sales/customer service representatives	≥92%	C4
	Length of time to resolve disputes	≤4 h	C5
Conformance with customer requests	% of baselined projects with a plan	≥90%	C6
	% customer requests satisfied	≥90%	C7

Customer Objectives	Measures	Targets	KPI
Increase customer base	Customer lifetime value ($)	Baseline	C8
	Share of wallet (%) [1]	≥25%	C9
	Retention %	≥80%	C10
	Win-back percent	≥85%	C11
	New acquisitions/current number of customers	≥10%	C12
	Rate of defection	≤3%	C13
Enhance customer-facing systems	Average number of searches per order/query	Baseline	C14
	Average number of support calls per order/query	Baseline	C15
	Average elapsed time to select product and select an order	Baseline	C16
	Average elapsed time to search website	Baseline	C17
	Number of steps required to select and purchase	Baseline	C18
	Average time to answer incoming phone call	Baseline	C19
	% availability of customer facing applications	≥98%	C20
	Average cost to service each customer's transaction	Baseline	C21
Support internal customers	% better decisions	≥90%	C22
	% time reduction in making decisions	≥90%	C23
	Average time to answer a support phone call	Baseline	C24

[1] Compare to competition using service such as http://www.lexisnexis.com/marketintelligence.

Internal Business Processes Objectives	Measures	Targets	KPI
Improve data quality	Forms inputted	Baseline	I1
	Data entry error rate	≤3%	I2
	Age of current data	Baseline	I3
	% of employees who have up-to-date data	≥98%	I4
Improve balance between technical and strategic activities	% of time devoted to maintenance	≤20	I5
	Strategic project counts	Baseline	I6
	% of time devoted to ad hoc activities	≤15%	I7
Increase product quality and reliability	% reduction in demand for customer support	≥25%	I8
	Number of end user queries handled	Baseline	I9
	Average time to address an end user problem	≤4 h	I10
	Equipment downtime	≤1%	I11
	Mean time to failure	≤1000 h	I12
	% remaining known product faults	≤5%	I13
	% of projects with lessons learned in database	≥95%	I14
	Fault density [1]	≤3%	I15
	Defect density[2]	≤3%	I16
	Cumulative failure [3]	Baseline	I17
	Fault days number [4]	≤1	I18
	Functional test coverage [5]	≥95%	I19
	Requirements traceability [6]	≥98%	I20
	Maturity index [7]	≥1	I21
	% of conflicting requirements	≤5%	I22
	Test coverage [8]	≥92%	I23
	Cyclomatic complexity [9]	≤20	I24
	% of project time allocated to quality testing	≥15%	I25

Internal Business Processes Objectives	Measures	Targets	KPI
Reduce risk	% definitional uncertainty risk [10]	≤10%	I26
	% technological risk [11]	≤45%	I27
	% developmental risk [12]	<10%	I28
	% nonalignment risk [13]	≤4%	I29
	% service delivery risk [14]	≤5%	I30
	Number of fraudulent transactions	≤1%	I31
	% of systems that have risk contingency plans	≥95%	I32
	% of systems that have been assessed for security breaches	≥95%	I33
Improve processes	% resources devoted to planning and review of product development activities	≥25%	I34
	% resources devoted to R&D	Baseline	I35
	Average time required to develop a new product/service	Baseline	I36
	Person-months of effort/project	Baseline	I37
	% requirements fulfilled	≥90%	I38
	Pages of documentation	Baseline	I39
	% of on-time implementations	≥97%	I40
	% expected features delivered	>98%	I41
	Average time to provide feedback to the project team	≤1 day	I42
	Project development time	≥50%	I43
	% project backlog	≤10%	I44
	% project cancellation rate	≤20%	I45
	Support personnel to development personnel ratio	≥35%	I56

Internal Business Processes Objectives	Measures	Targets	KPI
Enhance resource planning	Number of supplier relationships	Baseline	I47
	Decision speed	<5 days	I48
	Paperwork reduction	≥10%	I49
Monitor change management	Number of change requests per month	Baseline	I50
	% change to customer environment	Baseline	I51
	Changes released per month	Baseline	I52
Enhance applications portfolio	Age distribution of projects	Baseline	I53
	Technical performance of project portfolio [15]	Baseline	I54
	Rate of product acceptance	≥95%	I55

[1] Faults of a specific severity/thousand.

[2] Total number of unique defects detected.

[3] Failures per period.

[4] Number of days that faults spend in the system from their creation to their removal.

[5] Number of requirements for which test cases have been completed/total number of functional requirements.

[6] Number of requirements met /number of original requirements.

[7] Number of functions in current delivery—(adds + changes + deletes)/number of functions in current delivery.

[8] (implemented capabilities/required capabilities)*(capabilities tested)/total capabilities)*100%

[9] Cyclomatic complexity equals the number of decisions plus one. Cyclomatic complexity, also known as V(G) or the graph theoretic number, is calculated by simply counting the number of decision statements. A high cyclomatic complexity denotes a complex procedure that is hard to understand, test, and maintain. There is a relationship between cyclomatic complexity and the "risk" in a procedure.

[10] Low degree of project specification. Rate risk probability from 0% to 100%.

[11] Use of bleeding edge technology. Rate risk probability from 0% to 100%.

[12] Lack of development skillsets.

[13] Resistance of employees or end users to change. Rate probability of risk from 0% to 100%.

[14] Problems with delivering system—for example, interface difficulties. Rate risk probability from 0% to 100%.

[15] Rate on a scale of 1 to 2 with 1 being unsatisfactory and 2 being satisfactory.

Learning and Growth Objectives	Measures	Targets	KPI
Create a quality workforce	% of employees meeting mandatory qualification standards	≥95%	L1
	% of voluntary separations	≥98%	L2
	% of leaders' time devoted to mentoring	≥45%	L3
	% of employees with certifications	≥54%	L4
	% of employees with degrees	≥75%	L5
	% of employees with three or more years of experience	≥75%	L6
	Average appraisal rating	Baseline	L7
	Number of employee suggestions	Baseline	L8
	% expert in currently used technologies	≥95%	L9
	Rookie ratio [1]	≤10%	L10
	% expert in emerging technologies	≥75%	L11
	Proportion of support staff	≥35%	L12
	Availability of strategic information	≥100%	L13
	Intranet searches	Baseline	L14
	Average years of experience with team	Baseline	L15
	Average years of experience with language	Baseline	L16
	Average years of experience with software	Baseline	L17
	% of employees whose performance evaluation plans are aligned with organizational goals and objectives	≥98%	L18

Create a quality workforce	% conformity with HR road map as a basis for resource allocation	≥95%	L19
	% of critical positions with current competency profiles and succession plans in place	≥98%	L20
	% number of Net meetings	≥20%	L21
	Number of new templates, procedures, tools to increase productivity	Baseline	L22
Increase employee satisfaction	% of employees satisfied with the work environment	≥98%	L23
	% of employees satisfied with the professionalism, culture, values, and empowerment	≥98%	L24
	Employee overtime	Baseline	L25
	Employee absenteeism	Baseline	L26
	Discrimination charges	Baseline	L27
	Employee grievances	Baseline	L28
	Tardiness	Baseline	L29
	Number of employee suggestions implemented	Baseline	L30
	% in-house promotions	≥90%	L31
Enhance employee training	% of technical training goals met	≥90%	L32
	Number of training sessions attended per employee	Baseline	L33
	Training budget as a percentage of overall budget	≥20%	L34
	Frequency of use of new skills	≥85%	L35
Enhance R&D	Research budget as a percentage of budget	≥35%	L36
	Number of quality improvements	Baseline	L37
	Number of innovative processes deployed	Baseline	L38
	% of R&D directly in line with business strategy	≥98%	L39

Enhance R&D	Number of technologies owned or possessed by company	Baseline	L40
	Number of new patents generated by R&D	Baseline	L41
	Number of patentable innovations not yet patented	Baseline	L42
	Number of patents protecting the core of a specific technology or business area	Baseline	L43
	Number of entrepreneurs in company [2]	Baseline	L44
	% of workforce that is currently dedicated to innovation projects	≥5%	L45
	Number of new products, services, and businesses launched	Baseline	L46
	% of employees who have received training in innovation	≥5%	L47
Social software engineering	Number of wikis	Baseline	L48
	Number of blogs	Baseline	L49
	Number of group workspaces	Baseline	L50
	Number of collaborative project plans	Baseline	L51
	Number of collaborative spreadsheets	Baseline	L52
	Number of teams using social software engineering	Baseline	L53
	Number of team members using social software engineering	Baseline	L54
	Maturity of collaboration	Baseline	L55
	Degree of communication efficiency	Baseline	L56
	Collaborative lessons learned	Baseline	L57

[1] Rookie means new, inexperienced, or untrained personnel.

[2] Number of individuals who previously started a business.

Appendix G—Glossary

Advocacy: Creating a movement of "net-fluencers" to influence conversation, actions, or motives in support of one's objective.

Aggregation: Gathering and remixing content from blogs and other websites that provide RSS feeds; typically displayed in an aggregator such as Bloglines or Google Reader, or directly on your desktop using software (often also called a *newsreader*). Beneficial for breaking news, CNN has effective tools such as these. Digg and Reddit are examples of aggregator sites.

Ajax (asynchronous JavaScript and XML): A development technique for creating interactive web applications.

Alerts: Search engines, such as Google, allow you to specify words, phrases, or tags that you want checked periodically, with results of those searches returned to you by e-mail.

API (application programming interface): A source code interface (a set of routines, protocols, and tools for building software applications) that a computer system or program library provides to support requests for services from a computer program.

Archive: Collections of earlier items usually organized by week or month. You may still be able to comment on archived items.

Audio Video Interleaved (AVI): A Microsoft Corporation multimedia video format. It uses waveform audio and digital video frames (bitmaps) to compress animation.

Authenticity: The sense that something or someone is "real." Blogs enable people to publish content, and engage in conversations, that show their interests and values, and so help them develop an authentic voice online. Agencies should always be transparent and authentic while online.

Avatar: A graphical image that represents a person within the new media arena. You can build a visual character with the body, clothes, behaviors, gender, and name of your choice. This may or may not be an authentic representation.

Back channel communications: Private e-mails or other messages sent by the facilitator or between individuals during public conferencing. They have a significant effect on the way that public conversations go.

Badges and buttons: Graphics embedded into a web page (similar to a widget, and sometimes called one); they link to online content elsewhere, and typically serve as content syndication tools, to lead someone to content on another site.

Bandwidth: The capacity of an electronic line, such as a communications network or computer channel, to transmit bits per second (bps).

Blog: Websites with dated items of content in reverse chronological order, self-published by bloggers. Items (posts) may have keyword tags associated with them; they are usually available as feeds and often allow commenting. Blogs may be moderated by the host or may allow any material to be posted.

Blogosphere: The totality of blogs on the Internet, and the conversations taking place within that sphere.

Blogroll: A list of sites displayed in the sidebar of a blog, showing what the blogger reads regularly.

Bookmarking: A web-based service that lets users create and store links; saving the address of a website or item of content, either in your browser, or on a social bookmarking site like Delicious. If you add tags, others can easily find your research, too, and the social bookmarking site becomes an enormous public library.

Bulletin boards: The early vehicles for online collaboration, where users connected with a central computer can post and read e-mail-like messages.

Categories: Prespecified ways to organize content. Example: a set of keywords that you can use but not add to when posting on a site.

Champion: An enthusiast or group of enthusiasts who can get conversations started by posting messages, responding to others, or helping them.

Chat: A website interaction among a number of people who add text items one after the other into the same space at (almost) the same time. A place for chat, a chatroom, differs from a forum because conversations happen in "real time," similar to face-to-face.

Cloud computing: The use of applications hosted across the Internet by an independent service provider. An example of cloud computing is Google Docs, in which the word processing program is accessible through a web browser, and the content in the document resides in Google's servers.

Community, online: A group of people who communicate mainly through the Internet.

Community building: The process of recruiting potential community or network participants to help them find shared interests and goals, use the technology, and develop useful conversations.

Computing performed over the Internet: Cloud computing is the use of Internet-based services to support a business process. Cloud services typically have the following characteristics:

In the future, we will not have or need our data or software programs on our own personal computers: they will be floating around on a server somewhere, accessible via the Internet. The term *cloud* is used as a metaphor for the Internet, based on how the Internet is depicted sometimes in computer network diagrams. In cloud computing, resources are provided as a service over the Internet. Cloud computing services usually provide common business applications online that are accessed from a web browser, while the software and data are stored on the servers. Cloud computing encompasses any free or subscription-based or pay-per-use service that works over the Internet. You use what you need. Examples of cloud computing include

Google Docs—A free, web-based word processor, spreadsheet, presentation, and form application offered by Google. Documents, spreadsheets, forms, and presentations can be created within the application itself, imported through the web interface, or sent via e-mail. They can also be saved to the user's computer in a variety of formats or saved to the Google servers. Collaboration between users is also a feature of Google Docs. Documents can be shared, opened, and edited by multiple users at the same time. In the case of spreadsheets, users can be notified of changes to any specified regions via e-mail.

Zoho—A competitor of Google Docs. Web Office programs for personal use for free, some costs for "Professional Versions."

Conference, online: The conversations of people involved in a web forum, often organized around topics, threads, and themes.

Constructives: The science of applying new media viral mapping to a specific public affairs issue to determine a projected outcome; educating readers on projected paths.

Content management systems: Software suites that offer the ability to create static web pages, document stores, blogs, wikis, and other tools.

Conversation: The currency of social networking; an exchange of information through blogging, commenting, or contributing to forums.

Cookie: Information (in this case, URLs, web addresses) created by a web server and stored on a user's computer. This information lets websites keep a history of a user's browsing patterns and preferences. People can set up their browsers to accept or not accept cookies.

Copyright: A form of intellectual property that gives the author of an original work exclusive rights for a certain time period in relation to that work, including its publication, distribution, and adaptation.

Crowdsourcing: The collective skills and enthusiasm of those outside an organization who can volunteer their time to contribute content and solve problems.

Creative Commons: A not-for-profit organization and licensing system that offers creators the ability to fine-tune their copyright, spelling out the ways in which others may use their works.

Cyberculture: A collection of cultures and cultural products that exist on and made possible by the Internet, along with the stories told about these cultures and cultural products.

Digital story: A short personal nonfiction narrative composed on a computer, often for publishing online or publishing to a DVD, told from the narrator's point of view.

Domain name: A method of identifying computer addresses. Your e-mail address has a domain address. If there is a ".edu" at the end of your e-mail address, that means your account is affiliated with an educational institution. A ".com" extension means the account is business related, and a government account has a ".gov" suffix.

E-mail lists: Important networking tools offering the ability to "starburst" a message from a central postbox to any number of subscribers, and for them to respond.

Embedding: The act of inserting video or photos to a website or e-mail.

Enterprise 2.0: An entire new suite of emergent technologies—wikis, blogs, tagging, etc.—within the business environment.

Facilitator: Someone who helps people in an online group or forum manage their conversations.

Feed: The means by which you can read, view, or listen to items from blogs and other RSS-enabled sites without visiting the site, by subscribing and using an aggregator or newsreader.

Flash: Animation software used to develop interactive graphics for websites as well as desktop presentations and games.

Folksonomy: A folksonomy is a system of classification derived from the practice and method of collaboratively creating and managing tags to annotate and categorize content; this practice is also known as collaborative tagging, social classification, social indexing, and social tagging. See tag.

Forum: A discussion area on websites where people can post messages or comment on existing messages asynchronously (that is, independently of time or place).

Friends: Contacts whose profile you link to in your profile, thereby creating your network. On some sites, people have to accept the link; in others, they do not.

FOAF: FOAF is an acronym of "friend of a friend." It is a machine-readable ontology describing persons, their activities, and their relations to other people and objects. Anyone can use FOAF to describe him or herself. FOAF allows groups of people to describe social networks without the need for a centralized database.

Groups: Collections of individuals with some sense of unity through their activities, interests, or values. They are bounded: you are in a group, or you are not. They differ from networks, which are dispersed, and defined by nodes and connections.

Hyperlink: Text, images, or graphics that, when clicked with a mouse (or activated by keystrokes), will connect the user to a new website. The link is usually obvious, such as underlined text or a "button" of some type, but not always.

Instant messaging (IM): Chatting with one other person using an IM tool such as AOL Instant Messenger, Microsoft Live Messenger, or Yahoo! Messenger. The tools let a user show availability for a chat. Instant messaging can be a good alternative to e-mails for a rapid exchange. Problems arise when people in a group are using different IM tools that do not connect.

iPod: Apple's portable media player (music, books, pictures, video).

iPod Touch: It is a portable media player, personal digital assistant, and Wi-Fi mobile platform designed and marketed by Apple Inc.

Kindle: Amazon's Kindle is a software and hardware platform for reading electronic books (e-books), developed by Amazon.com. Three hardware devices, known as "Kindle," "Kindle 2," and "Kindle DX" support this platform, as does an iPhone application called "Kindle for iPhone."

Listening: Setting up searches that monitor blogs to determine when an organization receives a mention or reference; also, the art of skimming feeds to the blogosphere to find out what topics bubble up.

Listserv: A list of e-mail addresses of people with common interests. Software enables people who belong to a list to send messages to the group without typing a series of addresses into the message header.

Lurker: A person who reads but does not contribute or add comments to forums. The "one-percent rule-of-thumb" says that one percent of people contribute new content to an online community, another nine percent comment, and the rest lurk.

Malware: Malicious software designed to infiltrate a computer without the owner's informed consent. The expression covers a variety of forms of hostile, intrusive, or annoying software or program code. The term "computer virus" is sometimes used as a catchall phrase to include all types of malware, including true viruses.

Mashups: Mixes of technology, audio, video, and maps that combine several tools to create a new web service. For example, a mashup would be a Google map showing average housing prices drawn from a city assessor's online database.

Micro-blog: Extremely short blog posts in the vein of text-messaging. The messages are available to anyone or to a restricted group that the user chooses. Twitter, a popular micro-blog client, allows for posts of up to 140 characters, uploaded and read online or through instant messaging or mobile devices via text-messaging.

MP3 players: A digital audio player (DAP), more commonly referred to as an MP3 player, is a consumer electronics device that has the primary function of storing, organizing, and playing audio files (music, audio books, etc.). Some DAPs are also referred to as *portable media players* as they have image-viewing and/or video-playing support. MP3 refers to a patented digital audio encoding format and is the most common audio format for consumer audio storage, as well as the standard of digital audio compression for the transfer and playback of music on digital audio players.

Networks: Structures defined by nodes and the connections between them. In social networks, the nodes are people, and the connections are the relationships that they have. Networking is the process by which you develop and strengthen those relationships.

Newsgroup: An Internet "site" centered on a specific topic or course. Some newsreader software can "thread" discussion, so there can be various topics centered on a central theme.

Newsreader: Website or desktop tool that acts as an aggregator, gathering content from blogs and similar sites using RSS feeds so you can read the content in one place, instead of having to visit different sites.

Ontology: An ontology is a formal representation of knowledge as a set of concepts within a domain, and the relationships between those concepts. It is used to reason about the entities within that domain, and may be used to describe the domain.

Open-source software: Software available under a license that permits users to study, change, and improve the software, and to redistribute it in modified or unmodified form. Open source describes a broad general type of software license that makes source code available to the general public with relaxed or nonexistent copyright restrictions. It is an explicit "feature" of open source that it may put no restrictions on the use or distribution by any organization or user. Open source software (OSS) projects are built and maintained by a network of volunteer programmers.
Examples of Open Source Software
Productivity: Open Office, Neo Office
ILS: Evergreen. Koha, OPALS, Open Biblio
OS: Linux
Browser: Firefox

Peer-to-peer: Direct interaction between two people in a network. In that network, each peer connects to other peers, opening the opportunity for further sharing and learning.

Permalink: The address (URL) of an item of content. Example: a blog post, rather than the address of a web page with lots of different items. You will often find it at the end of a blog post.

Phishing: The criminally fraudulent process of attempting to acquire sensitive information such as usernames, passwords, and credit card details by masquerading as a trustworthy entity in an electronic communication. Communications purporting to be from popular social websites commonly try to lure the unsuspecting public. Phishing typically occurs by e-mail or instant messaging. It often directs users to enter details at a fake website whose look and feel are almost identical to the legitimate one. Even when using server authentication, it may require tremendous skill to detect that the website is fake.

Photo-sharing: Uploading images to a website such as Flickr, Picasa, SmugMug, BubbleShare, and Photobucket, adding tags, and offering people the opportunity to comment or even re-use your photos if you add an appropriate copyright license.

Podcast: A series of digital media files (either audio or video) that are released episodically and downloaded through web syndication. The mode of delivery differentiates podcasts from other ways of accessing media files over the Internet, such as simple download or streamed webcasts. Special client software applications known as *podcatchers* (e.g., iTunes, Zune, Juice, and Winamp) are used to automatically identify and download new files in a series when they are released, by accessing a centrally maintained web feed that lists all files associated with the series. New files are thus downloaded automatically and stored locally on the user's computer or other device for offline use, giving simpler access to episodic content.

Post: Item on a blog or forum.

Presence online: Availability for contact by instant messaging, Voice-Over IP, or other synchronous methods of communication; also, the degree to which an individual's name shows up in an online search.

Profiles: Information that users provide about themselves when signing up for a social networking site. As well as a picture and basic information, such information may include personal and business interests, a "blurb" and tags to help people search for like-minded people.

Remixing: The process of taking separate items of content, identified by tags and published through feeds, and combining them in different ways.

RSS: "Really Simple Syndication," which allows subscribers to receive content from blogs and other social media sites, delivered through a feed.

Shockwave: A three-dimensional (3D) animation technology format.

Sharing: The process of offering other people the use of text, images, video, bookmarks, or other content by adding tags, and applying copyright licenses that encourage use of content.

Smartmob: A gathering of users for an activity or event as a result of an online connection or network.

Smartphones: A smartphone is a mobile phone offering advanced capabilities, often with PC-like functionality. There is no industry standard definition of a smartphone. Many smartphones are phones with advanced features such as e-mail, Internet, and e-book reader capabilities. Some are miniature computers that have phone capability. Examples are the iPhone, Blackberry, and Google Android.

Social network analysis: SNA views social relationships in terms of network theory consisting of *nodes* and *ties* (also called *edges*, *links*, or *connections*). Nodes are the individual actors within the networks, and ties are the relationships between the actors. The resulting graph-based structures are often very complex. There can be many kinds of ties between the nodes. Research in a number of academic fields has shown that social networks operate on many levels, from families up to the level of nations, and play a critical role in determining the way problems are solved, organizations are run, and the degree to which individuals succeed in achieving their goals.

Social networking sites (SNS): Online communities where users can create profiles and socialize with others, using a range of social media tools including blogs, video, images, tags, lists of friends, forums, and messages. A social network service focuses on building online communities of people who share interests and/or activities, or who are interested in exploring the interests and activities of others. Most social network services are web based and provide a variety of ways for users to interact, such as e-mail and instant messaging services.

Facebook—http://www.facebook.com. Facebook users can join networks organized by city, workplace, school, and region. People can also add friends and send them messages, and update their personal profiles to notify friends about themselves. The website's name refers to the paper facebooks depicting members of a campus community that some US colleges and preparatory schools give to incoming students, faculty, and staff as a way to get to know other people on campus. Facebook is targeted to the college-age levels and was started at Harvard University. The website is free to users and generates revenue from advertising, including banner ads.

MySpace—http://www.myspace.com. MySpace is an interactive, user-submitted network of friends, personal profiles, blogs, groups, photos, music, and videos for teenagers and adults internationally. MySpace was overtaken internationally by its main competitor Facebook in April 2008, based on monthly unique visitors. MySpace operates solely on revenues generated by advertising as its user model and possesses no paid-for features for the end user.

Twitter—http://www.twitter.com. Twitter is a free social networking and micro-blogging service that enables its users to send and read other users' updates known as *tweets*. Tweets are text-based posts of up to 140 characters in length that are displayed on the user's profile page and delivered to other users who have subscribed to them (known as *followers*). Users can send and receive tweets via the Twitter website, Short Message Service (SMS), or external applications. The service is free to use over the Internet, but using SMS may incur phone service provider fees.

LinkedIn—http://www.linkedin.com. LinkedIn is an interconnected network of experienced professionals from around the world, representing 170 industries and 200 countries. It is a business-oriented social networking site. The purpose of the site is to allow registered users to maintain a list of contact details of people they know and trust in business.

Second Life—http://secondlife.com. Second Life (SL) is a 3D virtual world accessible via the Internet. A free client program called the Second Life Viewer enables its users, called *Residents*, to interact with each other through avatars. Residents can explore, meet other residents, socialize, participate in individual and group activities, and create and trade virtual property and services with one another, or travel throughout the world, which residents refer to as the grid.

Streaming media: Video or audio intended to be listened to online but not stored permanently.

Tag: A keyword added to a blog post, photo, or video to help users find related topics or media. The activity of labeling resources of interest is known as *tagging*. See folksonomy.

Threads: Strands of conversation.

Tiny URL: A web service that provides short aliases for redirection of long URLs.

Trackback: A facility for other bloggers to leave a calling card automatically, instead of commenting. "Blogger A" may write on "Blog A" about an item on "Blogger B's" site, and through the trackback facility leave a link on B's site back to A. The collection of comments and trackbacks on a site facilitates conversations.

Transparency: The ability to enhance searching, sharing, self-publishing, and commenting across networks to find out what is going on in any situation where online activity occurs.

Troll: A hurtful, but possibly valuable person who, for whatever reason, is both obsessed by and offended by everything you write on a blog.

URL: Unique Resource Locator is the technical term for a web address like

Video sharing: The process of sharing videos and making them available for others to view and comment on. Video sharing sites let viewers "embed," or display others' video on their own sites. Examples include YouTube, Blip. tv, and Vimeo.

Virtual worlds: Online places such as Second Life, where you can create a representation of yourself (an avatar) and socialize with other residents. Basic activity is free, but you can buy currency (using real money) in order to purchase "land" and trade with other residents. Some organizations use Second Life to run discussions, virtual events, and fundraising.

Web 2.0: A term coined by O'Reilly Media in 2004 to describe blogs, wikis, social networking sites, and other Internet-based services that emphasize collaboration and sharing, rather than less interactive publishing (Web 1.0). It is associated with the idea of the Internet as a platform.

Widget: "Window gadget," a stand-alone application that can be embedded in other applications, such as a website or a desktop, or viewed on a PDA. A widget may help accomplish missions such as subscribing to a feed, doing a specialist search, or even making a donation. For example, a widget might link to a display of the latest news and weather, a map program, or photos.

Whiteboard: The online equivalent of a write-on/wipe-off glossy surface; a tool that lets one write or sketch on a web page.

Wiki: A web page with an editing capability that lets users contribute to a body of information. The best-known example is Wikipedia, an encyclopedia created by thousands of contributors across the world. Once people have appropriate permissions (set by the owner), they can create pages and add to and alter existing pages.

WMA: Windows Media Audio (WMA) is an audio data compression technology developed by Microsoft. It is a proprietary technology that forms part of the Windows Media framework. It was conceived as a competitor to the popular MP3 and RealAudio codecs.

Worm: A self-replicating computer program that uses a network to send copies of itself to other nodes (computers on the network) without any intervention by the user. Unlike a virus, it does not need to attach itself to an existing program. Worms nearly always harm the network, if only by consuming bandwidth, whereas viruses corrupt or devour files on a targeted computer.

XML: "Extensible Markup Language," which is a system for organizing and tagging elements of a document so that the document can be transmitted and interpreted between applications and organizations. Human readable XML tags define "what it is," and HTML defines "how it looks." XML allows designers to create their own tags.

Zune: (Microsoft) and SanDisk's *Sansa View, Clip,* and *Fuze* are other popular MP3 players.

Appendix H—Worker Study Results

Question 1: What are the cultural reasons that employees resist the sharing of knowledge?

Age, education, ethnicity, gender, and tenure within the company and industry were examined to determine if these factors affected the sharing of knowledge.

Table H.1 summarizes the cultural reasons the participants suggested for knowledge-sharing problems in their respective companies. None of the study participants felt that tenure, either organizational or within the industry, impacted knowledge sharing. Of the remaining cultural factors, education had a moderate impact, while ethnicity and age had the most pronounced effect on knowledge sharing.

While most study participants indicated that there were no significant knowledge-sharing problems related to age, some interesting perspectives were uncovered. Mature, less educated participants felt that younger colleagues did not adequately share knowledge. Participant seven, who was over 50 and did not complete college, clearly articulated this: "Some younger people are not personable. There is no respect. They don't even say 'hello' to me in the hall."

Two out of the 21 participants emphasized the concept of respect. While this was only casually mentioned by 19% of the other participants, respect—or lack thereof—has the potential of being an important factor in knowledge sharing.

Participant 14, also a senior manager with an advanced degree in computer science, confirmed the fact that age might be a variable to be considered in knowledge sharing. The participant noted, "Age-wise we're fairly homogeneous so we really don't have knowledge-sharing problems." Nineteen percent of the participants observed that older employees had more problems in sharing and obtaining knowledge for their own use. Participant 19, a computer engineer, shared this insight, "Knowledge is power and people are trying to hold onto some of their advantage over other employees. I think older people have this problem more."

Table H.1 Cultural Factor Summary

Cultural factor	Number of sources: (%)	Number of references: (%)
Ethnicity	8 (38%)	13 (29%)
Education	3 (14%)	4 (8%)
Age	7 (33%)	8 (18%)
Gender	2 (10%)	3 (7%)
Tenure, organization	0	0
Tenure, industry	0	0

Participant 5, a senior manager in his fifties, noted that some older employees might not be familiar with modern technologies and, thus ran the risk of being kept out of the knowledge-sharing loop. "I have my phone. I use it as a phone. I don't text. People in their 20s and 30s are texting like crazy. The younger crowd is more technically involved. There is definitely a risk for people over 50 for being kept out of the loop. I see them struggling."

Advanced degrees were held by 57% of the participants in the study. The majority of participants, some 86%, indicated that education had little to do with knowledge sharing. Participant 8, the CEO of the case study firm, said, "I had several people working for me with advanced degrees. There were no problems with knowledge sharing. What's important is you're only as good as your last project. When the guy stops hitting home runs, he's fired. What matters here is how good you are—not the degrees you have."

There were dissenters, however. Participant 19 noted that those with higher educations shared more. "If you work with someone who has less than a bachelor's degree, they might want to share less because that's just their upbringing, and they might feel more threatened."

Ethnicity was a difficult subject for many of the participants. Some feared being labeled as a racist if they articulated their true feelings. Many of the participants were located in culturally diverse metropolitan areas and felt that there were few real knowledge-sharing problems related to this level of diversity, aside from the language barriers. However, 24% of the participants did note problems in this area.

Participant 7, who worked in a company located in the part of New York labeled by the press as the most diverse in the United States, said, "We have a diverse workforce. However, knowledge sharing is impeded by inability to speak proper English. It's just hard to understand them. You can't get a point across." The same participant added, "With different ethnicities, there is no common ground, so it is hard to share information with them."

Common ground was a recurring theme in the discussion. Participant 9, a nonmanagerial employee who did not complete college, had this to say about her diverse workplace: "In terms of the comfort factor, if you have different cultures trying to get along it could put up a barrier because you don't feel comfortable relating. In terms of knowledge sharing, there has to be some sort of comfort factor that you will be understood when you are trying to share."

Some of the participants pointed to the reticence to communicate in some cultural groups. Asians were singled out on two occasions. Participant 10, a senior project manager who is pursuing a doctorate, said, "Some cultures may be more reticent to communicate. Just a natural quietness. Sometimes I run into some folks of Asian background that tend to be less communicative. But that's just my experience."

The cultural factors studied included (a) ethnicity, (b) education, (c) age, (d) gender, and (e) tenure. Tenure within the organization or industry had no effect on knowledge sharing. On the other hand, the research demonstrated that education did somewhat impact knowledge sharing. While 86% of participants felt that education did not impact knowledge sharing, some of the participants felt that the higher the educational level, the more likely it was that the person would share knowledge. Consequently, the lower the educational level, the less likely persons would share knowledge, possibly due to fear that they would lose the only thing that made them valuable to the company.

The research uncovered a more definite relationship between age and knowledge sharing and ethnicity and knowledge sharing. 33% of the participants felt that there was a divide between older and younger workers, with the younger workers less willing to share with older workers. 19% of the participants indicated that senior workers, who tended to be more mature in years, felt threatened by younger workers and, as a result, did not share knowledge with them. As Participant 17 put it, "they don't want to be taken over."

Participant 5 brought up an interesting issue concerning the fact that younger people might be more technologically adept. For example, younger people tend to use text messaging to stay in constant communication. Like many of the older participants, Participant 5 preferred face-to-face and e-mail communication and feared that his lack of "technological savvy" in terms of communication mediums might keep him out of the loop.

The research found that ethnicity was a factor in knowledge sharing. The ability to understand what was being communicated and cultural mores in terms of the way different groups communicated, as well as work ethics, were cited as barriers to knowledge sharing by the participants.

Trust, comfort, and respect figured prominently in the interviews. The participants uniformly asserted that these three factors needed to be present in the cultural mix if knowledge sharing were to be successful in their organizations.

Question 2: What are the organizational reasons that employees resist the sharing of knowledge?

Table H.2 maps the participants against the various organizational factors examined in the study. Number of sources indicates the number of participants who mentioned this factor. The number of references indicates the number of times the factor was brought up during the interview.

Ten percent of the participants indicated that they withheld knowledge due to job security issues. However, 19% mentioned that they knew of others who had this problem. Participant 16, a chief technology officer with a master's degree, had this to say: "Technology people are often not the best in terms of sharing knowledge or communicating. My team members do have that problem. I think it's job security—they haven't been trained or led to believe that it's important to do that. It's a lot of desire to keep things to themselves because then they have this particular power over others."

It was understandable that office politics would figure prominently in the discussions. More than 38% of the participants mentioned politics in their interview sessions. Participant 1 summed this up nicely by stating simply that "knowledge is power."

Two aspects of politics are fear and control. Participant 18 stressed that sharing "knowledge opens people up and makes them vulnerable ... it might open me up to criticism." Participant 13, a senior manager pursuing his doctorate, continued this thought: "In some cases, people may hesitate because of the political arena ... so to speak. They may be fearful to speak up about something that others may not agree with ...They might be afraid that what they say will not be well received by others—whether it's someone above them or just their colleagues."

Thus, fear was a factor, fear of disagreements or fear of looking foolish. Control was the most common aspect of corporate politics. Participant 12, a computer

Table H.2 Organizational Factor Summary

Organizational factors	Number of sources (%)	Number of references (%)
Job security	4 (19%)	7 (7%)
Metrics, use of	1 (4%)	1 (1%)
Organizing	2 (9%)	3 (3%)
Politics	8 (38%)	10 (10%)
Time	7 (33%)	7 (7%)
Organizational, general	19 (90%)	44 (44%)
IT support	15 (71%)	23 (23%)

engineer with a master's degree, summed up the thoughts of most participants. "There are egos involved. There are control freaks—someone wants absolute control so they keep information from others."

Perhaps the most corrosive political problem preventing knowledge sharing was a work environment which, as Participant 9, put it "has a survivor mentality." She remarked: "People do not want to share between departments. There is a definite 'survivor' type feeling. They do things to make themselves look good. I think it's much healthier for us to work together and share information, but we can't. We are wary about giving other departments information, because they'll utilize it to make us look bad."

As Participant 9 observed, corporate politics was influenced by management. Participant 15 explained it this way: "In a small company, it comes from the CEO. The CEO creates that kind of culture. In a larger company, it's more departmental because people don't have that sort of visibility. Who is the top guy or woman that this person's career is influenced by, that's the person whose culture that they create drives those sorts of behaviors."

As Participant 15 so aptly observed, it was management that set the tone for effective knowledge sharing within the organization. However, as Participant 4, a project manager with a master's degree, phrased it, "I'm not real sure if management really recognizes their responsibility or that there may be a problem."

33% of the participants indicated that their managements did not actively support knowledge management practices. As Participant 10 explained, "Corporate sees a different world. It's just perspective. You can't appreciate or understand something you can't perceive."

Some participants viewed management as the principal problem. As Participant 9 put it: "The head of the company was hired to bring back the money. He has pets, shows favoritism. He is very political. He is playing one group against the other. He comes across as wanting all of this. He seems very interested in a good culture and sharing. But he's really interested in playing the game. He is just interested in looking good with the Board of Directors—so that his contract will be extended. We are very fragmented. I find out much of my information third hand. The head of the company comes across as very involved. He wants all of this Kumbaya. He wants all this knowledge sharing—openness. That's his philosophy. But he doesn't implement it."

Participant 14 talked about management's inertia and the ad hoc nature of any attempts at knowledge sharing. "The company could benefit from officially supporting knowledge sharing. I don't know why there is a problem. Some of it may be political. Some of it may be because it's never been done. Senior management is aware of it, they just don't do it. There was some talk, but nothing happens. There's a level of inertia. It's mentioned and then there's not really a follow through. If it were going to be organizational wide, it should be top down, bottom up. There is no pilot program. No one leading it. It's just kind of ad hoc."

Even when management supported knowledge sharing, there were other factors that needed to be overcome if employees were to share knowledge effectively. 29% of the participants brought up the subject of time constraints. Participant 13 described this problem. "Time limitations are a definite factor. People are busy. They've got other priorities. It's difficult to have a structure that's ongoing that brings people out of their daily routine that gets them talking and sharing."

Participant 20 best summed it up by saying that knowledge sharing was impeded by "sleep deprivation" caused by too much work. Participant 3, a CEO and holder of a doctorate, linked the problems of time to the problems of effective organizing. "No problem in doing this but staff has problems organizing stuff, making it available, always time issues, what's the priority."

Most organizations maintain a variety of databases. Those practicing knowledge management might also have a multiple of knowledge bases. Organizing these for effective knowledge sharing could be a challenge, although less than 10% of the participants indicated that this represented a major hurdle. Participant 12 asserted that the notion of knowledge silos was a problem, leading to redundant information and work efforts: "Two weeks ago I went to a meeting. This room had a bunch of poster boards in there. I said, hey, this is just what we're working on. I talked to one of my colleagues. I said, you know about that project up there. Isn't it the same thing that we're doing, I said, but why weren't we collaborating? I am not sure what the barrier is. They were a totally different group. But why weren't we collaborating? We are working in silos."

Only one of the participants worked at a company that emphasized knowledge sharing. Participant 16 described it this way: "We have a department called Center for Leadership and Organizational Excellence. Knowledge sharing is their charter. It's ingrained in the culture. All managers are required to take certain training that explains the importance of knowledge sharing and how do they have to promote it to their direct reports."

Participant 15, whose company did not actively promote knowledge sharing, had advice for management on how to promote effective knowledge sharing within the organization: "One way they do this is by tying people's business goals together. In my organization people get compensated and they get bonuses and their bonuses are based on certain metrics. And I think that the best way to promote the sharing of information is to tie people's metrics together down to the line item. If I get compensated for something and a peer that I collaborate with doesn't, he might not share information with me or seek information from me. By tying people's goals together you get the best cooperation."

All of the participants indicated that one of the major ways organizations could promote effective knowledge sharing was by providing technologies to assist in this area. Most of the participants indicated that their organizations provided some of these technologies. Participant 4 talked about his company's use of intranet-based technologies to support this effort. "Managers have web pages where they can post solutions to problems. This way we can all be on the same page and knowing what each other are doing."

A variety of collaborative technologies was being used, including Microsoft Sharepoint, Centra for whiteboarding and video, and WebEx for video-enhanced distributed meetings and document sharing. In spite of the wealth of technology available, other participants indicated that their organizations were not particularly forward thinking in this area. Participant 18 said, "We're so behind the curve that we needed to have a meeting on how to share your Calendar in Outlook. I would like a more intuitive and user-friendly knowledge-sharing product."

Other participants described how post 9/11 security concerns had forced departments to take stringent measures at the request of management. As Participant 12, emphasized: "There's a whole lot of ill feelings between the people that run the computer networks and the computer users because they put the network security in place as if computers are used for one purpose—word processing and e-mail. It doesn't really facilitate engineering and science. The security restrictions have gotten bad since 9/11. However, if this system ever did get used, it would be very valuable as much of the information cannot be found in any book. Computer networks are great, but this is where the barrier has been put up. When 9/11 happened, they put this big barrier up. They took away all of the file sharing. We went from Ethernet to sneakernet. No chat. Period. That's just a no-no. We don't have collaborative technologies. We have to pass files around via e-mail."

There are a variety of organizational factors that either support or impede effective knowledge sharing within an organization. These include (a) job security, (b) use of metrics, (c) organizing, (d) office politics, (e) lack of time, (f) organizational, management issues, and (g) IT support. 19% of the participants indicated that the issue of job security was twofold: (a) fear of losing face if others disagreed or one provided incorrect information; and (b) the desire to control a particular situation or people by sharing or withholding information.

Office politics was another factor discussed by 38% of the participants. It could have a corrosive effect, particularly if management spearheaded the political problem or overlooked it. As Participant 15 put it, "who is the top guy or woman that this person's career is influenced by, and that's the person whose culture drives those sorts of behaviors."

Lack of time and the inability to organize properly the vast information stores these organizations possess were also cited as factors that inhibited the effective sharing of knowledge by 29% of the participants. Participant 15 advised that the only way knowledge sharing could be effective was to add it to the goals of the organization and to measure its use.

It was organizational issues related to management that generated the most discussion. 33% of the participants stressed that many of those in charge of companies did not effectively promote knowledge sharing. Some did not endorse it at all (i.e., by omission) and some paid it lip service but did not provide the support required for this effort. One notable exception, Participant 16, stated that knowledge sharing was engrained in his company's corporate culture and pointed to a department created just for this purpose.

All of the participants discussed the technology tools in use at their organizations. These ran the gamut from e-mail to collaborative whiteboards. Some of the participants pointed out problems in using these technologies, including high-level security infrastructures, which precluded easy sharing of files and "being behind the curve" in the use of technologies.

Question 3: What are the key reasons employees list for not wanting to share their expertise?

Questions 1 and 2 enumerated the general cultural and organizational factors that impeded or enhanced effective knowledge sharing within an organization. Question 8 in the interview attempted to elicit the key reasons for knowledge-sharing problems. Many of them were addressed in the discussions in the preceding sections and are diagrammed in Figure H.1.

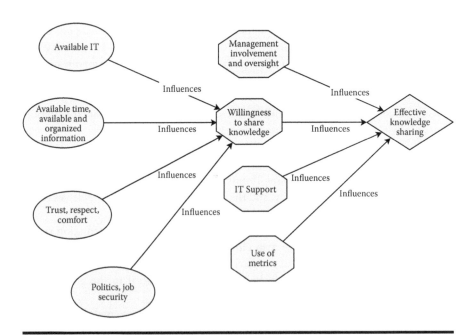

Figure H.1   Key factors affecting knowledge sharing.

A variety of factors affected the willingness to share knowledge in the sample population. Workers first needed to feel secure in their jobs. They needed to know that the act of sharing knowledge with their co-workers would not diminish their job in any way. Perhaps, more importantly, office politics had the potential to become a barrier for effective collaboration and knowledge sharing, diminishing any eagerness toward knowledge sharing. One participant even mentioned the survivor-type mentality in her office, an allusion to the popular television where teams are pitted against teams.

Trust, respect, and comfort were mentioned as variables that also affected the tendency toward willingness to share knowledge. It was stated that workers needed to trust and respect their co-workers. Given the diversity of the modern organization, one of the most important factors that seemed to affect willingness to share knowledge was the level of comfort in dealing with others. If there were a language or cultural barrier, that level of comfort did not effectively exist, thereby, diminishing the level of effective knowledge sharing.

More than a few of the participants in the sample indicated that they simply did not have sufficient time to share knowledge; they were too busy getting their base-level work completed. Several of the participants also complained about the lack of knowledge organization within their companies. Essentially, they felt that it was difficult to find the information they needed so that they could effectively collaborate and share knowledge.

Lack of available information technology assets was another factor in affecting willingness to share knowledge. Modern collaborative software, such as lessons learned databases, wikis, and other technologies were simply not available to them. One of the participants complained about the post 9-11 enforced security restrictions that effectively rendered his network useless.

Willingness to share knowledge, discussed in the last section, is just one of four factors that affect effective knowledge sharing. The other three factors are (a) management involvement and oversight, (b) IT support, and (c) use of metrics.

Many of the participants indicated that their senior management was not actively involved in promoting knowledge management within the company; in fact, knowledge management was not mentioned at all. Other participants indicated that their senior managers stated they supported knowledge management but did little else to promote it or did little to integrate it into the organization's performance management and measurement programs. One participant suggested that one way a company could promote a more effective knowledge sharing atmosphere was to utilize metrics to measure how it was used, when it was used, and how effective it was.

Finally, IT support was seen as critical to effective knowledge sharing. In some instances, the IT department was seen as the barrier, effectively limiting what information could be shared across teams and among members of teams. In other cases, IT was castigated for not providing modern technologies that supported knowledge sharing (e.g., wikis, whiteboards, etc.).

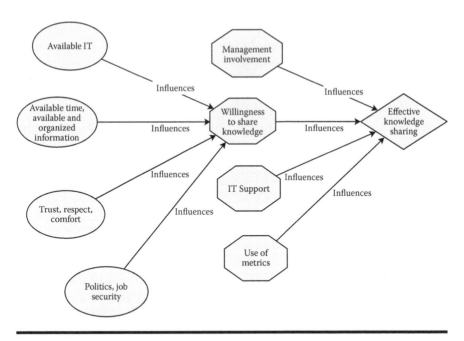

Figure H.2 Technology desired and in use in sample organizations.

Figure H.2 lists the technologies being used by the participants and the technologies that they desired to use.

It was noted that face-to-face (F2F) is still the predominant method of knowledge sharing with e-mail coming in a close second. Participant 19 summed up the general feeling on use of face-to-face communication, "I might be old-fashioned in that I just like face-to-face. There are just more nuances that can be given face-to-face. You can see if the person is receiving it and understanding it properly that way."

Although everyone in the sample was using e-mail, some complained about the problems of doing so, as Participant 3 mentioned, "E-mails have problems. Communicating orally and through e-mail can be very time-consuming depending on the people who are on the team. They get files lost, and they have to send again. Timeliness is a barrier."

Participant 8 agreed with this assessment: "I don't like e-mail because so many misunderstandings take place on e-mail. How one-dimensional it is. Because people walk away from the opposite impression of what was meant. Many people don't read e-mails and then they miss the point. They don't get the inflection. They don't get the sarcasm. You got to have the back and forth."

Chat was less popular than expected, although many project leaders used it with their younger project teams, but not without some complaints. Participant 3 had this to say about chat: "What I find a little difficult with chat is that sometimes you are overlapping your thoughts. You are asking a question, while the other person is answering the last question. Or you're making a comment, while the other person is making another comment. Might be transferring the wrong knowledge."

However, in all cases, technology was a fundamental component of the way information was transferred within these organizations. In many cases, the participants recommended more cutting-edge technologies, such as blogs and wikis, although none of them seemed to be aware of the many knowledge-sharing technologies and techniques available to them. Information technology (IT) support, therefore, can be said to be a critical factor in effective knowledge sharing.

The research uncovered a moderate relationship between education and knowledge sharing. While the majority of participants felt that education did not impact knowledge sharing, some of the participants felt that the higher the educational level, the more likely it was that the person would share knowledge. The lower the educational level, the less likely the person would share knowledge, possibly due to fear that they could lose the only thing that made them valuable to the company.

The research uncovered a more definite relationship between age and knowledge sharing and ethnicity and knowledge sharing. Some participants felt that there was a divide between older and younger workers, with the younger workers less willing to share with older workers. Other participants indicated that senior workers, who tended to be more mature in years, felt threatened by younger workers and, as a result, did not share knowledge with them. As one participant put it, "They don't want to be taken over."

Another participant brought up an interesting issue concerning the fact that younger people might be more technologically adept. For example, younger people used text messaging to stay in constant communication. Like many of the older participants, this participant preferred face-to-face and e-mail communications and feared that his lack of "technological savvy" in terms of communication mediums might keep him out of the loop.

The research found that ethnicity was somewhat a factor in knowledge sharing. The ability to understand what was being communicated and cultural mores in terms of the way different groups communicated, as well as work ethic, were cited as barriers to knowledge sharing by the participants.

Trust, comfort, and respect figured prominently in the interviews. The participants uniformly asserted that these three factors needed to be present in the cultural mix if knowledge sharing were to be successful in their organizations.

It was expected that corporate culture would have an impact on willingness to share knowledge. There was a wide variety of variables possible for this relationship: trust, management commitment, involvement, perception, rewards, leadership, resources provided, job title, tenure, and others.

The study found that there was a variety of organizational factors that either supported or impeded effective knowledge sharing within an organization. These included (a) job security, (b) use of metrics, (c) organizing (d) office politics, (e) lack of time, (f) organizational and management issues, and (g) IT support.

Several of the participants indicated that the issue of job security was twofold, including fear of losing face if others disagreed or one provided incorrect information and the desire to control a particular situation or people by sharing or withholding information.

Office politics was another factor discussed by many of the participants. Politics could have a corrosive effect, particularly if management spearheaded the political problem or overlooked it. As Participant 15 phrased it, "Who is the top guy or woman that this person's career is influenced by, and that's the person whose culture drives those sorts of behaviors."

Lack of time and inability to organize the vast information stores these organizations possess were also cited as factors that inhibited the effective sharing of knowledge. Participant 15 advised that the only way knowledge sharing could be effective was to add it to the goals of the organization and to measure its use.

Organizational issues related to management generated the most discussion. The research found that many of those in charge of companies did not effectively promote knowledge sharing. Some did not endorse it at all (i.e., by omission) and some paid it lip service but did not provide the support required for this effort. One notable exception, Participant 16, stated that knowledge sharing was engrained in his company's corporate culture and pointed to a department created just for that purpose.

All of the participants pointed to the technology tools in use at their organizations. These ran the gamut from e-mail to collaborative whiteboards. Some of the participants pointed out problems in using these technologies, including high-level security infrastructures that precluded easy sharing of files and "being behind the curve" in the use of technologies.

It was also expected that IT support would have an impact on willingness to share knowledge. There is a tendency to reduce knowledge complexity artificially with the use of technologies for knowledge management. It has also been found that there is a positive knowledge sharing culture due to the presence of technology.

The study found that IT support did, indeed, have an impact on the willingness to share knowledge. The study found a distinction between willingness to share knowledge and effective knowledge sharing, as shown in Figure H.3.

A variety of factors affected the willingness to share knowledge in the sample population. Workers first needed to feel secure in their jobs. They needed to know that the act of sharing knowledge with their co-workers would not diminish their job in any way. Perhaps, more importantly, office politics had the potential to become a barrier to effective collaboration and knowledge sharing, diminishing any eagerness toward knowledge sharing. One participant even mentioned the survivor-type mentality in her office, an allusion to the popular television where teams were pitted against teams.

Trust, respect and comfort were mentioned as variables that also affected a tendency towards willingness to share knowledge. It was stated that workers needed to trust and respect their co-workers. Given the diversity of the modern organization, one of the most important factors that seemed to affect willingness to share

	Technology Desired	*Technology Used*
Participant 1	0	f2f, online forums, email, wiki
Participant 10	blogs	email, wiki
Participant 11	wiki	f2f, bulletin board
Participant 12	0	email
Participant 13	0	f2f email, chat, whiteboard
Participant 14	wiki, repository	f2f
Participant 15	whiteboard	Sharepoint, intranet, email, cellphone
Participant 16	0	f2f, email
Participant 17	0	f2f, whiteboard
Participant 18	0	email, chat, WebEx
Participant 19	0	f2f, email, chat, intranet
Participant 2	0	email, web-based conferences, f2f
Participant 20	0	email
Participant 21	0	email
Participant 3	wiki	chat
Participant 4	0	f2f, email, web pages
Participant 5	0	f2f, email, conference calls
Participant 6	0	chat
Participant 7	0	phone, email
Participant 8	0	f2f
Participant 9	0	email, f2f, shared drive

Figure H.3   Key factors affecting knowledge sharing.

knowledge was the level of comfort in dealing with others. If there were a language or cultural barrier, that level of comfort did not effectively exist, thereby, diminishing the level of effective knowledge sharing.

More than a few of the participants in the sample indicated that they simply did not have sufficient time to share knowledge; they were too busy getting their base-level work completed. Several of the participants also complained about the lack of knowledge organization within their companies. Essentially, they felt that it was difficult to find the information they needed so that they could effectively collaborate and share knowledge.

Lack of available information technology assets was another factor in affecting willingness to share knowledge. Modern collaborative software, such as lessons learned databases, wikis and other technologies, were simply not available to them. One of the participants complained about the post-9/11 enforced security restrictions that effectively rendered his network useless.

Willingness to share knowledge was just one of four factors that affected effective knowledge sharing. The other three factors were: (a) management involvement and oversight, (b) IT support, and (c) use of metrics.

Many of the participants indicated that their senior management was not actively involved in promoting knowledge management within the company (i.e., knowledge management was not mentioned at all). Other participants indicated that their senior managers stated that they supported knowledge management but did little else to promote it or to integrate it into the organization's performance management and measurement programs. One participant suggested that one way a company could promote a more effective knowledge sharing atmosphere was to utilize metrics to measure how it was used, when it was used and how effective it was.

Finally, IT support was seen as critical to effective knowledge sharing. In some instances, the IT department was seen as the barrier, effectively limiting what information could be shared across teams and among members of teams. In other cases, IT was castigated for not providing the modern technologies that supported knowledge sharing (e.g., wikis, whiteboards, etc.). It should be noted, however, that some participants indicated that IT fully supported the move into these technologies. IT support, therefore, could be a critical factor in effective knowledge sharing.

The expectations for knowledge management, and by definition knowledge sharing, are that it would be able to improve growth and innovation; productivity and efficiency reflected in cost savings; customer relationships; employee learning, satisfaction, and retention; and management decision making. Knowledge sharing could meet these goals if it were embedded in the organization using a bottom-up approach, rather than a top-down approach. Top-down approaches were usually forced upon employees and, hence, resisted or, at least, ignored. The bottom-up approach is somewhat akin to viral marketing, where one person becomes enthusiastic about a product or service and tells someone who tells someone else. By providing the tools, methodologies, training, and support on a unit or departmental level, employees are encouraged to capture, share, and archive their knowledge for the good of the organization.

However, knowledge management needs to have a focus. A number of techniques can be used to disseminate knowledge-sharing practices:

1. Do not force people to adapt. They must be self-motivated.
2. Change the job of knowledge professionals. Enable everyone to carry on the task of knowledge management.

3. Consider localized knowledge bases. There is no reason why employees cannot store their domain of knowledge in their own private databases. Respect the privacy and confidentiality of people's personal information. People do not like to share what gives them their own personal competitive edge.
4. Help people connect to experts inside and outside the organization.
5. The current emphasis on a Balanced Scorecard and performance management and measurement might also be used as a lever to further embed knowledge sharing within an organization. A Balanced Scorecard had four perspectives to define a set of objectives, measures, targets, and initiatives to achieve the goals of that perspective. While the learning and growth perspective was a natural fit for knowledge sharing, the remaining perspectives should also be considered. Adding goals, metrics, and others for knowledge sharing activities is a sure way to get these departments at least to consider usage within the department.

Appendix 1: Selected Participant Quotes

Age

Sometimes people who are older versus younger… there might be problem. It's … a problem of respect. Someone who works with someone that they don't respect probably wouldn't share information with them, wouldn't want to help them. They don't respect or personally like them.

Education and Intelligence

There are pretty normal people on the team, but they don't have the same educational level. It is a factor—there is one person, in particular, on the team who is almost uneducated in her view of things. She doesn't have a degree, but is working on it. I see it as a problem in that her world knowledge is limited. She sometimes does things that are sneaky. She'll say I am going to do that and then doesn't do it correctly.

I'm being very frank. I have to label this as arrogance on my part. If I think you're stupid, I don't think you are really going to understand and appreciate this. I am only going to share what I think you need to know.

Ethnicity

I haven't noticed any problems due to age or ethnicity, except in the case of Asians, who play it close to the vest.

I think that foreign work ethic is such they tell you one thing and try to give you something else. They share very little information … . In that part of the world, there are no lies. There's only a positive truth and a negative truth. As long as the negative truth comes to a positive, it's okay.

Job Security

There are people who know something about the system, and they don't share it because of job security. I am guilty of this. I may not share information with a colleague because I want to be the one that brings it up in the meeting on Monday.

Organizing Data

It seems like there are so many different places where people have to go to find stuff. We're in the process of doing a consolidation and putting it on Sharepoint, but it's a tough transition right now. We're learning this product. They call it New Source. Trying to get all information on Sharepoint so people don't have to go to multiple destinations. So much knowledge within organization, people in every tenure are learning stuff everyday, so it does take a while to get up to speed to find out where the knowledge is in the organization. They are trying to use Sharepoint to do this. No master index now but creating it now with New Source.

Power

I have noticed that people have problems sharing with me. I always assumed that the reason was to protect their position. In other words, "knowledge is power." If they give away their knowledge, they give away their power. That was my working assumption. My peers and I would discuss, "why are they so reluctant to share information with us." It was because they were protecting the keys to the kingdom. This was usually the older employees, who had a lot of seniority and a lot of knowledge. They didn't want to be taken over.

Technology

Participant 11, a senior manager with a doctorate, agreed. "IT has to be humanized and untextualized. I know it makes me a minority because everyone is texting today. I prefer systems that allow for exchanges in more than just text.

Tools

They do a good job of providing the technology tools to support knowledge sharing and looking forward down the road. We focus a lot on identifying particular types of tools. We're looking at these tools ourselves. We evaluate them. If this turns out to be a beneficial tool, we recommend this to IT.

Appendix I—
Computer Use Policy

In consideration of being authorized by _____ (hereinafter referred to as "Company") to use and access Company computers, communications facilities, internal and external social networks, and resources (hereinafter referred to as "Company facilities and resources'), I agree to comply with the conditions set forth in paragraphs (a) through (j) as follows

(a) Use of and access to Company facilities and resources is provided only for Company business. I will use or access Company facilities and resources only in ways that are cost-effective and in the Company's best interest. I will not attempt to use or access resources or data that I have not been authorized to use or access.

(b) When a user ID is assigned to me, I will change the password so that it is not easily guessed. I will not share, write down, electronically store (without strong encryption), or otherwise disclose the password, authentication code, or any other device associated with any user ID assigned to me. I will take precautions to ensure that no other person makes use of any Company facilities and resources with any of my user IDs.

(c) All data stored on or originating from, and all communications transmitted or received using, Company facilities and resources are considered the property of the Company. Such data and communications are subject to monitoring or review by authorized personnel designated by Company Management. The term "private" as referred to in operating systems, application software, or electronic mail does not refer to personal privacy of an individual's data or mail. I also acknowledge that my use of or access to Company facilities and resources may be monitored at any time to assure that such use or access is in compliance with these conditions.

(d) Company information in any form shall be safeguarded. I will not copy, or distribute to others, any Company-sensitive information except as authorized. I will not upload, publish, transmit, or otherwise disclose any such

317

information concerning the Company, its operations and activities, on or through non-Company networks without prior approval of authorized Company Management.

(e) I will respect and observe the customs, traditions, and laws of the _____ and other countries where _____ has computer assets. I will not use Company facilities and resources to access or attempted access any computer data or computer site, or send or knowingly receive any electronic transmission that contains political, religious, pornographic, indecent, abusive, defamatory, threatening, illegal, or culturally offensive materials. I will report any such material with the source of the site name of such material to the concerned organization.

(f) I will not use Company facilities and resources for unauthorized access to, interference with or disruption of any software, data, hardware, or system available through Company facilities and resources. I will use standard Company procedures to check all downloaded files for viruses or destructive code prior to using the files on Company facilities and resources.

(g) I will not copy or download any material or any portion thereof protected by copyright without proper authorization from the copyright owner.

(h) I will not connect or use any channel of communication not authorized in compliance with Company policy and guidelines. For any situation in which I am uncertain of what behavior is expected of me in regard to using or accessing company facilities and resources, I will contact the concerned organization.

(i) I will not utilize unauthorized Internet access connections.

(j) I acknowledge that any violations of the above paragraphs (a) through (i) may result in disciplinary action including loss of access to Company facilities and resources, termination of my employment, my contract or my employer's contract, legal action, or other measures, as appropriate.

Acknowledgment

I acknowledge that I have read and understood the _____ Computer Use Policy as set of forth above and I shall abide by them while using or accessing company Computer and Communication facilities and resources.

Employee Name	Signature	Date

Appendix J—Best Practices Security Checklist

General

	Vulnerability	Description Criteria	Documentation Criteria	Demonstration Criteria
1	**Does the vendor have a documented and provable security policy for IT?** List of Items to be included 1. Statement of purpose 2. Organization structure 3. Physical security 4. Hiring and termination procedures 5. Data classification 6. Access control 7. Operating systems 8. Hardware and Software 9. Internet use 10. E-mail 11. Technical support 12. Virus protection, firewall, VPN, remote access 13. Backups and disaster recovery 14. Intrusion detection and incident response 15. Personnel security 16. Software development 17. Outsourcing (offshore) 18. Help desk development	Does not have a policy or cannot describe policy = **0** Can describe policy = **1**	Does not have a policy, or policy is not documented or documented but does not include any of the noted items = **0** Documented and includes 1–9 of 18 items = **1** Documented and included 10–18 items = **2**	Does not have a policy, or site cannot demonstrate policy = **0** Site can demonstrate policy but does not include any of the noted items = **1** Site can demonstrate policy, and it includes 1–9 of 18 items = **2** Site can demonstrate policy, and it includes 10–18 of 18 items = **3**
	Score			

2	Is this policy reviewed and updated on a regular basis? Question to ask 1. How often is the policy updated?	Does not have a policy or cannot describe review and update process = **0** Can describe review and update process = **1**	Does not have a policy, or policy review and update is not documented = **0** Can provide documentation for review and update to be completed less frequently than yearly = **1** Can provide documentation for review and update to be completed yearly or more frequently = **2**	Not applicable	
		Score			
3	**Does the vendor have management buy-in to security?**	Does not have a corporate security policy with management approval or cannot describe their corporate security policy = **0** Can describe their corporate security policy = **1**	Does not have a corporate security policy with management approval or cannot provide documentation of their corporate security policy = **0** Can provide documentation of their corporate security policy = **2**	Not applicable	
		Score			

Access Control

	Vulnerability	Description Criteria	Documentation Criteria	Demonstration Criteria
4	**Is the application PKI enabled for the client?**	Application is not PKI enabled for the client= **0** Can describe how their application uses PKI for their client = **1**	Cannot provide documentation that describes application PKI enabled for the client = **0** Can provide documentation the application uses PKI = **2**	Cannot demonstrate the application is PKI enabled = **0** Can demonstrate the application uses PKI = **2**
		Score		
5	**Is the application PKI enabled for the server and configured to require PKI for authentication?**	Application is not PKI enabled for server and configured to require PKI for authentication = **0** Can describe how their application is PKI enabled for the server and configured to require PKI for authentication = **1**	Application is not PKI enabled for server and configured to require PKI for authentication or cannot provide documentation = **0** Can provide documentation application is PKI enabled for the server and configured to require PKI for authentication = **2**	Application is not PKI enabled for the server and configured to require PKI for authentication or cannot demonstrate = **0** Can demonstrate the application is PKI enabled for the server and configured to require PKI for authentication = **2**
		Score		

				Score
6	**Does the vendor have robust revocation checking?**	Does not have robust revocation checking = **0** Does have robust revocation checking = **1**	Do not have robust revocation checking or cannot provide documentation = **0** Can provide documentation = **2**	Do not have robust revocation checking or cannot demonstrate = **0** Can demonstrate process = **3**	
7	**Is there a registration process for new users?** Question to ask 1. Is the registration process provided to new users?	Does not have registration process for new users = **0** Does have registration process for new users = **1**	Does not have registration process for new users, or process is not documented = **0** Can provide documentation, but it is not provided to new users = **1** Can provide documentation, and it is provided to new users = **2**	Does not have registration process for new users or cannot demonstrate registration process = **0** Can demonstrate new user registration process = **3**	

	Vulnerability	Description Criteria	Documentation Criteria	Demonstration Criteria	
8	**Does the vendor have an access request form?**	Does not have a form = **0**	Does not have a form or cannot provide form = **0**	Does not have a form or cannot provide form = **0**	
	List of Items to be included	Can describe form = **1**	Can provide blank form, and it contains all of the asterisked items = **1**	Can provide completed form, and it contains all of the asterisked items = **1**	
	1. * Type of request (initial, modification, deactivation)				
	2. * System name		Can provide blank form, and it contains all of the asterisked items and all of the non-asterisked items = **2**	Can provide completed form, and it contains all of the asterisked items and 1–4 of the 7 non-asterisked items = **2**	
	3. System location				
	4. * Date				
	5. * Name				
	6. Social security number/ employee number				
	7. * Organization			Can provide completed form, and it contains all of the asterisked items and 5–7 of the 7 non-asterisked items = **3**	
	8. Phone number				
	9. * E-mail address				
	10. Job title				
	11. Physical address				
	12. * Citizenship				
	13. User agreement				
	14. * Justification for access/need to know				
	15. * Type of access				
	16. * Supervisor approval				
	17. * Security manager verification				
	18. * Verification of need to know				
	Score				

| 9 | Does the vendor have a role-based policy for user access?

Questions to ask
1. Do administrators have an account for administrator work only and have an additional account for other purposes?
2. Are administrator privileges only granted to administrators and not to all users?
3. Are limits put on each user who has access to the application?
4. Are user privileges based on need-to-know?
5. Are permissions periodically reviewed to include superusers? | Does not have a role-based policy for user access or cannot describe their role-based policy = **0**

Can describe their role-based policy for user access = **1** | Does not have a role-based policy for user access or cannot provide documentation or can provide documentation but the documentation includes answers to only 1–2 of questions = **0**

Can provide documentation, and the documentation includes answers to 3–4 of questions = **1**

Can provide documentation, and the documentation includes answers to all of the 5 questions = **2** | Does not have a role-based policy for user access or cannot demonstrate their policy = **0**

Can demonstrate the answers to 1–2 of 5 questions = **1**

Can demonstrate the answers to 3–4 of 5 questions = **2**

Can demonstrate the answers to 5 of questions = **3** |
| **Score** | | | |

		Description Criteria	Documentation Criteria	Demonstration Criteria	
	Vulnerability	*Description Criteria*	*Documentation Criteria*	*Demonstration Criteria*	
10	**Is there a process for checking for inactive and terminated users?**	Does not have a process for checking for inactive and terminated users or cannot describe process = **0** Can describe their process for checking for inactive and terminated users = **1**	Does not have a process for checking for inactive and terminated Users, or the process is not documented = **0** Can provide documentation for a manual process = **1** Can provide documentation for an automated process = **2**	Does not have a process for checking for inactive and terminated users, or the process cannot be demonstrated = **0** Can demonstrate manual process = **2** Can demonstrate automated process = **3**	
			Score		

11	What is the period for revocation of users (the length of the contract, one year or whichever comes first)? Question to ask 1. What is the length of the revocation period?	Does not have a period for revocation of users or cannot describe period of revocation = **0** Can describe period for revocation of users = **1**	Does not have a period for revocation of users or cannot provide documentation = **0** Can provide documentation for revocation of users, and the period is less frequently than the length of the contract or one year = **1** Can provide documentation for revocation of users, and the period is the length of the contract, or one year or more frequently = **2**	Does not have a period for revocation of users or cannot demonstrate that users are revoked = **0** Can demonstrate the revocation of users, and the period is less frequently than the length of the contract or one year = **2** Can demonstrate the revocation of users, and the period is the length of the contract, or one year or more frequently = **3**
	Score			

	Vulnerability	Description Criteria	Documentation Criteria	Demonstration Criteria
12	**Does the vendor have a strong password policy?** List of Items to be included 1. A minimum of nine characters 2. Includes at least one uppercase alphabetic character 3. Includes at least one lowercase alphabetic character 4. Includes at least one non-alphanumeric (special) character 5. Includes at least one numeric character 6. Expires after 60 days 7. Is different than the previous 10 passwords used 8. Is changeable by the administrator at any time 9. Is changeable by the associated user only once in a 24-hour period (for human user accounts) 10. Is not changeable by users other than the administrator or the user with which the password is associated	Does not have a password policy or cannot describe policy = **0** Can describe their password policy = **1**	Does not have a password policy, or policy is not documented = **0** Can provide documentation for their policy, and it includes 1–5 of listed items = **1** Can provide documentation for their policy, and it includes 6–10 of listed items = **2**	Does not have a password policy or cannot demonstrate their policy = **0** Can demonstrate their policy, and it includes 1–4 of listed items = **1** Can demonstrate their policy, and it includes 5–7 of listed items = **2** Can demonstrate their policy, and it includes 8–10 of listed items = **3**
	Score			

13	**Does the vendor permit the use of default accounts, default passwords, community strings, or other default access control mechanisms?**	Uses default access control mechanisms or cannot describe the prohibition of these mechanisms = **0** Can describe how they do not use default access control mechanisms = **1**	Uses default access control mechanisms or cannot provide documentation for prohibiting these mechanisms = **0** Can provide documentation that no default access control mechanisms are used = **2**	Uses default access control mechanisms or cannot demonstrate that these are not in use = **0** Can demonstrate that no default access control mechanisms are used = **3**
		Score		
14	**Does the vendor permit the use of shared accounts?**	Permits shared accounts or cannot describe how shared accounts are not permitted = **0** Can describe how shared accounts are not permitted = **1**	Permits shared accounts or cannot provide documentation that prohibits shared accounts = **0** Can provide documentation that prohibits shared accounts = **2**	Permits shared accounts or cannot demonstrate that no shared accounts are used = **0** Can demonstrate that no shared accounts are used = **3**
		Score		

Confidentiality

	Vulnerability		Description Criteria	Documentation Criteria	Demonstration Criteria	
15	**Does the vendor utilize appropriate file permissions on sensitive data?** Question to ask 1. Are file permissions based on roles and need to know?		Does not have appropriate file permissions on sensitive data or cannot describe their file permissions on sensitive data = **0** Can describe their file permissions, and they are appropriate for sensitive data = **1**	Does not have appropriate file permissions on sensitive data or cannot provide documentation on sensitive data file permissions = **0** Can provide documentation that system file permissions are appropriate for sensitive data = **1** Can provide documentation that system file and application file permissions are appropriate for sensitive data = **2**	Does not have appropriate file permissions on sensitive data or cannot demonstrate file permissions on sensitive data = **0** Can demonstrate that system file permissions are appropriate for sensitive data = **2** Can demonstrate that system file and application file permissions are appropriate for sensitive data = **3**	
		Score				

#	Question			Score
16	Are authentication credentials stored in an encrypted format?	Authentication credentials are not stored in encrypted format or cannot describe how encryption is used to store authentication credentials = **0** Can describe how authentication credentials are stored in encrypted format = **1**	Authentication credentials are not stored in encrypted format or cannot provide documentation of the requirement = **0** Can provide documentation that authentication credentials are stored in encrypted format = **2**	Authentication credentials are not stored in encrypted format or cannot demonstrate that authentication credentials are stored in encrypted format = **0** Can demonstrate that authentication credentials are stored in encrypted format = **3**	
				Score	
17	Is SSL used with sensitive web traffic?	Cannot describe how SSL is used = **0** Can describe how SSL is used with sensitive web traffic = **1**	SSL is not used for sensitive web traffic= **0** Can provide documentation that SSL is used with unclassified, sensitive web traffic = **2**	SSL is not used for sensitive web traffic or cannot demonstrate how it is used = **0** Can demonstrate that SSL is used with sensitive web traffic = **3**	
				Score	

	Vulnerability	Description Criteria	Documentation Criteria	Demonstration Criteria	
18	**Is SSL used to protect sensitive data and data in transit?**	SSL is not used to protect sensitive data and data in transit or cannot describe how it is used = **0** Can describe how SSL is used to protect sensitive data and data in transit = **1**	SSL is not used to protect sensitive data and data in transit or cannot provide documentation that states this requirement = **0** Can provide documentation that SSL is used to protect sensitive data and data in transit = **2**	SSL is not used to protect sensitive data and data in transit or cannot demonstrate this requirement = **0** Can demonstrate that SSL is used to protect sensitive data and data in transit = **3**	
		Score			
19	**Are the authentication credentials encrypted during transmission?**	Authentication credentials are not encrypted during transmission or cannot describe how they are encrypted = **0** Can describe how authentication credentials are encrypted during transmission = **1**	Authentication credentials are not encrypted during transmission or cannot provide documentation of this requirement = **0** Can provide documentation that authentication credentials are encrypted during transmission = **2**	Authentication credentials are not encrypted during transmission or cannot demonstrate this requirement = **0** Can demonstrate that authentication credentials are encrypted during transmission = **3**	
		Score			

20	Does the vendor maintain separation of data to prevent disclosure of information?	Does not maintain separation of data or cannot describe how data will be separated = **0** Can describe how they will maintain separation of data = **1**	Does not maintain separation of data or cannot provide documentation requiring separation of data = **0** Can provide documentation that vendor does maintain separation of data = **2**	Does not maintain separation of data or cannot demonstrate the separation of data = **0** Can demonstrate that vendor does maintain separation of data = **3**	
		Score			

Integrity

21	Does the vendor have a trust mark or site seal to validate users have reached the vendor site?	Does not have a trust mark or site seal or cannot describe their trust mark or site seal = **0** Has a trust mark or site seal = **1**	Does not have a trust mark or site seal, or this requirement is not documented = **0** Can provide documentation that vendor has a trust mark or site seal = **2**	Does not have a trust mark or site seal or cannot show their trust meal or site seal = **0** Can show that vendor has a trust mark or site seal = **3**	
		Score			

	Vulnerability		Description Criteria	Documentation Criteria	Demonstration Criteria	
22	**Are the documents loaded to the vendor site scanned for viruses prior to posting?**		Does not virus scan documents prior to posting or cannot describe their scanning process = **0** Can describe their process for virus scanning documents prior to posting = **1**	Does not virus scan documents prior to posting, or process is not documented = **0** Can provide documentation that vendor does virus scan documents prior to posting = **2**	Does not virus scan documents prior to posting or cannot demonstrate scanning = **0** Can demonstrate that vendor does virus scan documents prior to posting = **3**	
		Score				
23	**Are virus signatures updated at least every 14 days?** Question to ask 1. Is the process manual or automated?		Virus signatures are not updated at least every 14 days, or vendor cannot describe update process = **0** Can describe process used to update virus signatures at least every 14 days = **1**	Virus signatures are not updated at least every 14 days, or update process is not documented = **0** Can provide documentation that virus signatures are updated at least every 14 days using a manual process = **1** Can provide documentation that virus signatures are updated at least every 14 days using an automated process = **2**	Virus signatures are not updated at least every 14 days, or update process cannot be demonstrated = **0** Can demonstrate that virus signatures are updated at least every 14 days using a manual process = **2** Can demonstrate that virus signatures are updated at least every 14 days using an automated process = **3**	
		Score				

24	Does the vendor scan the server for viruses on a regular basis? Question to ask 1. How often does the vendor scan for viruses?	Does not scan for viruses on a regular basis or cannot describe scanning process = **0** Can describe scanning process and how frequently scanning is done = **1**	Does not scan for viruses on a regular basis or cannot provide documentation of scanning process = **0** Can provide documentation that vendor scans for viruses less frequently than weekly = **1** Can provide documentation that vendor scans for viruses weekly or more frequently = **2**	Does not scan for viruses on a regular basis or cannot demonstrate scanning = **0** Can demonstrate that vendor scans for viruses less frequently than weekly = **2** Can demonstrate that vendor scans for viruses weekly or more frequently = **3**	
		Score			

	Vulnerability		Description Criteria	Documentation Criteria	Demonstration Criteria	
25	**Does the vendor scan the server for spyware on a regular basis?** Question to ask 1. How often does the vendor scan for spyware?		Does not scan for spyware on a regular basis or cannot describe scanning process = 0 Can describe process used for scanning for spyware and how frequently scanning is completed = 1	Does not scan for spyware on a regular basis or cannot provide documentation of process = 0 Can provide documentation that vendor scans for spyware less frequently than weekly = 1 Can provide documentation that vendor scans for spyware weekly or more frequently = 2	Does not scan for spyware on a regular basis or cannot demonstrate scanning process = 0 Can demonstrate that vendor scans for spyware less frequently than weekly = 2 Can demonstrate that vendor scans for spyware weekly or more frequently = 3	
		Score				

| 26 | **Does the vendor scan the server for adware on a regular basis?**

Question to ask
1. How often does the vendor scan for adware? | Vendor does not scan for adware on a regular basis or cannot describe scanning process = **0**

Vendor can describe process used to scan for adware and how frequently scanning is completed = **1** | Vendor does not scan for adware on a regular basis or cannot provide documentation of scanning = **0**

Can provide documentation that vendor scans for adware less frequently than weekly = **1**

Can provide documentation that vendor scans for adware weekly or more frequently = **2** | Vendor does not scan for adware on a regular basis or cannot demonstrate scanning process = **0**

Can demonstrate that vendor scans for adware less frequently than weekly = **2**

Can demonstrate that vendor scans for adware weekly or more frequently = **3** | |
| | | | | **Score** | |

Availability

Vulnerability	Description Criteria	Documentation Criteria	Demonstration Criteria
27 **Does the vendor have a policy for backups?** List of Items to be Included 1. Schedule for regular backups 2. Backups to be stored off-site 3. Recovery plan 4. Clearly defined activities and responsibilities of individuals 5. Policy should be tested annually 6. Personnel trained annually 7. Backups should maintain separation of data	Does not have a policy for backups or cannot describe backup policy = **0** Vendor can describe policy for backups = **1**	Does not have a policy for backups or cannot provide documentation of policy, or policy does not include any of the items listed = **0** Can provide documentation that vendor has policy, and it includes 1–3 of listed items = **1** Can provide documentation that vendor has policy, and it includes 4–7 of listed items = **2**	Does not have a policy for backups or cannot demonstrate backups = **0** Can demonstrate that vendor has policy, and it includes 1–2 of listed items = **1** Can demonstrate that vendor has policy, and it includes 3–4 of listed items = **2** Can demonstrate that vendor has policy, and it includes 5–7 of listed items = **3**
	Score		

28	**Does the vendor have a documented, executable process for backups?** Question to ask 1. Is the process manual or automated?	Does not have a backup process or cannot describe the process = **0** Can describe backup process = **1**	Does not have a backup process or cannot provide documentation of their backup process = **0** Can provide documentation of the manual backup process = **1** Can provide documentation of the automated backup process = **2**	Does not have a backup process or cannot demonstrate backup process = **0** Can demonstrate the manual backup process = **2** Can demonstrate the automated backup process = **3**
		Score		

	Vulnerability	Description Criteria	Documentation Criteria	Demonstration Criteria	
29	**Does the backup process include operating system files?** Question to ask 1. Is the process manual or automated?	Backup process does not include operating system files or cannot describe process = **0** Can describe backup process, and it includes operating system files = **1**	Backup process does not include operating system files or cannot provide documentation of process = **0** Can provide documentation of the manual backup process that includes operating system files = **1** Can provide documentation of the automated backup process that includes operating system files = **2**	Backup process does not include operating system files or cannot demonstrate process = **0** Can demonstrate the manual backup process that includes operating system files = **2** Can demonstrate the automated backup process that includes operating system files = **3**	
		Score			

30	**Does the backup process include user data?** Question to ask 1. Is the process manual or automated?	Backup process does not include user data or cannot describe process = **0** Can describe backup process, and it includes user data = **1**	Backup process does not include user data or cannot provide documentation of process = **0** Can provide documentation of the manual backup process = **1** Can provide documentation of the automated backup process = **2**	Backup process does not include user data or cannot demonstrate process = **0** Can demonstrate the manual backup process = **2** Can demonstrate the automated backup process = **3**	
		Score			
31	**Is the backup process tested on a regular basis?**	Backup process is not tested on a regular basis or cannot describe test of backup process = **0** Can describe backup process being tested on a regular basis = **1**	Backup process is not tested on a regular basis or cannot provide documentation of testing backup process = **0** Can provide documentation that backup process is tested on a regular basis = **2**	Backup process is not tested on a regular basis or cannot demonstrate that backup process has been tested on a regular basis = **0** Can demonstrate that backup process is tested on a regular basis = **3**	
		Score			

	Vulnerability		Description Criteria		Documentation Criteria		Demonstration Criteria	
32	Are the results of the backup process verified?		Backup process results are not verified or cannot describe verification process = **0** Can describe verification of backup process = **1**		Backup process results are not verified or cannot provide documentation of verification of backups = **0** Can provide documentation that backup process results are verified = **2**		Backup process results are not verified or cannot demonstrate verification of backup process = **0** Can demonstrate that backup process results are verified = **3**	
		Score						
33	Are the backups stored off-site?		Backups are not stored off-site or cannot describe where backups are stored= **0** Can describe off-site storage of backups = **1**		Backups are not stored off-site or cannot provide documentation that requires backups to be stored off-site = **0** Can provide documentation that backup are stored off-site = **2**		Backups are not stored off-site or cannot demonstrate that backups are stored off-site = **0** Can demonstrate that backup are stored off-site = **3**	
		Score						

34	**Does the vendor have a restore and recovery process?** Things to consider 1. Restore and recovery node 2. High availability failover Question to ask 1. Is the process manual or automated?	Does not have a restore and recovery process or cannot describe their process = **0** Can describe their restore and recovery process = **1**	Does not have restore and recovery process or cannot provide documentation of this process = **0** Can provide documentation of manual restore and recovery process = **1** Can provide documentation of automated restore and recovery process = **2**	Does not have a restore and recovery process or cannot demonstrate their process = **0** Can demonstrate manual restore and recovery process = **2** Can demonstrate automated restore and recovery process = **3**	
		Score			
35	**Is the restore and recovery process tested on a regular basis?**	Does not test their restore and recovery process or cannot describe testing their process = **0** Can describe testing of restore and recovery process = **1**	Does not test their restore and recovery process or cannot provide documentation of this process = **0** Can provide documentation of the testing of restore and recovery process = **2**	Does not test their restore and recovery process or cannot demonstrate this process = **0** Can demonstrate the testing of restore and recovery process = **3**	
		Score			

	Vulnerability		Description Criteria	Documentation Criteria	Demonstration Criteria	
36	Have the results of the recovery and restore process been verified?		Results are not verified or cannot describe verification process = 0 Can describe verification of results = 1	Results are not verified or cannot provide documentation of verification process = 0 Can provide documentation that results have been verified = 2	Results are not verified or cannot demonstrate verification of results = 0 Can demonstrate that results have been verified = 3	
		Score				

37	Does the application support a maximum number of concurrent users based on contract requirements without impact to availability of application? Things to consider 1. Scalability	Application does not have maximum number of concurrent users or cannot describe maximum number of concurrent users = 0 Can describe that application does have a maximum number of concurrent users = 1	Application does not have maximum number of concurrent users or cannot provide documentation of this number = 0 Can provide documentation that application has maximum number of concurrent users, but maximum number is not scalable = 1 Can provide documentation that application has maximum number of concurrent users, and maximum number is scalable = 2	Application does not have maximum number of concurrent users or cannot demonstrate the maximum number of concurrent users = 0 Can demonstrate that application has maximum number of concurrent users, but this maximum number is not scalable = 2 Can demonstrate that application has maximum number of concurrent users, and this maximum number is scalable = 3
	Score			

	Vulnerability	*Description Criteria*	*Documentation Criteria*	*Demonstration Criteria*	
38	**Does the application limit the maximum number of concurrent sessions per user?**	Application does not have a maximum number of concurrent sessions per user or cannot describe maximum number = 0 Can describe that application has maximum number of concurrent sessions per user = 1	Application does not have a maximum number of concurrent sessions per user or cannot provide documentation = 0 Can provide documentation that application has maximum number of concurrent sessions per user = 2	Application does not have a maximum number of concurrent sessions per user or cannot demonstrate the maximum number sessions = 0 Can demonstrate that application has maximum number of concurrent sessions per user = 3	
		Score			
39	**Does the vendor have an alternative power supply or uninterruptible power supply in support of the application and data transmissions?**	Vendor does not have alternative or uninterruptible power supply or cannot describe alternative power supply = 0 Can describe their alternative or uninterruptible power supply = 1	Vendor does not have alternative or uninterruptible power supply or cannot provide documentation of power supply = 0 Can provide documentation of alternative or uninterruptible power supply = 2	Vendor does not have alternative or uninterruptible power supply or cannot demonstrate this power supply = 0 Can demonstrate alternative or uninterruptible power supply = 3	
		Score			

					Score
40	**Does the vendor provide the appropriate level of redundancy of all application components based on contract requirements?**	Does not provide appropriate redundancy or cannot describe redundancy = 0 Can describe how they provide appropriate redundancy = 1	Does not provide appropriate redundancy or cannot provide documentation of redundancy = 0 Can provide documentation of appropriate redundancy = 2	Does not provide appropriate redundancy or cannot demonstrate redundancy = 0 Can demonstrate appropriate redundancy = 3	
					Score
41	**Does the vendor utilize a system performance monitoring tool to analyze performance in real time?**	Does not utilize system performance tool or cannot describe how they use this tool = 0 Can describe how they utilize a system performance tool = 1	Does not utilize system performance tool or cannot provide documentation of utilizing tool = 0 Can provide documentation of a system performance tool = 2	Does not utilize system performance tool or cannot demonstrate this tool = 0 Can demonstrate a system performance tool = 3	

Non-repudiation

	Vulnerability	*Description Criteria*	*Documentation Criteria*	*Demonstration Criteria*	
42	**Does the vendor use cryptography to implement encryption, key exchange, digital signature, and hash?**	Does not use cryptography or cannot describe how it used in their application = **0** Can describe how they use cryptography = **1**	Does not use cryptography or cannot provide documentation of using cryptography in their application = **0** Can provide documentation of cryptography = **2**	Does not use cryptography or cannot demonstrate use of cryptography = **0** Can demonstrate use of cryptography = **3**	
		Score			
43	**Does the vendor perform auditing?** List of Items to be included 1. Operating system 2. Application 3. Web server 4. Web services 5. Network devices 6. Database 7. Wireless	Does not perform auditing or cannot describe how they perform auditing = **0** Can describe their auditing process = **1**	Does not perform auditing or cannot provide documentation requiring auditing = **0** Can provide documentation of auditing, and auditing includes 1–3 of listed items = **1** Can provide documentation auditing, and auditing includes 4–7 of listed items = **2**	Does not perform auditing or cannot demonstrate auditing = **0** Can demonstrate auditing, and auditing includes 1–2 of listed items = **1** Can demonstrate auditing, and auditing includes 3–4 of listed items = **2** Can demonstrate auditing and auditing includes 5–7 of listed items = **3**	
		Score			

44	**Does the vendor audit both success and failure of logon attempts to the application?**	Does not audit both success and failure of logon attempts to the application or cannot describe how they audit these events = **0** Can describe how they audit both success and failure of logon attempts to application = **1**	Does not audit both success and failure of logon attempts to the application or cannot provide documentation of auditing both events = **0** Can provide documentation of auditing both success and failure of logon attempts to application = **2**	Does not audit both success and failure of logon attempts to application or cannot demonstrate auditing of these events = **0** Can demonstrate of auditing both success and failure of logon attempts to application = **3**
	Score			

	Vulnerability		Description Criteria	Documentation Criteria	Demonstration Criteria	
45	**Does the vendor have a policy for reviewing audit logs?** Things to consider 1. Frequency of review (daily, weekly)		Does not have policy for reviewing audit logs or cannot describe their policy = **0** Can describe their policy for reviewing audit logs = **1**	Does not have policy for reviewing audit logs or cannot provide documentation of policy = **0** Can provide copy of policy for reviewing audit logs, and reviews are completed less frequently than daily = **1** Can provide copy of policy for reviewing audit logs, and reviews are completed daily or more frequently = **2**	Does not have policy for reviewing audit logs or cannot demonstrate policy = **0** Can demonstrate reviewing logs, and reviews are done less frequently than weekly = **1** Can demonstrate reviewing logs, and reviews are completed weekly or more frequently but less frequently than daily = **2** Can demonstrate reviewing logs, and reviews are completed daily or more frequently = **3**	
		Score				

| 46 | **What events does the vendor log?**
List of Items to be included
1. Audit all failures
2. Successful logon attempt
3. Failure of logon attempt
4. Permission changes
5. Unsuccessful file access
6. Creating users and objects
7. Deletion and modification of system files
8. Registry key/kernel changes | Does not audit or vendor's auditing does not include any of the listed items or cannot describe what events are audited = **0**
Can describe events audited = **1** | Does not audit or vendor's auditing does not include any of the listed items or cannot provide documentation of events in log = **0**
Can provide documentation for auditing, and it includes auditing 1–4 of items = **1**
Can provide copy of policy for auditing, and it includes auditing 5–8 of items = **2** | Does not audit or vendor's auditing does not include any listed items or cannot demonstrate events in log = **0**
Can show audit log, and log contains 1–2 of listed items = **1**
Can show audit log, and log contains 3–4 of listed items = **2**
Can show audit log, and log contains 5–8 of listed items = **3** |
| **Score** | | | | |

	Vulnerability	Description Criteria	Documentation Criteria	Demonstration Criteria
47	**What events does the application log?** List of Items to be included 1. Startup and shutdown 2. Authentication 3. Authorization/permission granting 4. Actions by trusted users 5. Process invocation 6. Controlled access to data by individually authenticated user 7. Unsuccessful data access attempt 8. Data deletion 9. Data transfer 10. Application configuration change 11. Application of confidentiality or integrity labels to data 12. Override or modification of data labels or markings 13. Output to removable media 14. Output to a printer	Application does not audit or cannot describe what application is logging = **0** Can describe what application audit = **1**	Application does not audit or cannot provide documentation for application auditing = **0** Can provide documentation for application auditing, and it includes auditing 1–7 of listed items = **1** Can provide documentation for application auditing, and it includes auditing 8–14 of listed items = **2**	Application does not audit or cannot demonstrate what application is logging = **0** Can show application audit log, and log contains 1–5 of listed items = **1** Can show application audit log, and log contains 6–10 of listed items = **2** Can show application audit log, and log contains 11–14 of listed items = **3**
	Score			

Protection

#	Question				Score
48	Does the vendor follow some type of guidance to secure the vendor computing and network infrastructure?	Follows no guidance for securing their computing and network infrastructure or cannot describe what guidance they follow = 0 Follows guidance for securing their computing and network infrastructure and can describe what that guidance is = 1	Follows no guidance for securing their computing and network infrastructure or cannot provide documentation of guidance = 0 Can provide copy of guidance, but it does not include defense in depth = 1 Can provide copy of guidance, and it includes defense in depth = 2	Follows no guidance for securing their computing and network infrastructure or cannot demonstrate guidance = 0 Can demonstrate their security guidance, but it does not include defense in depth = 2 Can demonstrate their security guidance, and it includes defense in depth = 3	
49	Does the vendor employ a firewall?	Does not employ firewall or cannot describe their firewall = 0 Does employ firewall and can describe their firewall = 1	Does not employ firewall or cannot provide documentation of employing firewall = 0 Can provide documentation of employment of firewall = 2	Does not employ firewall or cannot demonstrate employment of firewall = 0 Can demonstrate employment of firewall = 3	

	Vulnerability	Description Criteria	Documentation Criteria	Demonstration Criteria	
50	**Are the firewall ACLs set to deny by default, allow by exception?**	Does not have firewall ACLs set to deny by default, allow by exception or cannot describe their firewall ACLs = **0** Has firewall ACLs set to deny by default, allow by exception and can describe their ACLs = **1**	Does not have firewall ACLs set to deny by default, allow by exception or cannot provide documentation of firewall ACLs = **0** Can provide documentation of firewall ACLs, but they are not set to deny by default, allow by exception = **1** Can provide documentation of firewall ACLs, and they are set to deny by default, allow by exception = **2**	Does not have firewall ACLs set to deny by default, allow by exception or cannot demonstrate their firewall ACLs = **0** Can demonstrate firewall ACLs, but they are not set to deny by default, allow by exception = **2** Can demonstrate firewall ACLs, and they are set to deny by default, allow by exception = **3**	
				Score	

					Score
51	**Does the vendor deploy and monitor network intrusion detection tools?**	Does not deploy and monitor network intrusion detection tools = 0 Vendor does deploy and monitor network intrusion detection tools = 1	Does not deploy and monitor network intrusion detection tools = 0 Can provide documentation for deploying and monitoring network intrusion detection tools = 2	Does not deploy and monitor network intrusion detection tools = 0 Can demonstrate that network intrusion detection tools have been deployed and are monitored = 3	
52	**Does the vendor deploy and monitor host-based intrusion detection tools?**	Does not deploy and monitor host-based intrusion detection tools or cannot describe their use of host-based intrusion detection tools = 1 HIDs = 0 Can describe their use of host-based intrusion detection tools = 1	Does not deploy and monitor host-based intrusion detection tools or cannot provide documentation of deployment and monitoring = 0 Can provide documentation for deploying and monitoring host-based intrusion detection tools = 2	Does not deploy and monitor host-based intrusion detection tools or cannot demonstrate their HIDs = 0 Can demonstrate that host-based intrusion detection tools have been deployed and are monitored = 3	Score

	Vulnerability		Description Criteria	Documentation Criteria	Demonstration Criteria	
53	**Does the vendor have strong two-factor authentication for management/admin traffic?** Things to consider 1. Something you have 2. Something you are 3. Something you know		Does not have strong two-factor authentication for management/admin traffic or cannot describe their two-factor authentication = 0 Can describe their strong two-factor authentication for management/admin traffic = 1	Does not have strong two-factor authentication for management/admin traffic or cannot provide documentation of their strong two-factor authentication = 0 Can provide documentation for strong two-factor authentication for management/admin traffic = 2	Does not have strong two-factor authentication for management/admin traffic or cannot demonstrate two-factor authentication = 0 Can demonstrate strong two-factor authentication for management/admin traffic = 3	
		Score				
54	**Does the vendor have a patch management process?**		Does not have patch management process or cannot describe their process = 0 Can describe their patch management process = 1	Does not have patch management process or cannot provide documentation for patch management process = 0 Can provide documentation for patch management process = 2	Does not have patch management process or cannot demonstrate patch management process = 0 Can demonstrate patch management process = 3	
		Score				

#	Question	Score			
55	**What is the vendor's patch management process?** Question to ask 1. Does the vendor subscribe to the application vendor hardware/software notification sites for the latest patch notifications? 2. Is there a schedule for applying patches? 3. Are patches tested before applying to productions? 4. Is the severity of the vulnerability considered during determination of the timeliness of applying the patch?		Does not have patch management process or cannot describe their patch management process = **0** Vendor can describe their patch management process = **1**	Does not have patch management process or cannot provide documentation of their patch management process = **0** Can provide documentation of their patch management process, and it addresses 1–2 of questions = **1** Can provide documentation of their patch management process, and it addresses 3–4 of questions = **2**	Does not have a patch management process or cannot demonstrate their patch management process = **0** Can demonstrate their patch management process, and it addresses 1–2 of questions = **2** Can demonstrate their patch management process, and it addresses 3–4 of questions = **3**
		Score			
56	**Does the vendor have a verification process for ensuring patches have been applied?**		Does not have verification process or cannot describe their verification process = **0** Can describe their verification process = **1**	Does not have verification process or cannot provide documentation of verification process = **0** Can provide documentation which requires verification that patches have been applied = **2**	Does not have verification process or cannot demonstrate patches have been applied = **0** Can demonstrate patches have been applied = **3**
		Score			

	Vulnerability	Description Criteria	Documentation Criteria	Demonstration Criteria	
57	Does the vendor perform security self-assessments on a regular basis? Question to ask 1. How often does the vendor perform self-assessments?	Does not perform self-assessments or cannot describe self-assessment process = **0** Does perform self-assessments = **1**	Does not perform self-assessments or cannot provide documentation of self-assessment requirement = **0** Can provide documentation requiring self-assessments to be performed less frequently than monthly = **1** Can provide documentation requiring self-assessments to be performed monthly or more frequently = **2**	Does not perform self-assessments or cannot demonstrate their self-assessment process = **0** Can demonstrate self-assessments are performed, and they are completed less frequently than monthly = **2** Can demonstrate self-assessments are performed, and they are completed monthly or more frequently = **3**	
				Score	

#	Question				Score
58	**Are self-assessment results reviewed on a regular basis?**	Does not review self-assessment results or cannot describe review or self-assessment results = **0** Can describe review self-assessment results = **1**	Does not review self-assessment results or cannot provide documentation of review of results = **0** Can provide documentation that requires review of self-assessment results = **2**	Does not review self-assessment results or cannot demonstrate review of self-assessment results = **0** Can demonstrate review of self-assessment results = **3**	
59	**Does the vendor require sanitation of equipment and media prior to disposal?**	Does not require sanitation of equipment and media prior to disposal or cannot describe sanitation process = **0** Can describe the sanitation of equipment and media prior to disposal = **1**	Does not require sanitation of equipment and media prior to disposal or cannot provide documentation of sanitation = **0** Can provide documentation of sanitation of equipment and media prior to disposal = **2**	Does not require sanitation of equipment and media prior to disposal or cannot demonstrate sanitation = **0** Can demonstrate sanitation of equipment and media prior to disposal = **3**	

	Vulnerability		Description Criteria	Documentation Criteria	Demonstration Criteria	
60	Does the vendor's security policy and process contain guidance for maintaining and monitoring a baseline configuration?		Does not have guidance for baseline configuration or cannot describe their baseline configuration = 0 Can describe their guidance for baseline configuration = 1	Does not have guidance for baseline configuration or cannot provide documentation of guidance = 0 Can provide documentation of baseline configuration = 2	Does not have guidance for baseline configuration or cannot demonstrate baseline configurations = 0 Can demonstrate baseline configuration = 3	
		Score				
61	Does the vendor have a process in place to routinely verify baseline configuration?		Does not have process for routinely verifying baseline configuration or cannot describe process = 0 Can describe process for routinely verifying baseline configuration = 1	Does not have process for routinely verifying baseline configuration or cannot provide process documentation = 0 Can provide process documentation that requires routine verification of baseline configuration = 2	Does not have process for routinely verifying baseline configuration or cannot demonstrate the process= 0 Can demonstrate process for verifying baseline configuration = 3	
		Score				

62	Does the vendor employ a baseline configuration tool?	Does not employ baseline configuration tool or cannot describe their baseline configuration tool = **0** Can describe employment of baseline configuration tool = **1**	Does not employ baseline configuration tool or cannot provide documentation of employment of a baseline configuration tool = **0** Can provide documentation that requires using a baseline configuration tool = **2**	Does not employ baseline configuration tool or cannot demonstrate employment of baseline configuration tool = **0** Can demonstrate using a baseline configuration tool = **3**
	Score			

Detection

	Vulnerability	Description Criteria	Documentation Criteria	Demonstration Criteria
63	**Does the vendor's security policy contain guidance for regularly scheduled routine security audits performed by an external party?** List of Items to be included 1. Operating systems 2. Web servers 3. Browsers 4. Web services 5. Database 6. Network sensors 7. Firewalls 8. Applications 9. Wireless	Does not contain guidance for regularly scheduled routine security audits performed by an external party or cannot describe policy = **0** Can describe security policy, and it contains guidance for regularly scheduled routine security audits performed by an external party = **1**	Does not contain guidance for regularly scheduled routine security audits performed by external party or cannot provide documentation of policy = **0** Can provide a copy of security policy that requires routine security audits performed by external party, but policy does not include all of listed items = **1** Can provide a copy of security policy that requires routine security audits performed by external party, and policy does include all of listed items = **2**	Does not contain guidance for regularly scheduled routine security audits performed by external party or cannot demonstrate policy = **0** Can demonstrate security policy that requires routine security audits performed by external party, but policy includes only operating systems = **1** Can demonstrate security policy that requires routine security audits performed by external party, but policy includes operating systems but not all of listed items = **2** Can demonstrate security policy that requires routine security audits performed by external party, and policy includes all of listed items = **3**
	Score			

64	Does the vendor perform verification of their perimeter router policies?	Does not perform verification of their perimeter router policies or cannot describe verification process = 0 Can describe verification of their perimeter router policies = 1	Does not perform verification of their perimeter router policies or cannot provide documentation of verification = 0 Can provide documentation that requires performing verification of perimeter router policies less frequently than monthly = 1 Can provide documentation that requires performing verification of perimeter router policies monthly or more frequently than monthly = 2	Does not perform verification of their perimeter router policies or cannot demonstrate verification = 0 Can demonstrate verification of their perimeter router policies, and verification is done less frequently than quarterly = 1 Can demonstrate verification of their perimeter router policies, and verification is done quarterly or less frequently than monthly = 2 Can demonstrate verification of their perimeter router policies, and verification is done monthly or more frequently than monthly = 3
	Question to ask 1. How often does the vendor perform verification of their perimeter router policies?			
		Score		

	Vulnerability		Description Criteria	Documentation Criteria	Demonstration Criteria	
65	**Is the vendor firewall or network sensor configured to alert for unauthorized access attempts and privilege escalation?**		Firewall/network sensor is not configured to alert or cannot describe how firewall/network sensor is configured to alert = **0** Can describe how firewall/network sensor is configured to alert for unauthorized access attempts and privilege escalation = **1**	Firewall/network sensor is not configured to alert or cannot provide documentation on how firewall/network sensor is configured to alert = **0** Can provide documentation on how firewall/network sensor is configured to alert = **2**	Firewall/network sensor is not configured to alert or cannot demonstrate how firewall/network sensor is configured to alert = **0** Can demonstrate how firewall/network sensor is configured to alert = **3**	
		Score				

66	Does the vendor routinely check that no new ports, protocols, or services are activated without approval by the configuration management board?	Does not routinely check that no PPS are activated without approval or cannot describe checking process = 0 Can describe process for routinely checking that no new PPS are activated without approval = 1	Does not routinely check that no PPS are activated without approval or cannot provide documentation of checking process = 0 Can provide documentation for routinely checking that no new PPS are activated without approval = 2	Does not routinely check that no PPS are activated without approval or cannot demonstration of checking process = 0 Can demonstrate checking that no new PPS are activated without approval = 3
			Score	
67	Does the vendor comply with ports, protocols, and services guidance?	Does not comply with the guidance or cannot describe how they do comply = 0 Can describe how they comply with the guidance = 1	Does not comply with the guidance or cannot provide documentation on how they do comply = 0 Can provide documentation on how they do comply = 2	Does not comply with the guidance or cannot demonstrate how they do comply = 0 Can demonstrate on how they do comply = 3
			Score	

	Vulnerability		Description Criteria	Documentation Criteria	Demonstration Criteria	
68	**Does the vendor's security policy require routine review of HIDs, NIDs, and firewall rules for accuracy, efficiency, and their ability to withstand new attacks?** Question to ask 1. How often are reviews completed?		Does not require routine review of HIDs, NIDs, and firewall rules or cannot describe policy with this requirement = **0** Can describe how they routinely review HIDs, NIDs, and firewall rules = **1**	Does not require routine review of HIDs, NIDs, and firewall rules or cannot provide policy with this requirement = **0** Can provide documentation on how they routinely review HIDs, NIDs, and firewall rules, but review is performed less frequently than monthly = **1** Can provide documentation on how they routinely review HIDs, NIDs, and firewall rules, but review is performed monthly or more frequently than monthly = **2**	Does not require routine review of HIDs, NIDs, and firewall rules or cannot demonstrate the policy with this requirement = **0** Can demonstrate how they routinely review HIDs, NIDs, and firewall rules, but review occurs less frequently than quarterly = **1** Can demonstrate how they routinely review HIDs, NIDs, and firewall rules, but review occurs quarterly or more frequently than quarterly but less frequently than monthly = **2** Can demonstrate how they routinely review HIDs, NIDs, and firewall rules. but review occurs monthly or more frequently than monthly = **3**	
		Score				

Reaction

69	Does the vendor have a documented incident response program?	Does not have documented incident response program or cannot describe incident response program = 0 Can describe incident response program = 1	Does not have documented incident response program or cannot provide documentation of incident response program = 0 Can provide documentation of the incident response program = 2	Does not have documented incident response program or cannot demonstrate the incident response program = 0 Can demonstrate incident response program = 3
		Score		

	Vulnerability	Description Criteria	Documentation Criteria	Demonstration Criteria
70	**Does the vendor have a documented incident response policy?** List of Items to be included 1. Statement of management commitment 2. Purpose and objectives of policy 3. Scope of policy 4. Definition of computer incident and their consequences 5. Organizational structure 6. Roles, responsibilities, and level of authority 7. Prioritization or severity rating of incident 8. Performance measures 9. Methods of secure communication 10. Reporting and contract forms	Does not have documented incident response policy or cannot describe incident response policy = **0** Can describe incident response policy = **1**	Does not have documented incident response policy, or incident response policy does not include any of listed items or cannot provide incident response policy = **0** Can provide incident response policy, and it includes 1–5 of listed items = **1** Can provide incident response policy, and it includes 6–10 of listed items = **2**	Does not have documented incident response policy, or incident response policy does not include any of listed items or cannot demonstrate incident response policy = **0** Can demonstrate incident response policy, and it includes 1–3 of listed items = **1** Can demonstrate incident response policy, and it includes 4–7 of listed items = **2** Can demonstrate incident response policy, and it includes 8–10 of listed items = **3**
	Score			

| 71 | **Does the vendor have documented incident response procedures?**

List of Items to be included
1. Standard operating procedures (SOP)
2. Identification of incident
3. Reporting of incident
4. Actions to be taken
5. Containment of incident
6. Eradication of incident
7. Recovery of incident
8. Contact information
   a. Internal parties
   b. External parties
9. List of threats to guard against and respond to
10. Incident reporting forms (internal)
11. Incident reporting forms (external)
12. Equipment list
13. Checklists | Does not have documented incident response procedures or cannot describe incident response procedures = **0**

Can describe incident response procedures = **1** | Does not have documented incident response procedures or cannot provide documentation of incident response procedures = **0**

Can provide incident response procedures, and it includes 1–7 of listed items = **1**

Can provide incident response procedures, and it includes 8–15 of listed items = **2** | Does not have documented incident response procedures or cannot demonstrate incident response procedures = **0**

Can demonstrate incident response procedures, and it includes 1–5 of listed items = **1**

Can demonstrate incident response procedures, and it includes 6–10 of listed items = **2**

Can demonstrate incident response procedures, and it includes 11–15 of listed items = **3** |
| | **Score** | | | |

	Vulnerability	Description Criteria	Documentation Criteria	Demonstration Criteria
72	**Are the incident response procedures published in hard copy?**	Are not published in hard copy or cannot describe requirement for publishing in hard copy = 0 Can describe requirement for incident response procedures to be published in hard copy = 1	Are not published in hard copy or cannot provide documentation of requirement for publishing in hard copy = 0 Can provide hard copy of the incident response procedures = 2	Are not published in hard copy or cannot demonstrate publishing in hard copy = 0 Can demonstrate publishing hard copy of incident response procedures = 3
		Score		
73	**Are the incident response procedures published on the intranet or some shared media?**	Are not published on intranet or some shared media or cannot describe requirement for publishing on intranet or some shared media = 0 Are published on intranet or some shared media = 1	Are not published on intranet or some shared media or cannot provide documentation of requirement for publishing on intranet or some shared media = 0 Can provide documentation of requirement for publishing on intranet or some shared media = 2	Are not published on intranet or some shared media or cannot demonstrate that procedures are published on intranet or some shared media = 0 Can demonstrate that procedures are published on intranet or some shared media = 3
		Score		

| 74 | **Is the incident response policy reviewed and updated on a regular basis?**

Question to ask

1. How often is the review an update? | Is not reviewed and updated or cannot describe process for reviewing and updating policy = **0**

Can describe how policy is reviewed and updated = **1** | Is not reviewed and updated or cannot describe process for reviewing and updating policy = **0**

Can describe process for reviewing and updating policy, and process performed less frequently than yearly = **1**

Can describe process for reviewing and updating policy, and process performed yearly or more frequently than yearly = **2** | Is not reviewed and updated or cannot demonstrate process for reviewing and updating policy = **0**

Can demonstrate process for reviewing and updating policy, and process has been performed less frequently than yearly = **2**

Can demonstrate process for reviewing and updating policy, and process has been performed yearly or more frequently than yearly = **3** | |
| | | | **Score** | | |

	Vulnerability	Description Criteria	Documentation Criteria	Demonstration Criteria	
75	**Is initial incident response training provided to user community?**	Is not provided to users or cannot describe the requirement for providing initial training to user = **0** Can describe their requirement for providing initial incident response training to user = **1**	Is not provided to users or cannot provide documentation of providing initial training to user = **0** Can provide documentation of providing initial incident response training to user = **2**	Is not provided to users or cannot demonstrate providing initial training to user = **0** Can demonstrate providing initial incident response training to user = **3**	
	Score				

76	Is refresher incident response training provided periodically to user community? Question to ask 1. How often is training provided?	Is not provided to users or cannot describe requirement for providing refresher training to user = **0** Can describe requirement for providing refresher incident response training to user = **1**	Is not provided to users or cannot provide documentation of providing refresher training to user = **0** Can provide documentation of providing refresher incident response training to user, and training is provided less frequently than yearly = **1** Can provide documentation of providing refresher incident response training to user, and training is provided yearly or more frequently than yearly = **2**	Is not provided to users or cannot demonstrate providing refresher training to user = **0** Can demonstrate providing refresher incident response training to user, and training is provided less frequently than yearly = **2** Can demonstrate providing refresher incident response training to user, and training is provided yearly or more frequently than yearly = **3**
	Score			

Vulnerability	Description Criteria	Documentation Criteria	Demonstration Criteria

77 **Is there an incident response reporting mechanism in place?**
 	
 List of Items to be included
 1. Who discovered the incident
 2. How incident was recognized
 3. Nature of incident
 4. When did the incident occur
 5. When was the incident detected
 6. What is the impact to clients
 7. Who was involved
 8. What evidence was recovered
 9. Where did the incident occur
 10. Affected computer information
 11. Why it happened
 12. How it occurred
 13. Team activities
 14. Who was notified
    a. Internal
    b. External
 15. Resolution
	Does not have incident response reporting mechanism or cannot describe incident response reporting mechanism = **0**
	
	 Can describe incident response reporting mechanism = **1**
		Does not have incident response reporting mechanism or cannot provide documentation of incident response reporting mechanism = **0**
		
		 Can provide documentation of incident response reporting mechanism, and it includes 1–8 of listed items = **1**
		
		 Can provide documentation of incident response reporting mechanism, and it includes 8–16 of listed items = **2**
			Does not have incident response reporting mechanism or cannot demonstrate incident response reporting mechanism = **0**
			
			 Can demonstrate reporting mechanism, and it includes 1–6 of listed items = **1**
			
			 Can demonstrate reporting mechanism, and it includes 7–11 of listed items = **2**
			
			 Can demonstrate reporting mechanism, and it includes 12–16 of listed items = **3**

Score			

78	**Is the incident response reporting mechanism on a computer database, paper, or both?**	Is not database, paper, or both or cannot describe their requirement for reporting mechanism to be on database, paper, or both = **0**	Is not database, paper, or both or cannot provide documentation of their requirement for reporting mechanism to be on database, paper, or both = **0**	Is not provided to users or cannot demonstrate providing initial training to user = **0**	
		Can describe their requirement for reporting mechanism to be on database, paper, or both = **1**	Can provide documentation of reporting mechanism to be on paper only = **1**	Can demonstrate reporting mechanism to be on paper only = **1**	
			Can provide documentation of requirement for reporting mechanism to be on paper and database = **2**	Can demonstrate reporting mechanism to be on database only = **2**	
				Can demonstrate reporting mechanism to be on paper and database = **3**	
			Score		

	Vulnerability	Description Criteria	Documentation Criteria	Demonstration Criteria	
79	Are the incident response reports sent to management on a regular basis? Question to ask 1. How often are reports sent to management?	Are not sent to management on regular basis or cannot describe how reports are sent to management on regular basis = **0** Can describe how reports are sent to management on regular basis = **1**	Are not sent to management on regular basis or cannot provide documentation of requirement for reports to be sent to management on regular basis = **0** Can provide documentation of requirement for reports to be sent to management on regular basis, and reports are sent less frequently than monthly = **1** Can provide documentation of requirement for reports to be sent to management on regular basis, and reports are sent monthly or more frequently than monthly = **2**	Are not sent to management on regular basis or cannot demonstrate requirement for reports to be sent to management on regular basis = **0** Can demonstrate requirement for reports to be sent to management on regular basis, and reports are sent yearly or less frequently than yearly = **1** Can demonstrate requirement for reports to be sent to management on regular basis, and reports are sent quarterly or less frequently than quarterly but more frequently than yearly = **2** Can demonstrate requirement for reports to be sent to management on regular basis, and reports are sent monthly or less frequently than monthly but more frequently than quarterly = **3**	
			Score		

80	Are the incident response procedures tested periodically through exercises or simulations? Question to ask 1. How often are the procedures tested?	Are not tested periodically or cannot describe how procedures are not tested periodically = 0 Can describe how procedures are tested periodically = 1	Are not tested periodically or cannot provide documentation on how procedures are tested periodically = 0 Can provide documentation on how procedures are tested periodically, and procedures are tested less frequently than monthly = 1 Can provide documentation on how procedures are tested periodically, and procedures are tested monthly or more frequently than monthly = 2	Are not tested periodically or cannot demonstrate how procedures are tested periodically = 0 Can demonstrate how procedures are tested periodically, and procedures are tested and procedures are tested yearly or less frequently than yearly = 1 Can demonstrate how procedures are tested, and procedures are tested quarterly or less frequently than quarterly but more frequently than yearly = 2 Can demonstrate how procedures are tested, and procedures are tested monthly or less frequently than monthly but more frequently than quarterly = 3
	Score			

	Vulnerability	Description Criteria	Documentation Criteria	Demonstration Criteria	
81	**Does the incident response team include members from all key functional areas?** List of Items to be included 1. Senior management 2. Human resources/personnel 3. Information technology/information security 4. Technical staff members 5. Budget or finance	Does not have members from all key functional areas or cannot describe who is on the incident response team = **0** Can describe who is on the incident response team = **1**	Does not have members from all key functional areas or cannot provide documentation for who is on team = **0** Can provide documentation of who is on the incident response team, and it includes 1–3 of the listed items = **1** Can provide documentation of who is on the incident response team, and it includes 4–5 of the listed items = **2**	Does not have members from all key functional areas or cannot demonstrate who is on team = **0** Can demonstrate who is on the incident response team, and it includes 1–2 of the listed items = **1** Can demonstrate who is on the incident response team, and it includes 3–4 of the listed items = **2** Can demonstrate who is on the incident response team, and it includes 5 of the listed items = **3**	
		Score			

Configuration Management

		Score	Does not exist, or it does not include all of the items or cannot describe the configuration management plan = 0 Can describe the configuration management plan, and it includes all of the items = 1	Does not exist, or it does not include all of the items or cannot provide documentation of the configuration management plan = 0 Can provide documentation of the configuration management plan = 2	Does not exist, or it does not include all of the items or cannot demonstrate the configuration management plan = 0 Can demonstrate the configuration management plan = 3
82	Does the configuration management plan include hardware, operating system, utility software, communication, network device changes, application, and facilities?				

	Vulnerability	Description Criteria	Documentation Criteria	Demonstration Criteria	
83	**Does the configuration management plan contain the necessary items?** List of Items to be included 1. Identify the configuration change 2. Contain an approval process 3. Review the configuration change 4. Schedule the configuration change 5. Track the implementation of the configuration change 6. Track system impact of the configuration change 7. Record and report configuration change to the appropriate party 8. Back out plan if the configuration change does not work as planned 9. Provide for minutes of the meeting 10. Emergency change procedures 11. List of team members from key functional areas	Does not have configuration management plan or cannot describe configuration management plan = **0** Can describe configuration management plan = **1**	Does not have configuration management plan or cannot provide documentation of configuration management plan = **0** Can provide documentation of configuration management plan, and it includes 1–5 of listed items = **1** Can provide documentation of configuration management plan, and it includes 6–11 of listed items = **2**	Does not have configuration management plan or cannot demonstrate plan = **0** Can demonstrate configuration management plan, and it includes 1–4 of listed items = **1** Can demonstrate configuration management plan, and it includes 5–8 of listed items = **2** Can demonstrate configuration management plan, and it includes 9–11 of listed items = **3**	
				Score	

84	Is the configuration management process automated or manual?	Does not have configuration management process or cannot describe configuration management process = **0** Can describe configuration management process = **1**	Does not have configuration management process or cannot provide documentation of configuration management process = **0** Can provide documentation of configuration management process, and process is manual = **1** Can provide documentation of configuration management process, and process is automated = **2**	Does not have configuration management process or cannot demonstrate configuration management process = **0** Can demonstrate configuration management process, and process is manual = **2** Can demonstrate configuration management process, and process is automated = **3**
	Score			

Vulnerability Management

	Vulnerability	Description Criteria	Documentation Criteria	Demonstration Criteria
85	**Does the vendor's security policy contain guidance for regularly scheduled internal vulnerability audits?** Question to ask 1. How often are vulnerability audits performed?	Does not require regularly scheduled internal vulnerability audits or cannot describe the requirement = **0** Can describe the requirement for regularly scheduled vulnerability audits = **1**	Does not require regularly scheduled internal vulnerability audits or cannot describe the requirement = **0** Can provide documentation that requires regularly scheduled internal vulnerability audits, and audits are performed less frequently than monthly = **1** Can provide documentation that requires regularly scheduled internal vulnerability audits, and audits are performed monthly or more frequently than monthly = **2**	Does not require regularly scheduled internal vulnerability audits or cannot describe the requirement = **0** Can demonstrate requirement for regularly scheduled vulnerability audits, and audits are performed yearly or less frequently than yearly = **1** Can demonstrate requirement for regularly scheduled vulnerability audits, and audits are performed quarterly or less frequently than quarterly but more frequently than yearly = **2** Can demonstrate requirement for regularly scheduled vulnerability audits, and audits are

	Score			
86 Does the vendor utilize a network vulnerability scanner? Question to ask 1. How often is the network scanned?		Does not utilize network vulnerability scanner or cannot describe how their scanner is used = 0 Can describe how their scanner is used = 1	Does not utilize network vulnerability scanner or cannot provide documentation of how their scanner is used = 0 Can provide documentation of how their scanner is used, and scans are performed less frequently than monthly = 1 Can provide documentation of how their scanner is used, and scans are performed monthly or more frequently than monthly = 2	Does not utilize network vulnerability scanner or cannot demonstrate how their scanner is used = 0 Can demonstrate how their scanner is used, and scans are performed yearly or less frequently than yearly = 1 Can demonstrate how their scanner is used, and scans are performed quarterly or less frequently than quarterly but more frequently than yearly = 2 Can demonstrate how their scanner is used, and scans are performed monthly or less frequently than monthly but more frequently than quarterly = 3	performed monthly or less frequently than monthly but more frequently than quarterly = 3
	Score			

	Vulnerability		Description Criteria	Documentation Criteria	Demonstration Criteria	
87	**Are the results of the network vulnerability scans sent to management on a regular basis?**		Are not sent to management or cannot describe the requirement for network vulnerability scan results to be sent to management = **0** Can describe the requirement for network vulnerability scan results to be sent to management = **1**	Are not sent to management or cannot provide documentation of the requirement for network vulnerability scan results to be sent to management = **0** Can provide documentation of the requirement for network vulnerability scan results to be sent to management = **2**	Are not sent to management or cannot demonstrate the requirement for network vulnerability scan results to be sent to management = **0** Can demonstrate network vulnerability scan results to be sent to management = **3**	
		Score				

88	Is there a process in place to regularly correct discovered vulnerabilities and configuration discrepancies?	Does not have process to correct discovered vulnerabilities and configuration discrepancies, or cannot describe the process to correct discovered vulnerabilities and configuration discrepancies = **0** Can describe process to correct discovered vulnerabilities and configuration discrepancies = **1**	Does not have process to correct discovered vulnerabilities and configuration discrepancies, or cannot provide documentation of process to correct discovered vulnerabilities and configuration discrepancies = **0** Can provide documentation of process to correct discovered vulnerabilities and configuration discrepancies = **2**	Does not have process to correct discovered vulnerabilities and configuration discrepancies, or cannot demonstrate process to correct discovered vulnerabilities and configuration discrepancies = **0** Can demonstrate process to correct discovered vulnerabilities and configuration discrepancies = **3**	
			Score		

	Vulnerability		Description Criteria	Documentation Criteria	Demonstration Criteria	
89	Does the vendor have a verification process for ensuring vulnerabilities and configuration discrepancies have been corrected?		Does not have process for ensuring vulnerabilities and configuration discrepancies have been corrected or cannot describe correction process = **0** Can describe the vulnerability and configuration discrepancy correction process = **1**	Does not have process for ensuring vulnerabilities and configuration discrepancies have been corrected or cannot provide documentation of correction process = **0** Can provide documentation of the correction process = **2**	Does not have process for ensuring vulnerabilities and configuration discrepancies have been corrected or cannot demonstrate correction process = **0** Can demonstrate corrections have been made = **3**	
		Score				

90	Does the vendor routinely run a port scanning tool to ensure no new or unexpected ports, protocols, or services are discovered? Question to ask 1. How often are ports scanned?	Does not utilize port scanner to ensure no new or unexpected PPS are discovered or cannot describe how their scanner is used = **0** Can describe how their scanner is used = **1**	Does not utilize port scanner to ensure no new or unexpected PPS are discovered or cannot provide documentation of requirement to use a port scanner = **0** Can provide documentation of requirement to use port scanner, and scans are performed less frequently than monthly = **1** Can provide documentation of requirement to use port scanner, and scans are performed monthly or more frequently than monthly = **2**	Does not utilize port scanner to ensure no new or unexpected PPS are discovered or cannot demonstrate how their scanner is used = **0** Can demonstrate how their scanner is used, and scans are performed yearly or less frequently than yearly = **1** Can demonstrate how their scanner is used, and scans are performed quarterly or less frequently than quarterly but more frequently than yearly = **2** Can demonstrate how their scanner is used, and scans are performed monthly or less frequently than monthly but more frequently than quarterly = **3**	
				Score	

	Vulnerability	Description Criteria	Documentation Criteria	Demonstration Criteria	
91	**Is the vendor's application compliant with the ports, protocols, and services CAL?**	Is not compliant with the CAL or cannot describe how they are compliant = **0** Can describe how they are compliant with the PPS CAL = **1**	Is not compliant with PPS CAL or cannot describe how they are compliant = **0** Can provide documentation of compliancy with the PPS CAL = **2**	Is not compliant with PPS CAL or cannot describe how they are compliant = **0** Can demonstrate they are compliant with the PPS CAL = **3**	
		Score			
92	**Are the results of the port scans sent to management on a regular basis?**	Are not sent to management or cannot describe requirement for ports scan results to be sent to management = **0** Can describe requirement for port scan results to be sent to management = **1**	Are not sent to management or cannot provide documentation of the requirement for port scan results to be sent to management = **0** Can provide documentation of the requirement for port scan results to be sent to management = **2**	Are not sent to management or cannot demonstrate requirement for port scan results to be sent to management = **0** Can demonstrate port scan results to be sent to management = **3**	
		Score			

93	**What ports, protocols, and services are necessary for access to the application from outside the local enclave?**	Note PPS and Compliance statement here		
		Score		
94	**Does the vendor routinely run a web-scanning tool to check for new web vulnerabilities?**	Does not utilize web scanner to check for new web vulnerabilities or cannot describe how their web scanner is used = 0 Can describe how their web scanner is used = 1	Does not utilize web scanner to check for new web vulnerabilities or cannot provide documentation of requirement to scan web = 0 Can provide documentation of requirement to scan web, and scans are performed less frequently than monthly = 1 Can provide documentation of requirement to scan web, and scans are performed monthly or more frequently than monthly = 2	Does not utilize web scanner to check for new web vulnerabilities or cannot demonstrate how their web scanner is used = 0 Can demonstrate how their web scanner is used, and scans are performed yearly or less frequently than yearly = 1 Can demonstrate how their web scanner is used, and scans are performed quarterly or less frequently than quarterly but more frequently than yearly = 2 Can demonstrate how their web scanner is used, and scans are performed monthly or less frequently than monthly but more frequently than quarterly = 3
		Score		

	Vulnerability	Description Criteria	Documentation Criteria	Demonstration Criteria
95	**Are the results of the web scans sent to management on a regular basis?**	Are not sent to management or cannot describe requirement for web scan results to be sent to management = 0 Can describe the requirement for web scan results to be sent to management = 1	Are not sent to management or cannot provide documentation of requirement for web scan results to be sent to management = 0 Can provide documentation of requirement for web scan results to be sent to management = 2	Are not sent to management or cannot demonstrate requirement for web scan results to be sent to management = 0 Can demonstrate web scan results are sent to management = 3
	Score			
96	**Does the vendor routinely run a password-checking tool?**	Does not utilize password-checking tool or cannot describe how their password-checking tool works = 0 Can describe how their password-checking tool works = 3	Does not utilize password-checking tool or cannot provide documentation of requirement for tool = 0 Can provide documentation of requirement for password-checking tool, and it is run monthly or more frequently than monthly or they are using PKI = 3	Does not utilize password-checking tool or cannot demonstrate how their password-checking tool works = 0 Can demonstrate how their password-checking tool works, and it is run monthly or more frequently than monthly or they are using PKI = 3

#	Question				Score
97	**Are the results of the password-checking tool sent to management on a regular basis?**	Are not sent to management or cannot describe requirement for password-checking results to be sent to management = **0** Can describe requirement for password-checking results to be sent to management = **1**	Are not sent to management or cannot provide documentation of requirement for password-checking results to be sent to management = **0** Can provide documentation of requirement for password-checking results to be sent to management = **2**	Are not sent to management or cannot demonstrate requirement for password-checking results to be sent to management = **0** Can demonstrate password-checking results are sent to management = **3**	
98	**Does the vendor subscribe to the applicable vendor's security notification sites for the latest security vulnerabilities' notifications?**	Does not subscribe to security notification sites or cannot describe requirement for subscribing to security notification sites = **0** Can describe requirement for subscribing to security notification sites = **1**	Does not subscribe to security notification sites or cannot provide documentation of requirement for subscribing to security notification sites = **0** Can provide documentation of requirement for subscribing to security notification sites = **2**	Does not subscribe to security notification sites or cannot demonstrate they have subscribed to security notification sites = **0** Can demonstrate they have subscribed to security notification sites = **3**	

Personnel Security

	Vulnerability		Description Criteria	Documentation Criteria	Demonstration Criteria
99	**Does the vendor have a documented requirement for a background security investigation?** Question to ask 1. What type of background security investigation is required?		Does not have requirement for background security investigation or cannot describe their background security investigation = **0** Can describe their background security investigation = **1**	Does not have requirement for background security investigation or cannot provide documentation of requirement for background security investigation = **0** Can provide documentation of the requirement for background security investigation = **1**	Does not have background security investigation or cannot demonstrate background security investigation has been done = **0** Can demonstrate background security investigation has been done = **1**

	Score			
100 **Does the vendor perform background security investigations on a regular basis?** Question to ask 1. How frequently are background investigation performed?		Does not have background security investigation or cannot describe their background security investigation = **0** Can describe their background security investigation = **1**	Does not have background security investigation or cannot provide copy of background security investigation = **0** Can provide documentation of background security investigation, and investigation is performed less frequently than every 5 years = **1** Can provide documentation of background security investigation, and investigation is performed every 5 years or more frequently than every 5 years = **2**	Does not have background security investigation or cannot demonstrate background investigation has been done = **0** Can demonstrate security investigation has been done, and investigation is performed less frequently than every 5 years = **2** Can demonstrate security investigation has been done, and investigation is performed every 5 years or more frequently than every 5 years = **3**

	Vulnerability	Score	Description Criteria	Documentation Criteria	Demonstration Criteria
101	**Can the vendor prove they perform background security investigations?** Thing to consider 1. Is having a clearance a requirement in the statement of work?		Cannot prove they do background investigations = **0** Can prove they do background investigations = **2**	NA	NA
102	**Does the vendor's background security investigation include pertinent areas?** List of Items to be included 1. Does the hiring process restrict hiring a convicted felon? 2. Does the investigation cover participation or membership of subversive activities or groups? 3. Does the investigation research the credit background of the potential employee? 4. Does the hiring process require a drug screening test?		Does not require background security investigation, or they cannot describe their background investigation = **0** Can describe their background investigation = **1**	Does not require background security investigation, or they cannot provide documentation of their background investigation = **0** Can provide documentation of their background investigation, and it includes 1–2 of listed items = **1** Can provide documentation of their background investigation, and it includes 3–4 of listed items = **2**	Does not require background security investigation, or they cannot demonstrate their background investigation = **0** Can demonstrate their background investigation, and it includes 1–2 of listed items = **1** Can demonstrate their background investigation, and it includes 3 of listed items = **2** Can demonstrate their background investigation, and it includes 4 of listed items = **3**

	Score			
103 Are vendor personnel subject to a background check? List of Items to be included 1. System administrators 2. Help desk 3. Administrative personnel 4. Management 5. Janitorial staff		Are not subject to background check or cannot describe their background check = **0** Can describe their background check = **1**	Are not subject to background check or cannot provide documentation of their background check = **0** Can provide documentation of their background check, and system administrators and help desk are subject to background check = **1** Can provide documentation of their background check, and all 5 of listed items are subject to background check = **2**	Are not subject to background check or cannot demonstrate their background check = **0** Can demonstrate their background check, and system administrators and help desk are subject to background check = **1** Can demonstrate their background check, and system administrators, help desk, and management are subject to background check = **2** Can demonstrate their background check, and all 5 of listed items are subject to background check = **3**

	Score			
Vulnerability		*Description Criteria*	*Documentation Criteria*	*Demonstration Criteria*
104 **Does the personnel assigned to doing background checks have a security clearance?**		Do not have security clearance or vendor cannot describe requirement for these personnel to have clearance = 0 Can describe requirement for these personnel to have clearance = 1	Do not have security clearance or vendor cannot provide documentation of requirement for these personnel to have clearance = 0 Can provide documentation of requirement for these personnel to have clearance = 2	Do not have security clearance or vendor cannot demonstrate requirement for these personnel to have clearance = 0 Can demonstrate these personnel to have clearance = 3

Physical Security

	Score			
Vulnerability		*Description Criteria*	*Documentation Criteria*	*Demonstration Criteria*
105 **Is there access control at every physical access point to the vendor facility?**		Does not have access control at every access point or cannot describe how every physical access point has access control = 0 Can describe how every physical access point has access control = 1	Does not have access control at every access point or cannot provide documentation requiring access control at every physical access point = 0 Can provide documentation requiring access control at every physical access point = 2	Does not have access control at every access point or cannot demonstrate how every physical access point has access control = 0 Can demonstrate access control at every physical access point to the facility = 3

	Score			
106 Does the facility housing the equipment have a separate access control zone to restrict unauthorized personnel?		Does not have separate access control zone to restrict unauthorized personnel or cannot describe how their separate access control zone is used to restrict unauthorized personnel = 0 Can describe how their separate access control zone is used to restrict unauthorized personnel = 1	Does not have separate access control zone to restrict unauthorized personnel or cannot provide documentation of requirement of separate access control zone is used to restrict unauthorized personnel = 0 Can provide documentation of requirement of separate access control zone is used to restrict unauthorized personnel = 2	Does not have separate access control zone to restrict unauthorized personnel or cannot demonstrate how their separate access control zone is used to restrict unauthorized personnel = 0 Can demonstrate how their separate access control zone is used to restrict unauthorized personnel = 3

	Score	Vulnerability	Description Criteria	Documentation Criteria	Demonstration Criteria
107		**Does the facility housing the equipment have additional security measures (key control)?** Items to consider 1. Area is locked with a key lock when not manned. 2. All doors, either interior or exterior, have closed circuit television (CCTV)/motion detector. 3. Area is manned 24/7, or area is alarmed when not manned or area is locked with GSA approved lock when not manned.	Does not have additional security measures or cannot describe how their additional security measures = **0** Can describe how their additional security measures are present in facility housing equipment = **1**	Does not have additional security measures or cannot provide documentation requiring additional security measures = **0** Can provide documentation requiring additional security measures = **2**	Does not have additional security measures or cannot demonstrate their additional security measures = **0** Can demonstrate their additional security measures on facility housing equipment, and area is locked with key lock when not manned = **1** Can demonstrate their additional security measures on facility housing equipment, and all doors have CCTV/motion detector = **2** Can demonstrate their additional security measures on facility housing equipment, and area is manned 24/7 or area is alarmed when not manned or area is locked when not manned = **3**

	Score			
108 Does the facility have a disaster recovery plan? Question to ask 1. Is the plan developed, documented, and tested annually?		Does not have disaster recovery plan or cannot describe their disaster recovery plan = **0** Can describe how their disaster recovery plan = **1**	Does not have disaster recovery plan or cannot provide their disaster recovery plan = **0** Can provide their disaster recovery plan, but it is documented only = **1** Can provide their disaster recovery plan, and it is fully developed, documented, and tested annually = **2**	Does not have disaster recovery plan or cannot demonstrate their disaster recovery plan = **0** Can demonstrate their disaster recovery plan, but it is documented only = **2** Can demonstrate their disaster recovery plan, and it is fully developed, documented, and tested annually = **3**

	Score			
Vulnerability		*Description Criteria*	*Documentation Criteria*	*Demonstration Criteria*
109 Does the facility have environmental controls? Items to include 1. Fire suppression 2. Climate-controlled computer facility		Does not have environmental controls or cannot describe their environmental controls = **0** Can describe environmental controls = **1**	Does not have environmental controls or cannot provide documentation of their environmental controls = **0** Can provide documentation of their environmental controls, and it includes 1 of items listed = **1** Can provide documentation of their environmental controls, and it includes 2 of the items listed = **2**	Does not have environmental controls or cannot demonstrate their environmental controls = **0** Can demonstrate their environmental controls, and it includes 1 of items listed = **2** Can demonstrate environmental controls, and it includes 2 of items listed = **3**
	Score			

Security Awareness and Training

110	Do employees receive general security training? Questions to ask 1. Are training materials made available? 2. Is initial and annual training given and documented?	Does not have general security training or cannot describe their general security training = **0** Can describe their general security training = **1**	Does not have general security training or cannot provide documentation of their general security training = **0** Can provide documentation of their general security training, but it is only training materials made available = **1** Can provide documentation of their general security training, and it is includes initial and annual training, and the training is documented = **2**	Does not have general security training or cannot demonstrate their general security training = **0** Can demonstrate their general security training, but it is only training materials made available = **2** Can demonstrate their general security training, and it is includes initial and annual training, and the training is documented = **3**

Vulnerability	Score	Description Criteria	Documentation Criteria	Demonstration Criteria	
111 **Do privileged users receive additional security training specific to their duties?** Questions to ask 1. Are privileged users given additional training? 2. Do system administrators, security personnel, and other privileged users required to be certified?		Do not receive additional security training or cannot describe privileged users' additional training = **0** Can describe privileged users' additional training = **1**	Do not receive additional security training or cannot provide documentation of privileged users' additional training = **0** Can provide documentation of privileged users' additional training = **1** Can provide documentation of system administrators, security personnel, and privileged users' additional training = **2**	Does not have general security training or cannot demonstrate their general security training = **0** Can demonstrate privileged users' additional training = **2** Can demonstrate system administrators, security personnel, and privileged users' additional training = **3**	
	Score				

Index